Further ▮

A FEMINIST ETHIC Oʀ ▮

———————— ■ ————————

"This revised edition of Sharon Welch's *A Feminist Ethic of Risk* eschews a muddle-headed utopianism for an ethic of risk that recognizes the ambiguities that shape our moral lives and hopes. Welch explores our contemporary political contexts while carefully explaining how she, as a white feminist, draws on womanist methodology to prevent violations of human rights in the face of a collapse of moral vision and political will. Her goal, an admirable and ultimately practical one, is to craft an ethic that helps us learn on a daily basis how to live creatively, responsibly, and compassionately in the present."

Emilie M. Townes
Union Theological Seminary, New York

"Anyone interested in an ethic for life in our troubled world does well to read Welch's *A Feminist Ethic of Risk.* It retains importance because of its honest and hard-hitting recognition of and appreciation for the risk we embrace when we seek to act in responsible and just ways, taking as our starting premise accountability and openness to others. In this revised edition, Welch's insights into the current sociopolitical and cultural scene, and the complexity of intentions that have shaped our world, only serve further to enhance the importance of this book. My words of advice to those browsing through this book are simple: read it and read it again!"

Anthony B. Pinn, Macalaster College

"Sharon Welch has drunk from the wellsprings of survivors—womanists, Native Americans, white feminists—and offers us this cup of wisdom: what it takes to 'reconstitute the world' (Adrienne Rich). After I read this book I felt more clear-eyed and yet more hopeful than I have in years."

Susan Brooks Thistlethwaite
Chicago Theological Seminary

A Feminist Ethic of

RISK

Sharon D. Welch

Revised Edition

Fortress Press   Minneapolis

Excerpt from "In These Dissenting Times" from *Revolutionary Petunias and Other Poems,* copyright © 1973, 1970 by Alice Walker, reprinted by permission of Harcourt Brace Jovanovich, Inc.

From *The Salt-Eaters* by Toni Cade Bambara, copyright © 1980 by Toni Cade Bambara, reprinted by permission of Random House, Inc. Published in the U.K. by the Women's Press Ltd., London, 1982.

Excerpt from *The Chosen Place, The Timeless People* by Paule Marshall, copyright © 1984 by Paule Marshall, reprinted by permission of Joan Daves.

The lines from "Natural Resources" from *The Dream of a Common Language, Poems 1974, 1977,* by Adrienne Rich, are reprinted with the permission of the author and W.W. Norton & Company, Inc. Copyright © 1978 by W.W. Norton & Company, Inc.

Excerpt from "The Black Goddess" by Donna Kate Rushin, in *Home Girls: A Black Feminist Anthology,* Barbara Smith, ed., copyright © 1983 Donna Kate Rushin. Reprinted by permission of Kate Rushin and Kitchen Table: Women of Color Press, P. O. Box 908, Latham, NY 12110.

Excerpt from "Until We're Free" by Gioconda Belli from *Nicaragua in Revolution: The Poets Speak,* Bridget Aldaraca, Edward Baker, Ileana Rodriguez, Marc Zimmerman, eds. (Minneapolis: Marxist Educational Press, 1980). Reprinted by permission of Marxist Educational Press, 215 Ford Hall, University of Minnesota, Minneapolis, MN 55455.

Excerpt from *Let the Circle Be Unbroken* by Mildred D. Taylor. Copyright © 1981 by Mildred D. Taylor. Reprinted by permission of the publisher, Dial Books for Young Readers.

Excerpt from *Roll of Thunder, Hear My Cry* by Mildred D. Taylor. Copyright © 1976 by Mildred D. Taylor. Reprinted by permission of the publisher, Dial Books for Young Readers.

Excerpt from "The nature of this flower to bloom" (June Jordan in a personal letter, 1970). In *Revolutionary Petunias and Other Poems* by Alice Walker. Reprinted by permission of June Jordan.

Excerpt from *The Bluest Eye* by Toni Morrison. Copyright © 1970 by Toni Morrison. Reprinted by arrangement with Henry Holt and Company, Inc.

Interior design by Karen Buck
Cover design by David Meyer
Author photo by Roger Berg, Creative Photos

Library of Congress Cataloging-in-Publication Data
Welch, Sharon D.
   A feminist ethic of risk / Sharon D. Welch.—Rev. ed.
     p. cm.
   Includes bilbiographical references and index.
   ISBN 0-8006-3185-4 (alk. paper)
   1. Christian ethics. 2. Feminist ethics. 3. Social Ethics. 4. Feminist thoelogy. 5. American Fiction—Afro-American authors—History and criticism. 6. Feminism and literature—United States—History—20th century. 7. Women and literature—United States—History—20th century. 8. American fiction—Women authors—History and criticism. 9. American fiction—20th century—History and criticism. 10. Afro-American women in literature. 11. Social ethics in literature. 12. Risk in literature. I. Title.
BJ1275.W42 1989
241'.082—dc21   99-058931
                                                                                                              CIP

The paper used in this publication meets the minimum requirements of American National Standard for Information Sciences—Permanence of Paper for Printed Library Materials, ANSI Z329.48-1984.
Manufactured in the U.S.A.   AF-1-3185

04   03   02   01   00   1   2   3   4   5   6   7   8   9   10

For LaVonne

Contents

———— ■ ————

Acknowledgments

———— ■ ————

I am deeply grateful to the people whose challenge and support made this revision possible: my colleagues in the religious studies department at the University of Missouri: Jill Raitt, Bob Flanagan, Steve Friesen, Sue Crowley, Paul Johnson, Phillip Clart and Horace Griffin; colleagues with whom I have worked for social justice and racial justice: Helen Neville, Karen Debord, Diane Williams, Karen Touzeau, KC Morrison, Mable Grimes, Geta LeSeur, Carolyn Dorsey, Shirley Jordan, Jaci Goldberg, Aaron Thompson, Elaine Lawless, Meg Riley, Thandeka, William Jones, Anita Farber-Robertson, Mark Morrison-Reed, Jean Kapuscik, Theophus Smith, Carol Lee Sanchez, Gary Oxenhandler, Monica Naylor, and all the teachers I have worked with in seminars and workshops on multicultural education; my editor at Fortress Press, Michael West; and, most importantly, Jon Poses, whose commitment to world peace is a continual source of joy and inspiration.

Part One

CULTURED DESPAIR
AND THE DEATH OF
THE MORAL IMAGINATION

————— ■ —————

1

The Ethic of Control

─────────── ■ ───────────

What does it mean to act ethically in a world of expediency, to stand for justice in a world of exploitation, to act with compassion in a world of indifference, cynicism, and despair? How do we work for justice when it seems that only individual well-being is attainable, while collective social justice is unreachable?[1]

When I wrote this book in the 1980s, sexism, racism, economic injustice, and the imminent threat of nuclear war shaped the political horizon. The Cold War, and its attendant economic, moral, and psychological costs, seemed as immutable an aspect of our political landscape as the nation-state. With the collapse of the Soviet Union and the rejection of communism by Eastern European nations, our political situation has changed in significant ways. While the unimaginable has occurred—the Cold War has ended—political and economic threats to international and national justice remain. As Barbara Crossette writes of the hopes of many after the end of the Cold War: "The world expected peace. It found a new brutality."[2]

This last decade has seen a truly horrifying explosion of violence in Bosnia, Rwanda, the Sudan, Somalia, Kosovo, and East Timor. We are even threatened by a return to a nuclear arms race as India and Pakistan test nuclear weapons, and the United States considers, once again, developing "Star Wars," a national missile defense system.[3] Further, the "triumph of capitalism" has masked but not ameliorated the social injustices that plagued America and has arguably exacerbated them elsewhere.

How do we effectively respond to these threats to social justice, and to further violations of human rights? More importantly, how do we *prevent* violations of human rights, how do we prevent not only interstate conflict and wars of expansion, but intrastate armed conflict and civil war?

COMMUNICATIVE ETHICS

Threats to a society's collective well-being, justice, and even survival stem from many causes: natural disasters and limitations, the human exploitation of nature and of other people, the shortsightedness and ignorance of humanity, and, oddly enough, particular constructions of ethical responsibility. Our moral and political imagination is shaped by an ethic of control, a construction of agency, responsibility, and goodness which assumes that it is possible to guarantee the efficacy of one's actions. In this chapter, I claim that the root of much middle-class cynicism and despair is a specific construction of the good and of responsible action. I criticize a particular construction of responsibility, the ethic of control, and argue for an alternative construction of responsible action, the ethic of risk. In revising this book for a second edition, I have made changes that contextualize the work in terms of contemporary ethics and political concerns. In order to address our current political challenges, I have omitted the introduction and those portions of chapter 2 that analyzed the dynamics of the nuclear arms race and have replaced them with chapter 1. In this chapter, I describe the contributions of communicative ethics for an understanding of our current political challenges.

How do we learn to be moral? Where do we gain moral vision, insight, and courage? This book, in its original form and in its subsequent revision, recounts a journey, an exploration of the meaning of good and evil, right and wrong, and the ironic and sometimes tragic contours of that journey. The journey began with a recognition of moral failure—the collapse of political will and insight in face of enormous life-and-death struggles. The journey continued with the discovery of another tradition of moral wisdom that provided insight, clarity, and vision.

The original name of this book, *A Feminist Ethic of Risk*, is both accurate and misleading as a title for this journey. It is accurate in its naming of the process, the method of ethical reflection as feminist. It is wrong, however, in implying that the ethic of risk itself is feminist. It is not. It is an ethic expressed in the lives and writings of African American women and men, of womanist ethicists and novelists. To reflect this reality, the book would be more accurately titled simply *An Ethic of Risk*, an account of the foundational challenge to, and critique of, Euro-American ethics posed by womanist and African American male ethicists, and a response to that critique.

I approach political issues as a social ethicist, and from the perspective of communicative ethics. Social ethics, as concisely defined by Emilie Townes, is "a discipline [that] looks at social structures, processes and communities. . . . It also looks at socially shared patterns of moral judgments and behavior."[4] How do we discern, however, when those "socially shared patterns" are *themselves immoral,* finely textured masks for perpetuating power, alienation, and control? To see the fundamental flaws in shared systems of values and behaviors requires difference, a thorough engagement with other communities, with other systems of knowing and acting. This mutually self-critical engagement with difference is the work of communicative ethics. While I have learned much from Jürgen Habermas's description of the task of communicative ethics, I share with many feminists a strong critique of his understanding of the purpose and method of communicative ethics. This critique is developed more fully in chapter 7. It is enough now to point to three key elements in this redefinition of communicative ethics. First, with Jane Braaten, I claim that the goal of communicative ethics is community and solidarity, not justification and universal consensus.[5] Second, following womanist ethicists, I concur that key elements of community and solidarity are accountability and respect. Accountability entails recognition of wrongdoing and imbalances of power and leads to self-critical attempts to use power justly. Respect is not primarily sympathy for the other, but acknowledgment of the equality, dignity, and independence of others. We work *with,* not for, others.[6]

Third, what are the conditions of transformative communication? Garth Kasimu Baker-Fletcher describes a "three-in-one ethical norm" that allows us to interact critically and honestly.

Rather than merely tolerating others, Baker-Fletcher calls us to:

1. *Genuine interest* in the cultures, religions, and differences that compromise the globe, rather than the grasping and assimilative "curiosity" of Euro-dominators;
2. *Genuine nonvolatile confrontation,* where differences between cultures and groups cannot be overlooked, dismissed, or trivialized; and
3. *Genuine perseverance* in maintaining respect, dialogue, and communication, even after significant differences have been noted and addressed. [7]

Accepting Baker-Fletcher's challenge leads to a third modification of communicative ethics. In this reconstruction of communicative ethics, communicative ethics is not simply a matter of dialogue. Critical engagement requires action and reflection, action on issues of justice with (not for) members of another community, and serious attention to the history, art, literature, ethics, and philosophies of other communities. While there is dialogue, it is a dialogue informed by the primary tasks of working together and learning from the literature and history of the other community. It is in this regard that literature is valuable. I explore the nature of womanist literature more fully in chapter 2. At this juncture, however, it is crucial to note Katie G. Cannon's description of the value of womanist literature as a resource for constructive ethics: "The Black women's literary tradition is the best available literary repository for understanding the ethical values Black women have created and cultivated in their participation in this society."[8]

In this exercise in communicative ethics, I demonstrate what can be gained through working with and learning from African American activists and scholars. This work is a beginning point, and not a definitive piece, in many ways. First, there is much more to be learned by Euro-Americans through work with African Americans than is recounted here. Second, there is as much to be learned from a thorough engagement with other communities, from, for example, work with *mujerista* theologians and ethicists, Latino/Latina, Jewish, and Asian and Asian American activists and writers, activists and writers with disabilities, and for those of us Euro-Americans who are heterosexual, from gay and lesbian activists and writers.[9] I hope that this work will motivate a similar engagement with these, and other, traditions.

This particular view of social ethics and public policy emerges from an engagement with an African American critique of white ethical and political systems. From the perspective of this critique, it is clear that our military system, for example, is as much product of goodness as it is evil, as much a consequence of responsibility as it is of irresponsibility. Analyzing the forces that drive militarism leads us to a critique of what counts as goodness, what counts as responsible action in our culture. Likewise, the resort to military force is as much a product of goodness as it is of evil, as much a consequence of responsibility as it is of irresponsibility. Analyzing the forces that sustain a military economy and drive the use of military action leads us to a similar critique. Militarism is as much a fruit of what Western civilization regards as its best as it is of its worst.

This recognition leads to a peculiar mode of attributing blame and calling for change. When confronted with social evil, many people assert their good intentions, resist feeling guilty, and claim that they are actually decent people. My argument is that such good intentions are beside the point, for well-intentioned people are responsible for militarism. To point to that responsibility is not to deny anyone's goodness, anyone's fair intentions. The problem is deeper and more complex than a simple manifestation of either ignorance or malevolence. Our culture's definition of goodness will lead us again and again to the possibility of genocide and to the threat of war. What is required to prevent war, and to address other deep-seated forms of injustice, is a reversion of values. This involves taking one's desire to be moral as the motive for a thorough examination of the deadly consequences of particular values and reformulating what we mean by "responsible action" in light of the consequences of our culture's definitions of virtue.

The problem is that what counts as "responsible action" for the Euro-American middle class is predicated on an intrinsically immoral balance of power. We assume that to be responsible means that one can ensure that the aim of one's action will be carried out. This understanding of responsible action leads to a striking paralysis of will when faced with complex problems. It seems natural to many people, when faced with a problem too big to be solved alone or within the foreseeable future, simply to do nothing. If one cannot do everything to solve the problem of world hunger, for example, one does nothing and even argues against partial remedies as foolhardy and deluded.

While the forces leading to war have often seemed insurmountable, it is necessary for continued resistance to remember that there are alternative sets of values, alternative understandings of power. In my work with African American women and men, and through reading the literature of African American women and men, I find a fundamental challenge to the presuppositions of Western ethical theories. Much feminist and liberal ethical theory, by contrast, is concerned with the justification of the ends of moral action. Diane Meyers and Eva Kittay, for example, describe alternative constructions of the aim of moral reasoning, the morality of rights or the morality of care and responsibility:

> The morality of rights and formal reasoning is the one familiar to us from the liberal tradition of [John Locke], [Immanuel] Kant, and, most recently, [John] Rawls. It posits an autonomous moral agent who discovers and applies a set of fundamental rules through the use of universal and abstract reason. The morality of care and responsibility is an alternative set of moral concerns that [Carol] Gilligan believes she has encountered in her investigation of women's moral decision-making. Here, the central preoccupation is a responsiveness to others that dictates providing care, preventing harm, and maintaining relationships.[10]

In this book, I emphasize neither "rights" nor "care" as the basis of moral reasoning. Rather, from this exercise in communicative ethics, we gain a redefinition of virtue, of responsible action, that offers a challenge to both an ethic of rights and an ethic of care. Any ethical system can become coercive and self-deluding. The check to "caring" manipulation or control and the check to a justice that brackets the conditions of actual life is the same: accountability to others, an openness to critique and insight from other perspectives.[11] I am challenged by African American women and men to criticize the understandings of responsible action that distort the implementation of communally-accepted norms. This work complements, therefore, both variants of moral theory. After an understanding of rights or responsibilities has been reached, what thwarts sustained work to attain those ends?

As Beverly W. Harrison reminds us, liberation ethics requires pursuing many questions in addition to those of identifying norms for moral action:

Because liberation ethics assesses moral norms within a broader sociohistorical analytic frame, we are clear, as many contemporary moral philosophers are not, that identifying norms is only one dimension of moral reasoning. The perennial moral dilemmas that beset all human socio-ethical action are not resolved by narrow normative analyses. Identifying normative principles and weighing means in terms of their consistency with one's moral ends are elements in a liberation ethical process, not the whole of it.[12]

A liberation ethical process also includes a careful examination of what enables moral action and sustains political activism.

I describe an existing ethic of resistance, highlighting definitions of responsible action, in Part Two of this work. At the heart of this system of morality lies a different calculus of risk and an ethic of risk. Though it often seems to be mere powerlessness to those accustomed to the overweening power that we usually take to be constitutive of responsible action, the ethic of risk is actually an attempt to exercise and create another sort of power. The ethic of risk also has its theological correlate, a theology of divine immanence, that reinforces the ethic of risk and the passion for justice. I explore elements of this theology in chapter 8.

MILITARISM AND THE ETHIC OF CONTROL

In reading womanist literature and works by African American men, and in working with African American activists, we can encounter a foundational critique of white middle-class moral ideals and practices. These critiques reach to the heart of what sustains racism; these critiques also point to the cultural ideals and practices that vitiate our search for just means of responding to, and preventing, brutality and war.

Many Americans hoped that the end of the Cold War would bring a substantial "peace dividend," the investment of federal funds in domestic needs instead of nuclear and conventional weapons. While there was a measure of governmental support for economic conversion in the early 1990s, it had been rendered irrelevant by 1999 with the political pressure for increased military spending.[13] What happened to the peace dividend? Jonathan Feldman, Gregory Bischak, Lloyd Dumas, Fred Rose, and others have analyzed the many obstacles to implementing economic conversion: the inertia of defense planning, the use of military spending as a jobs program, the difficulty of converting from production for the U.S. Department of Defense to the different requirements of civilian production.[14] None of these barriers was insurmountable (Jonathan Feldman gives a thorough analysis of successful conversion), but the will to take on such challenges faltered in light of pressures to respond militarily to a host of new security threats.[15]

There have been many humanitarian crises in the past decade. Barbara Crossette gives a stark depiction of a few of the forms of brutality that compel outrage and the desire to act creatively and decisively:

> Around the world the crises pile up, and a collage of headlines does not make a pretty picture. In Kosovo, babies die of cold on hillsides where mothers have fled to save their lives. In Sierra Leone, madmen posing as a rebel army cut off the hands of teen-aged boys and trap families in their homes to torch them. Angolans shoot down relief planes. A defiant Saddam Hussein watches the United Nations drift helplessly without a policy. Haiti spirals back into chaos. And the chief judge of an international tribunal is stopped cold at Serbia's border when she tries to investigate crimes against humanity in Kosovo.
> Who's in charge here?[16]

To many people in the United States, it seems that force, and therefore more military spending, is the only effective response to brutality. John Hillen, for example, writing in *Foreign Affairs*, notes that "the most striking feature of this years' defense budget debate [1999] was that there was none."[17] Hillen is critical of "President Clinton's proposed $112 billion increase in military spending over the next six years" not because this increase is excessive but because it is not well-designed. Hillen argues that more spending is necessary. But rather than it's being designated for building weapons for "the wars [that the Army, Navy, and Air Force] would like to fight," Hillen believes we need spending that addresses the military forces required in new forms of conflict, "conflicts such as Somalia, Haiti, Bosnia and Kosovo [that] will be the order of the day."[18]

Who's in charge here? Hillen's answer: the United States, but ineffectually. Hillen claims that "in order to buttress an American foreign policy that is growing more imperial by the day, the Pentagon will need significantly increased defense spending—but the process must be fixed so that national security needs, not budgetary inertia, lead the way."[19]

Should America's foreign policy grow even more imperial? What alternatives do we have?

Some national-security experts decry America's concerns with international human rights. Edward Luttwak, for example, criticizes American support for military intervention simply because people are horrified by reports of torture, rape, mass killings, and forced dislocation of thousands of people in civil wars. "Today cease-fires and armistices are imposed on lesser powers by multilateral agreement—not to avoid great-power competition but for essentially disinterested and indeed frivolous motives, such as television audiences' revulsion at harrowing scenes of war."[20] Luttwack argues that these interventions prevent a lasting resolution of internal conflicts, a resolution only possible through war.[21]

Like Luttwak, Michael Hirsh doubts that humanitarian motives should be a cause for war. He analyzes the reasons for these recent violations of human rights, arguing that they are grounded, perversely, in the success of the American ideas of "Wilsonian idealism (democracy, international law, self-determination) and Friedmanian economics (open markets). . . . American ideas, having triumphed and then saturated the globe every bit as much as McDonald's hamburgers and Disney cartoons, have run amuck."[22] As Hirsh says, "Wilson's message of hope and principle has metastasized beyond Washington's control and helps explain why discontented ethnic and religious groups around the world, from the Kosovars to the Kurds, yearn quixotically for their own statehood. And why none of them, much to Washington's consternation, will give up the fight."[23]

Demands for independence are likely to increase, and with them, threats of internal violence and international instability. According to Hirsh, this leads the United States to value the maintenance of a stable status quo out of fear of the instability that accompanies demands for more democratic institutions and self-determination.

> The United States has become a nation of, by, and for the status quo. Washington simply does not want more devolution into statehood, and it wishes the idea of self-determination, as a motivating force , would quietly go away. The reason is obvious: There are some 5,000 ethnic groups in the world, and only 185

members of the U.N.; if all these groups went the way of the Kosovo Liberation Army, the wars would never stop. But in opposing such movements, we leave an odor of hypocrisy in our wake. All of which helps explain why it has proved so difficult to construct a coherent post-Cold War "vision."[24]

Given the instability caused by the success of American ideals, Hirsh raises the possibility of withdrawal from involvement in the affairs of other nations altogether. "One is tempted to conclude that it may be time for America the crusader state— historian Walter McDougall's term—to hang up its lance. It's become far too dangerous out there."[25]

Many other Americans acknowledge the dangers "out there," yet embrace the challenges of responding to them. Hirsh quotes Secretary of State Madeline Albright, for example, who is undaunted by the complexity of the challenges of fighting the undesired results of the success of our ideals. "Albright, when I asked her about the blowback problem, retorted that she'd rather be fighting our own ideas than fascism and tyranny."[26]

Like Albright, Joseph Nye Jr. argues that we should respond to the brutality of intrastate conflict. He concurs with William Perry and Ashton Carter that there are three types of legitimate threats to U.S. security:

> At the top of their new hierarchy they put "A list" threats like that the Soviet Union once presented to our survival. The "B list" features imminent threats to U.S. interests—but not to our survival—such as North Korea or Iraq. The "C list" includes important contingencies that indirectly affect U.S. security but do not directly threaten U.S. interests. . . . What is striking is how the 'C list' [Kosovo, Bosnia, Somalia, Rwanda, and Haiti] has come to dominate today's foreign policy agenda.[27]

Unlike those who decry our concern with humanitarian conflicts, Nye laments rather the shallowness of this concern, noting that it is often "a mile wide and an inch deep."[28] Similarly, David Rief, writing of the "precarious triumph of human rights," also warns of a further danger. "Human solidarity is a real fact of the world, but so is compassion fatigue, particularly in an era when press coverage of events is episodic, fickle and often trivializing."[29]

Given the shallowness of much humanitarian concern, Nye wonders if our commitment is deep enough to sustain involvement when success is not easily attained:

> Of course, acting on humanitarian values is appropriate. . . . But apparently simple cases like Somalia can turn out to be extremely difficult to resolve, and others, like Kosovo, are difficult from the start. . . . One of the direct effects of the Somalia disaster was America's failure (along with other countries) to support and reinforce the United Nations peacekeeping force in Rwanda that could have limited a true genocide in 1994.[30]

For now, many people throughout the world are revolted by the human and ecological costs of war and the revival of genocide. How, though, do we respond to further incidents of ethnic cleansing, to the brutal violations of the rights of women by the Taliban in Afghanistan, to the violation of human rights by the Chinese government? Is force the only option? As Nye states, "Polls show that the American people are neither isolationist nor eager to serve as the world's police. But finding a middle course is proving difficult and complex."[31]

Peace activists also deal with this dilemma. Michael Lerner describes the situation cogently. "Under almost every possible circumstance we at *Tikkun* have a predisposition to oppose armed force and to seek negotiations. But when we see acts of mass murder and genocide, the expulsion of hundreds of thousands of people from their homes, and acts of brutality and rape, we feel impelled to act."[32]

Many peace activists find ourselves in a dilemma: we are opposed to war because of its dire costs, yet there are victims in Bosnia, Rwanda, and Kosovo who need support and help. What can we do that is both just and effective? Noam Chomsky's answer is as clear and unambiguous in principle as it is unrealistic in practice.

> A standard argument for the bombing is that we had to do something: we could not simply stand by as the atrocities continued. That is never true. One choice, always, is to follow the Hippocratic principle: "First, do no harm." If you can think of no way to adhere to that elementary principle, then do nothing. There are always ways that can be considered. Diplomacy and negotiations are never at an end.[33]

The purity and absoluteness of this guideline to "do no harm" is a recipe for illusion and paralysis. Doing nothing *does harm*: our neutrality helps the oppressors more than the victims of oppression. Furthermore, any action has risks and unforeseen consequences. The results of diplomatic negotiations may involve cooperation with unjust parties; diplomacy and negotiations can also be used as a cover, a delaying tactic to give the semblance of involvement while people are being killed. Cynthia Enloe describes the problem clearly:

> People of very good will can often find themselves supporting things they feel are quite horrifying. You may not normally be in favor of military solutions, but you get stuck. For instance, I sometimes just go silent, because I'm horrified by events in Kosovo, but I can't think of what to do about them. . . . And it's that kind of silence that's often taken for popular support of a militarized solution. I should have been paying more attention in 1995, '96, and '97, when there were nonmilitary possibilities. I shouldn't let myself get to the point where I imagine there are only two possible stances: being passive in the face of Milosevic's injustices or supporting the NATO bombing.[34]

How can we avoid this dilemma? Enloe is right: in a military economy and with a diplomacy backed by military force, it is all too easy to wait to act until military action is the only possible effective response. How do we intervene earlier? What would those interventions be? What is a third way—a way that is neither isolationist nor interventionist? To move to nonmilitary responses to humanitarian crises requires a reordering of our economic systems and a revaluation of values—not moving from a military economy to a peace economy but from militarism to a culture and economy based on diplomacy, not war. This move requires a redefinition of responsible action, no longer ensuring the fulfillment of certain aims but setting in place a set of conditions for justice, flexibility, and responsiveness.

How do we know what to do, and what counts as "doing something" in response to injustice? The problem is intrinsic to our culture's concept of responsible action. Our understanding of "doing" (the expectation of certain results and of definitive responses) is dangerous in itself. The assumption of "doing something," which means controlling events and receiving a quick and predictable response, is both part of the problem and also prevents its resolution. It is difficult for us to imagine effective alternative responses to humanitarian crises because, as a culture, we are shaped by an ethic of control—the assumption that effective action is unambiguous, unilateral, and decisive.

Our current military system is predicated on a set of beliefs about the legitimacy and efficacy of military power. Seymour Melman describes the "master beliefs" that sustain a militarized national security policy, society, and economy:

> First, more armed forces mean more power, and military power can be made indefinitely large. (Accordingly, disarmament would spell powerlessness.) The second of these master beliefs is that "defense spending" boosts the economy. (Therefore, reducing military budgets would mean economic decline.) The third belief is that the war-making institutions provide protection against an evil, alien enemy. (Therefore, reversing the arms race means becoming vulnerable to pillage, enslavement.) . . . Subordinate to the master beliefs are a series of associated propositions. . . . The United States is intrinsically, morally good and the USSR morally evil.[35]

What would an alternative set of assumptions be? First, brutality will emerge again and again in human history. It will emerge in our own society and in other societies. This is in sharp contrast to Amitai Etzioni's arguments for a peace economy: he supported the conversion from war to peace but, in so doing, derided those who fear the irruption of new security threats: "And hired intellectuals produce rationales to justify continued high levels of military commitments in peace time: 'Who knows what the future will bring?' they write, 'You can never be too careful,' etc., ad nauseum."[36]

We cannot know what the future will bring. As Vojtech Mastny writes, "Although military threats to Europe have receded (happily), they have not disappeared. If the recent past is any indication, new ones will appear in unexpected forms. The alliance has not been good at anticipating such threats."[37] It is likely that humans will continue to seek to oppress each other. To think otherwise is to deny not only the events of the last century but also the events of our own history as a nation—our "ethnic cleansing" of American Indians and the enslavement of millions of African people.

Let us assume, therefore, that the tendency toward domination and brutality will remain in ourselves and in other nations. If so, the goal of "lasting peace" is illusory. This takes us far from Michael Glenna's evocation of human longing: "Ever since Athens founded the Delian League in 478 B.C. . . . humanity has striven to establish a structure for truly lasting peace, before conflict erupts—not after."[38]

Let us reframe this goal: Conflicts that endanger peace, that endanger justice, will occur. How can we establish and maintain institutions that do not presume to prevent such conflicts but rather respond to political disputes *before* they erupt into armed struggle? Our goal is not ensuring a "lasting peace" nor preventing all conflicts within or between nations. As a second assumption, then, let us adopt the goal of Global Action to Prevent War, an international coalition of peacemaking groups: not the abolition of war but putting in place institutions and processes that will make war "rare" rather than a daily occurrence.

> Global Action to Prevent War addresses the global problem of organized violence. The world also faces fundamental crises of poverty, human rights violations, environmental destruction, and discrimination based on race, gender, ethnicity, and religion. To meet these challenges, many efforts must be pursued: No single campaign can deal effectively with all of them—but efforts to address such global problems can and should complement and support one another. The Global Action program focuses on violent expressions of conflict, which obstruct efforts to get at the roots of conflict. Specifically, the program increases early warning and early action, such as mediation, to prevent the escalation of disputes into armed violence; it minimizes the mistrust fueled by arms races and offensive military strategies; it guards against genocide; and it builds commitment to the rule of law and the peaceful resolution of conflicts.[39]

To establish such structures, we need diplomatic institutions that are as well-funded and well integrated into our culture as the military system is now. We need a culture of diplomacy and institutions of nonviolent, diplomatic intervention. Hundreds of organizations, governmental and nongovernmental, are devoted to research and implementing nonviolent conflict resolution and peacemaking. What would it take to coordinate these efforts, as groups like Global Action are trying to do? What would it take to give these institutions the political clout, cultural power, and financial resources now held by the military?

Surely we can do more than carve out separate spaces for warring parties, to paraphrase Deborah Sontag. She writes of the end of utopian visions of multiethnic harmony in the Balkans, Northern Ireland, and the Middle East:

> There is a cold-blooded quality to the resolution of ethnic and territorial conflicts in today's world. Rosy visions of multi-ethnic harmony, often imposed by outsiders, have turned steely.... There does seem to be a change in the air, a new pragmatism that sees the hopeful dream of peace with harmony as naive, even as an obstacle to ending conflicts. Perhaps it is a kind of battle fatigue with peacemaking, too; conflicting peoples would just as soon carve out a conflict-free zone and be done with it.[40]

What else can be done? We need as much study of the strategies of conflict resolution as we have now of strategies for fighting war. What enables governmental leaders to reach an agreement? What enables their peoples to accept these agreements, supporting peace accords, rather than feeling betrayed by them? What are the stages and conditions in learning to coexist and share power? These issues are addressed now in research institutes, in departments of political science, in law schools that focus on mediation. Much is being done, yet more time and resources can be invested in nonviolent conflict resolution and in war prevention.

The third alternative assumption is that all of the participants in a conflict are flawed. There is no simple division between good and evil. While there may be at the moment considerably more violence by one party than another, all parties involved will face the threat of succumbing to revenge. Moreover, all are threatened with the delusion of confusing self-interests with moral purity or the good of the whole. Peacekeeping forces themselves, for example, need to be monitored and stopped from committing atrocities.[41]

Although alternatives to military power do exist, these forms of power can also be misused. In imagining effective responses to injustice in other countries, Nye addresses the "peculiar nature of American power" today. He argues that we have two sorts of power, what he calls "hard power" (a country's economic and military ability to buy and coerce) and "soft power" (the ability to attract through cultural and ideological appeal).[42]

Michael Howard has noted the "peculiarly American" use of 'soft' as a pejorative description of nonmilitary power.[43] Cynthia Enloe, Jill Stean, and many other feminist critics have analyzed the dangerously misleading gender connotations of this divide.[44] Let's avoid the slide into simplistic gender dualisms and refer to these two forms of power as what they are—coercion through military and economic power and the attraction of cultural power.

Nye himself describes the limits of coercive power and highlights the efficacy of cultural power:

> It is important that half a million foreign students want to study in the United States each year, that Europeans and Asians want to watch American films and TV, and that American liberties are attractive in many parts of the world. Our values are significant sources of soft power. Both hard and soft power remain vital, but in the information age soft power is becoming more compelling than ever before.[45]

Others have analyzed the global dominance of the United States. David A. Sanger, for example, describes America's "triple threat," power recognized by other nations, though unappreciated by many Americans: [46] "In the national self-image, America's pillars of global power—unparalleled financial clout, unmatched technological prowess and unchallenged military reach—are separate entities, bits of a far more fragile mosaic. Sure, times are good, but Americans don't *feel* particularly powerful now. . . ."[47]

Can we use the first two components of this power, "financial clout and technological prowess," effectively and responsibly? Can we use our cultural influence effectively and responsibly?

Before we move too quickly and uncritically to embrace cultural and economic power, however, we must remember two caveats: such power can be used to sustain an unjust social structure, and such power has its own costs and risks.

Let us examine the first caveat. Nye argues for stability as a level 'A' concern: "As a wealthy status quo power, the United States has an interest in maintaining international order."[48] But how can maintaining the status quo be a just goal in a world of gross inequalities in wealth and in access to goods for meeting basic human needs? Rather than decrying, as does Hirsh, the instability brought by these ideals or seeking stability uncritically, we can take Albright's challenge. The results of American cultural and economic power are intrinsically unpredictable and destabilizing: these are our problems now, just as fascism and tyranny were the challenges of earlier generations and other peoples.

There is a second caveat: nonmilitary expressions of power also have economic, ecological, and human costs. The ecological costs are clear: even if the world achieves a measure of peace through adoption of American consumer culture, can the ecosystem sustain such a depletion of natural resources? Also, what is the human loss in cultural diversity? Can our global linkages build on and incorporate more cultures than those of the United States? Furthermore, the use of economic and political sanctions can also have immense human costs, as is evident in the case of the sanctions against Iraq.[49]

These dangers do not mean that we should return to war. Nor do they mean that since we may do harm, we should do nothing. Rather, they propel us to a culture and economy of diplomacy and to an ethic of risk.

The fourth assumption is that change for the better, although not lasting, is possible. Citizens' groups have had a major role in moving the world toward more justice and toward the creation of institutions that can redress conflicts nonviolently. David Bernstein reminds us to "Consider recent events in which citizens' groups were major players: the defeat of apartheid in South Africa; the end of the dictatorship in Chile; the political transformation in the Philippines; the overthrow of Communist regimes in Central Europe; the creation of an international treaty prohibiting land mines; the establishment of an international criminal court."[50]

The current level of cooperation within some European countries can serve as a model for international relations. As Robert Hunter writes of the importance of NATO: "It . . . helps guarantee an achievement without precedent: the 15 nations of the [European Union] have abolished war as an instrument of relations with one another, and created what can be called a European Civil Space."[51]

Others have described this as an example of "security communities . . . groupings of states, tied together through common values and transnational links, that reject violent conflict resolution as unthinkable."[52] What makes such communities possible? Can they be formed even when there are substantial differences in values? We have much to learn about the creation and maintenance of such communities.[53]

Is such a leap—not only from military coercion to cultural, economic, and political power, but from the "moralism that justifies control" to an engagement with the world that accepts risk, ambiguity, and imperfection—possible?[54] How? Where do we get this vision of a culture based on diplomacy, not war? How do we work for such a vision? The ethic of risk and ambiguity does not have to be invented. It is clearly expressed in the lives and writings of many African Americans.[55]

THE ETHIC OF RISK

An alternative ethical, spiritual, and political vision can be found in womanist literature. The term *womanist* was coined by Alice Walker in 1983. This term has been embraced by scores of activists, theologians, and ethicists, and has accompanied a creative outpouring of artistic and scholarly work.[56] Katie G. Cannon argues that her goal as a womanist is scholarly—"to recast the very terms and terrain of religious scholarship"—and political:

> Each essay in this book is a challenge to systems of domination. Each contains an imperative for women and men of African ancestry to map out survival strategies in such a way that moral wisdom is communicated. Each is a call for action wherein the individual social-self as well as the larger collective community can break out of brutal cycles of misery and violence.[57]

Emilie Townes, a social ethicist, explores the power of womanist spirituality in her work in social ethics. Womanist spirituality, she says, "is the deep kneading of humanity and divinity into one breath, one hope, one vision. Womanist spirituality is not only way of living, it is a style of witness that seeks to cross the yawning chasm of hatreds and prejudices and oppressions into a deeper and richer love of God as we experience Jesus in our lives."[58] Like

Katie Cannon, Townes finds this spirituality in many sources. She sees it in the "moral wisdom of African American women" and finds it expressed in "autobiographies, speeches, novels, poems, sermons, testimonies, songs and oral histories."[59]

This moral tradition is found in the lives of many African American women and men. Garth Kasimu Baker-Fletcher, Peter J. Paris, James H. Cone, Dwight N. Hopkins and Anthony B. Pinn also explore the critical insights to be found in the lives of African American women and men.[60] Much of this ethical tradition is Christian, much is theistic, yet it is also expressed in what Pinn calls a "strong humanism." Pinn finds this strong humanism in some expressions of African American folk wisdom. In this tradition, "moral evil in the world is easily understood as the result of a misguided 'will to power' and nothing more."[61]

Unlike the theistic traditions analyzed and developed by most African American scholars of religion, the ethical wisdom that Pinn explores in this strand of African American culture works with the recognition that "there is no evidence of God's existence (no progress humans cannot easily take credit for and no suffering they are incapable of fostering)."[62] The response to oppression, though, is as complex and vital as that in the theistic strains of African American spirituality and ethics: "strong humanism seeks to combat oppression through radical human commitment to life and corresponding activity."[63]

In this ethical tradition, in both theistic and humanistic variants, we find a foundational critique of the white "will to power." We also find a creative vision of an alternative ethical system. Katie Cannon has developed a compelling critique of "dominant ethics," the ethics of Anglo-Protestant American society. She claims that "dominant ethics makes a virtue of qualities that lead to economic success—self-reliance, frugality, and industry. . . . Dominant ethics also assumes that a moral agent is to a considerable degree free and self-directing."[64] Cannon explores a moral wisdom created in the face of oppression—what are the possibilities of moral agency when one is not free?

In this struggle, we find not only an attempt to become free and successful (as defined by dominant ethics) but a redefinition of freedom, of success, and of responsible action.

This ethical tradition is refracted by racism in two ways: first, it emerges as a creative, communal response to individual acts of racism and to racist institutions. Second, it is not seen by many Euro-Americans because of racism. Emilie Townes raises this issue starkly; her focus is not just individual wrongdoing, but collective wrongdoing. As a womanist ethicist, she questions "the radical nature of oppression and devaluation of the self and the community in the context of structural evil."[65] Delores Williams, a womanist theologian, also highlights the continual presence of racism, and describes three "in-house strategies" to "retrieve and perpetuate the collective knowledge, wisdom and action Black people used as they tried to survive, to develop a productive quality of life and to be liberated from oppressive social, political, economic and legal systems."[66] In contrast to those who would maintain that racism no longer exists, these scholars and activists ground their work in resistance to the changing forms of racial injustice.[67]

The wisdom that emerges in resistance to racism is not an essential characteristic of all African Americans but a cultural and historical achievement of some communities and individuals in the face of oppression. This wisdom is not easily won, and this moral tradition can be lost. Delores Williams provides, therefore, specific strategies for how this tradition may be passed on in African American churches and communities.[68] Marcia Riggs and Garth Kasimu Baker-Fletcher analyze the loss of this tradition in the black middle class, and Emilie Townes addresses the varied forms of the loss of this spiritual heritage. Townes argues that the African American community is not immune to the loss of community and cooperation that shape much of American life.[69]

All of us are in this together; but some of us are *unaware* of an ethical heritage that can offer challenge and hope.[70] Cheryl Townsend Gilkes analyzes the way racism leads to this lack of awareness: "Embedded in a society whose material and symbolic dimensions are suffused with racism, African Americans are repeatedly dismissed as a people without a history and without defensible norms, values, customs, and traditions."[71] Gilkes states that we find in Alice Walker's fiction, for example, a "thick description of the social world of creative, resourceful and developing Black people [that] forms [a] subversive and critical ethnography."[72]

This literary, ethical, spiritual and philosophical tradition is compelling for two reasons: first, it offers a profound critique of the systemic and cultural distortions and costs of racism that whites need to hear and understand. Second, it provides narratives of engaged goodness: there are no heroic pretensions, no grand narratives of certain triumph but a life-affirming refusal to submit to cynicism, alienation, and despair.

The first reason is straightforward: there are differences in this tradition, new and challenging insights that people of my race and class need to hear. The second reason, though, has a different tone. These narratives, though startling in their critique of dominant power and ethics, are also as familiar as breath. This is the shape of "nonheroic goodness" that I have seen in my family, friends, and in parts of my communities. These are the textures of their moral and spiritual lives. These are not narratives of alienation, isolation, and suspicion but testimonies to the power of lives lived in connection and, from that connection, lives lived for justice, for beauty, for compassion. Karen Baker-Fletcher highlights the ethical power of this limited goodness in her analysis of Toni Morrison's novel *Beloved*:

> From Toni Morrison's writing I have learned the importance of honesty about human nature. There are no perfect people in her writing, no division of saints and sinners. There are simply people with both extraordinary traits and palpable flaws. . . . What is most important, it seems, is that we be ready to repent our tragic flaws and forgive them in others. . . . So, in *Beloved* an ordinary Ohio community is portrayed as rich in spirit and culture yet also flawed in its capacity for envy, ignorance and resentment. . . . It is important to consider disconnection from the earth and one another in a way that does not condemn or judge but that simply lifts up the reality of how tragic we can be. I write about our efforts and occasional successes at attaining justice not to exalt such events but to lift up our capacity for goodness. It is in such efforts and successes that I find hope. Morrison writes about tragic heroes. What her writings reveal for me is that we are all tragic heroes in a way.[73]

How do we learn from these stories that "lift up our capacity for goodness" and "lift up the reality of how tragic we can be?" This is the work of social ethics and of a redefined communicative ethics. Emilie Townes points out a key factor distorting the ethics of white Americans: comfortably embedded in the ethics and ethos of the dominant group, we do not have to hear the voices of others. If we remain in our own communities, doing social ethics only from within one set of socially shared values and behaviors, we do not see the partiality and immorality of those views and behaviors. Says Townes:

> Within each set of social relations in U.S. society and culture, there is an imbalance of power. Hegemony maintains this inequality and is seen as normal and right. Hegemony also works to keep the dominant group in power by promoting its own world view as neutral, universal, and moral. . . . In the oppression matrix in which the public/private realm split occurs, the structural and systemic character of the social inequalities must not be lost. . . . First, intent is not usually a factor. In other words, gender bias and discrimination is so integrated into our lives and our institutions that it becomes like breathing—present until we die. This grim reality means that it is easy for all of us to participate in oppressive practices and ideologies without consciously intending to do so.[74]

If we wish to break out of our self-justifying moral worlds, we must relinquish the justification of "intent." For the ethical issue here is precisely the disparity between intent and effect: we may well intend the good and yet perpetuate systems of injustice.

As we listen to other voices, we who are white can see the respect embodied therein, and learn to practice it ourselves. Townes describes womanist spirituality as one that respects the individual in the community. Drawing on Paule Marshall's novel *Praisesong for the Widow*, she describes the spirituality reflected in that novel: "Such spirituality tells us that each of us has worth, each of us has the right to have that worth recognized and respected, each of us has a right to be known for who we are. It holds us accountable to and with one another."[75]

Townes also calls all of us, people of color and whites, to accountability: "A key value we must regain is that of accountability. This means a respect-filled communal dialogue with a transclass base."[76] What does it mean, though, to be accountable? Aaron Thompson, sociologist and leader of diversity workshops, incorporates the practice of accountability into his diversity training work with police departments, faculty, students, and administrators. At the end of the workshop, the participants are told to keep a journal for a year, writing down *only their actions* in regard to issues of diversity and justice. This journal is not to focus on thoughts or feelings, but only on actions taken that reflect (or fail to reflect) their new understandings of justice for people of color, women, gays and lesbians, or people with disabilities.[77]

Accountability is not met by increasingly sophisticated analyses of structures of oppression. Accountability is not met by increasingly subtle and deep feelings of rage and/or sorrow because of injustice. *Accountability requires action*: the use of our power in concrete ways to implement the demands of justice. Thinking and feeling, no matter how profound and subtle, are not actions. They may *lead* to action, but in themselves they mean little. The actions that reflect accountability, are, of course, as varied and multiple as there are ways of being in the world: how we vote; where we give our money; how we make our money; what we say and do in relation to coworkers: whom we hire, whom we promote, whom we mentor; where we live; what public policies we support or oppose by demonstrating, writing, speaking out; what we teach our children, and more importantly, what we show our children about justice by how we use our time and resources.

If we open our eyes to this ethical tradition, what will we find? This is an ethic of celebration, a proud declaration that African American life cannot be reduced to victimization and oppression. Cheryl Kirk-Duggan describes the power of the blues "as signification, personification, and metaphor" in expressing "a celebratory, defiant survival."[78] As she puts it:

> The Blues enable Blues people to reckon with realities: life, death, sex, humor, sickness, transportation, movement, nature, suffering, humiliation, liberation and survival. Blues provide affirmation in the face of the absurdity of oppression. . . . Realism, irony, and humor allowed Blues people to critique religious hypocrisy or to offer parallel options.[79]

This is a literature, a tradition, that acknowledges in "communal lament" (Townes) the depth of injustice yet moves nonetheless to action and communal empowerment.[80] As Townes states, this is not a "success" ethic but an ethic grounded in the stories of those who did respond creatively to injustice:

> How often and in how many places have our ancestors gone before us and found a similar set of challenges? How did they respond? . . . This strength is not founded on certainty, but on trust and belief. Therefore this strength does not depend on a faith community or a faithful person "getting it right" or "being right." Rather its byword is faith. A spirituality of life that is social witness does not revolve around a success ethic that is

grounded in measurable gains and regrettable losses. Rather, it moves in the midst of degradation to proclaim the dignity of life. Such a strength measures its power in its ability to continually call forth hope and righteous agency.[81]

This hope does not deny the complexity of life and the difficulty of our choices. Rather we find here what Cheryl Townsend Gilkes finds in the writings of Alice Walker, "An engagement with the messiness of experience and the connectedness of that messiness to things that are also grand and glorious."[82]

These connections are not easily won, yet once found, they move us to a deep appreciation of life, history, the past, present, and future. Karen Baker-Fletcher writes of a this-worldly ethic, "a fullness of time in which past, present, and future are held together."[83] According to Townes, this ever-present Spirit calls us, not to sacrifice but to lives of empathy, love, responsibility, and accountability:

> As a moral virtue, empathy means that we put ourselves in the place of another. . . . We move away from "those people" and "they" language and behavior to "we" and "us" and "our" ways of living and believing. . . . This love, which is agapic and erotic, . . . is concerned for self and for others. It is a very interested love that questions self-sacrifice, self-denial, genocide, and other forms of annihilation that are often held, by our cultures, as greater goods or necessary evils. . . . We live our lives from the inside outward in such a manner that we begin to take on a deep responsibility for ourselves and a sense of accountability to others.[84]

Townes invites all of us, "peoples of color and white, male and female, young and old, to carry out a communal lament."[85] She also challenges all of us to live out our hopes, the "hope birthed from lament." This hope knows loss and vulnerability, yet loss and despair do not have the last word:

> But there is something about hope, when it is grounded in the divine, that is solid enough to sustain our lives and overcome skepticism and doubt. . . . We are led into a life of risk . . . hope leads us into an exodus that crosses and transcends human-made boundaries. When we truly believe in this hope, it will order and shape our lives in ways that are not always predictable, not always safe, rarely conventional. With hope, we do not give up, for we answer life *with* life. [86]

This hope also drives us to protest the costs of racism, sexism, and militarism. It moves us to seek new structures of power, new ways of meeting the threat of genocide and civil war. This ethic challenges us to live creatively with the disjunction between the clarity of our moral imperatives (justice, peace, equality) and the ambiguity of our efforts to implement those ideals in our economic and educational systems and in a foreign policy focused on diplomacy and cultural power rather than military force.

This ethic takes us far from the comfortable prayer of Reinhold Niebuhr: "God grant me the courage to change what I can, the serenity to accept what I cannot change, and the wisdom to know the difference." The drive of moral life is that we can never know the difference between that which we can change and that which we cannot. Our challenge is to move creatively in a very different sort of adventure, one whose prayer is more like this: "What improbable task, with which unpredictable results, shall we undertake today?" In trading an ethic of control for an ethic of risk, and in living out this ethos, we can neither undo the past nor control the future. But we can learn from the past, and we can live creatively, responsibly, and compassionately in the present.

2

Narratives of Healing and Transformation

———— ■ ————

Resistance movements in the United States have an uneven history. Times of great progress are rare, while significant setbacks are frequent. Much work has been done in analyzing patterns of social change, attempting to find causes of the surges of popular resistance that produced changes in labor and civil rights legislation, welfare increases, an end to the Vietnam War, and recognition of women's rights.[1]

While the international peace movement played a large role in the end of the Cold War, it was not successful in mobilizing wide-spread popular support for a peace dividend. Like many others who have worked for social change, activists in the peace movement have found it difficult to switch from political opposition to building alternative institutions. How do we reshape a militarized economy? How do we create institutions for non-military responses to political conflict? How do we redefine our cultural values, moving away from a glorification of heroic action as righteous violence against enemies to alternative visions of creativity and courage?

Similar challenges face South Africa and the countries of Eastern Europe: how do we sustain work for social justice in the face of partial victories and continued obstacles to social transformation? Once one form of government is overthrown, how do we actually create new economic, cultural, and political systems? How do we sustain political will and vision, not just for one campaign, but for generations?

THE DESPAIR OF
THE MIDDLE CLASS

The dilemma facing middle-class activists is worthy of special attention—the temptation of cynicism and despair once revolutionary fervor or youthful idealism is shaken by the intransigence of systems of oppression. It was easy, for example, for many Euro-American middle-class women to work for women's rights when our rage was new and our excitement at finding others who shared that rage and a vision of a new way of being was fresh. The women's movement now faces the problem of continuing when our rage is no longer new yet ever increases, when our vision is both more concrete and is still far from being actualized.

The feminist vision is more concrete because we have embodied it in our communities of women—in our collectives and caucuses and in women's newspapers, businesses, and health centers. With concreteness have come further challenges. We realize more fully the costs and difficulties of trying to live in ways that do not perpetuate systems of domination and exclusion. The feminist vision is also far from widespread actualization. Women are still oppressed throughout the world, and there is even evidence of a backlash of violence against women in the number of rapes and murders of women and the increasing violence against women depicted in mainstream pornography.[2]

It is often difficult to continue to work in the face of these problems. Different configurations of political and personal problems raise the temptation of despair. Former activists can become more concerned with immediate gratification and personal achievement than with social change. The liberal press—for example, the *Boston Globe* and the *New Republic*—reflects a popular mood of seasoned cynicism, well aware of the problems facing all of us, but also aware of the faults and limitations of attempts to address those problems. The immensity of the dilemma has destroyed hope. For not only is there awareness of the complexity and scale of social problems and the limitations of attempts to resolve them, an awareness essential for radical change, but this complexity has resulted in a failure of nerve.[3]

It is this failure of nerve—the inability to persist in resistance when problems are seen in their full magnitude that is of critical significance. The danger in the type of unending critique offered by many liberals and leftists is that critique itself will issue in only enervation and loss of will rather than serve as the foundation for more solidly critical work or for more sophisticated programs of education and resistance.

This inability to persist in resistance does not appear to be a universal problem, however. The temptation to cynicism and despair when problems are seen as intransigent is a temptation that takes a particular form for the middle class. This does not mean that those who are poor or working class are not damaged by or susceptible to despair. That obviously is not the case. But the despair of the affluent, the despair of the middle class has a particular tone: it is a despair cushioned by privilege and grounded in privilege. It is easier to give up on long-term social change when one is comfortable in the present—when it is possible to have challenging work, excellent health care and housing, and access to the fine arts. When the good life is present or within reach, it is tempting to despair of its ever being in reach for others and resort merely to enjoying it for oneself and one's family.

The cultured despair of the middle class is ideological: it masks the bad faith of abandoning social justice work for others when one is already the beneficiary of partial social change. It masks the ideological definition of moral action that leads to despair when easy solutions cannot be found. Becoming so easily discouraged is the privilege of those accustomed to too much power, accustomed to having needs met without negotiation and work, accustomed to having a political and economic system that responds to their needs.

It is not easy to recognize this class bias. The Marxist and revisionist Marxist analysis that would make these points clear is not common in the United States, not often taught in public schools, and not even common among most college students. Few middle-class activists are aware of the economic and political factors constitutive of our experience.

TESTIMONIES OF WISDOM

Far from reducing my dilemma, and much of that of the middle class, to a simple matter of growing into a "mature realism," in which one gives up on the hope of extensive social change, I wish to address the power of inadequate and dangerous models of maturity. To the extent that we still cling to the ideal of omnipotence—of a sovereign god or an all-wise, always successful father—we are trapped in our own role as oppressors, expecting a level of ease in action impossible in an interdependent world.

The problem is grave, but there are ways out. One such avenue is exemplified in the women's movement, as we have become, only through long struggle, a movement more inclusive of the pain and wisdom of women of all races and classes. It has not been easy for

Euro-American middle-class women to hear the concerns of women of color, of women who are poor or working class. Yet, to the extent that this has happened, the movement has become richer, deeper, and wiser. Euro-American women have much to learn from women of color. We can learn from and with each other while still remembering that we cannot speak for other women. I cannot speak for African-American women or offer a definitive interpretation of the moral tradition expressed in their lives and in their writing; I speak, rather, as a Euro-American and middle-class woman who has been deeply moved by the wisdom of black women. I find in my political and academic work with African-American women resources that bring healing and hope. I find in many of their lives, and reflected in their writings, a moral wisdom that I wish to study and to emulate, a tradition of strength and persistence that is one of the richest heritages of humankind. I speak of what I have learned from this heritage—the challenge it offers to me as a middle-class Euro-American woman and the hope that it brings as well. Working with African-American women has brought glimpses of the moral wisdom and strength that we all need in order to respond with honesty and persistence to the grave threats facing humankind.

This moral wisdom may be seen with special force through five novels. The first, Paule Marshall's *The Chosen Place, The Timeless People,* explores the various requirements for social transformation, focusing on the need for past and present evils to be seen and acknowledged by oppressors before long-lasting change can occur. The second is *The Bluest Eye* by Toni Morrison. The third and fourth novels are written for children, Mildred Taylor's *Roll of Thunder, Hear My Cry* and *Let The Circle Be Unbroken.* Taylor's novels express a moral wisdom in the unflinching recognition of the extent of social evil and in determined resistance to that evil, that I find challenging as an adult. The last novel, *The Salt-Eaters* by Toni Cade Bambara, examines the difficulty and opportunities of community-based work for social change in the current situation.

My interpretation of this ethical tradition is a response to the groundbreaking work of Katie G. Cannon. Cannon is an ethicist who describes "the moral wisdom found in the black women's literary tradition."[4] This literary tradition cannot be reduced to a few themes or a small number of literary styles. It is diverse, and the differences are as significant as the commonalities. Many African-American women and men have explored the diversity of this writing and the lives and experiences it reflects.[5] One literary critic finds the following commonalities in a collection of writings edited by Mary Helen Washington: "In each, we hear a black woman *testifying* about what the twin scourges of sexism and racism, merged into one oppressive entity, actually *do* to a human being, how the combination confines the imagination, puzzles the will and delimits free choice."[6] Washington names as well the forms of resistance reflected in the writing of black women:

> There are no women in this tradition hibernating in dark holes contemplating their invisibility; there are no women dismembering the bodies or crushing the skulls of either women or men; and few, if any, women in the literature of black women succeed in heroic quests without the support of other women or men in their communities.[7]

Although the themes of this literature are as diverse as the lives of its authors, the theme I address is not unrepresentative. Barbara Christian writes of "a persistent and major theme throughout Afro-American women's literature—our attempts to define and express our totality rather than being defined by others."[8] This common task is given particular shape by the social, political, and economic restrictions experienced by African-American women:

> But for Afro-American women, this natural desire has been powerfully opposed, repressed, distorted by this society's restrictions. For in defining ourselves, Afro-American women writers have necessarily had to confront the interaction between restrictions of racism, sexism, and class that characterize our existence, whatever our individual personalities, backgrounds, talents. Our words, in different shadings, call into question the pervasive mythology of democracy, justice, and freedom that America projects itself to be.[9]

African-American writers provide sharp critiques of the structures and costs of injustice and celebrate "the ability of human beings to transcend themselves, to actively change their condition."[10] Denunciations of evil and celebrations of resistance characterize the work of all the novelists examined here. One of Paule Marshall's reviewers, for example, John McCluskey, Jr., claims that her work embodies a "flexible and supple analysis" of suffering and resistance:

> It is just as harmful, of course, to restrict the description of the Black experience to unrelieved suffering, or, at the other extreme, to the continual miracle of collective triumph. It is both, and more. The art and the experience both deserve a more flexible and supple analysis which does not shy away from contradictions or seemingly eccentric social experiences or, further, from those areas where loyalties and betrayals blur.[11]

Paule Marshall states that "two themes [are] basic to her work: the encounter with the past and the need to reverse the present social order."[12] She describes the power and pain of the past and the struggle of black people to embrace this past in a way that leads to healing and transcendence. Eugenia Collier describes the way Marshall's concern with a healing embrace of the past is addressed in her novel *Praisesong for the Widow:*

> It [*Praisesong for the Widow*] links the Black individual with Black people worldwide, showing a vast multitude of people sharing a common past and, by necessity, a common future, in which the individual is made whole only by awareness and acceptance of this massive community. Here is the closing of the circle, the healing of the centuries-old hurt.[13]

Toni Cade Bambara's fiction explores a factor that enables and sustains transcendence: the ability of African-Americans to resist the multiple oppressions that cripple human life. Her work is carefully nuanced, acknowledging the defeats and costly victories of her people. She describes the tensions motivating her work:

> I despair at our failure to wrest power from those who have it and abuse it; our reluctance to reclaim our old powers lying dormant with neglect; our hesitancy to create new power in areas where it never before existed, and I'm euphoric because everything in our history, our spirit, our daily genius—suggests we do it.[14]

Bambara names the "givens" from which she works: the recognition that African-Americans "are at war"; the belief that "the natural response to oppression, ignorance, evil, and mystification is wide-awake resistance"; the belief that "the natural response to stress and crisis is not breakdown and capitulation, but transformation and renewal."[15] She says that her work is part of this natural resistance and renewal; her writing is a way of "participat[ing] in the empowerment of the community that names me."[16] Grounded in a community of resistance, Bambara writes stories of renewal and transformation:

> Stories are important. They keep us alive. In the ships, in the camps, in the quarters, fields, prisons, on the road, on the run, underground, under siege, in the throes, on the verge—the storyteller snatches us back from the edge to hear the next chapter. In which we are the subjects. We, the hero of the tales. Our lives preserved. How it was, how it be. Passing it along in the relay. That is what I work to do: to produce stories that save our lives.[17]

These stories, written "to save our lives," offer salvation and healing to Euro-Americans as well. Not written for us, but indicting us and our power, they offer the insight we need to stop our collective self-destruction, the abuse of power that threatens all life. In this literature I find an incisive portrayal of our Euro-American past, a past whose damage can be healed only as it is forthrightly confronted. While the critique of Euro-American power delineates the structures to be transformed, the transcendence of African-Americans—the rich heritage of empowerment, resistance, and renewal—offers models of how Euro-Americans who resist oppression can find courage to face the long struggle for justice.

In this account of the wisdom and strength of African-American women and men, I am self-consciously running the risk of romanticizing and simplifying a complex history. bell hooks and Mary Helen Washington warn of this danger, the tendency to see only the endurance and not the costs borne by black women.[18] Romanticism can be mitigated by remembering that the wisdom I extol was not attained easily or without cost. And, although there are moments of transcendence, oppression has destroyed the lives of millions of black women and men. It would be naive to ignore the immense costs of slavery, poverty, and discrimination.

From those courageously facing and struggling against an oppression they have not yet fully overcome, we can learn how we, too, can join the struggle against racism and persist in our work against other structural problems, problems that have as little chance of being easily overcome as does racism. This moral tradition exacerbates our understanding of the complexity of militarism and illuminates a heritage of imaginative resistance. Some black writers point to the connections between the threat of war and racism. Toni Cade Bambara and Paule Marshall indict white society for its dangerous attempts to control other nations and other people, its attempts to subsume the labor of others for its ends—an attempt that is justified by racism, and its attempts to subsume other nations to its purposes—an attempt that leads to the use of military force.

Although this literature enhances our sense of the complexity of the problems facing humankind, the overall tone is one of defiance, or, as Toni Cade Bambara puts it, "sheer holy boldness."[19] These writers express an ethic of risk, a definition of responsible action within the limits of bounded power. They describe the nature of responsible action when control is impossible and name the resources that evoke persistent defiance and resistance in the face of repeated defeats.

In this moral tradition action begins where much middle-class thought stops. The horizon of action is recognition that we cannot imagine how we will win. Acknowledgment of the immensity of the challenge is a given. There are no national and international programs, no particular strategies that can convincingly guarantee that the many forces and structures of exploitation can be stopped.

Such a situation calls for an ethic of risk, an ethic that begins with the recognition that we cannot guarantee decisive changes in the near future or even in our lifetime. The ethic of risk is propelled by the equally vital recognition that to stop resisting, even when success is unimaginable, is to die. The death that accompanies acquiescence to overwhelming problems is multidimensional: the threat of physical death, the death of the imagination, the death of the ability to care.[20]

Euro-Americans can draw a lesson from the writing of African-American women. Those who are oppressed have not all been defeated. Many African-American women and men manifest strength of character, insight, and analysis that we must learn from as we work against oppression. As we, too, resist the evil of racism, seeing its connections with other forms of structural oppression, we need to learn that failure to develop the strength to remain angry, in order to continually love and therefore to resist, is to die. The death we face is not as immediate as that faced by many African-Americans. The Euro-American who gives up the struggle against war or against racism does not face physical death. But the death that is experienced by those who turn from rage, who forgo resistance, is nonetheless real. It is the death of the imagination, the death of caring, the death of the ability to love. For if we cease resisting, we lose the ability to imagine a world that is any different than that of the present; we lose the ability to imagine strategies of resistance and ways of sustaining each other in the long struggle for justice. We lose the ability to care, to love life in all its forms. We cannot numb our pain at the degradation of life without numbing our joy at its abundance.

The ethic of risk is characterized by three elements, each of which is essential to maintain resistance in the face of overwhelming odds: a redefinition of responsible action, grounding in community, and strategic risk-taking. Responsible action does not mean the certain achievement of desired ends but the creation of a matrix in which further actions are possible, the creation of the conditions of possibility for desired changes.

Toni Cade Bambara, for example, writes in *The Salt-Eaters* of the value of combining political education with a study of African spiritual wisdom, finding in this combination the foundation for action that is aware of its likely impact within given political and economic structures and empowered by a spiritual tradition, a covenant with life, a commitment to respect and protect the forces of nature. She also writes of the possible long-term import of partial successes. A momentary gain, such as the creation of a school or clinic where the dignity of each person is no longer destroyed by racism, offers a concrete model of what is sought on a larger scale. Such achievements enlarge the imagination, offering glimpses of an equitable social structure. Momentary gains may encourage others to take the risk of developing their own strategies for resistance. Bambara writes of "sporting power" for others, freeing them to find their own power and exercise it in ways that cannot yet be imagined, specified, or predicted.[21]

Responsible action as the creation of a matrix for further resistance is sustained and enabled by participation in an extensive community. African-American women write of the power resident in communities that provide a haven offering support in struggle and constitute the context for a struggle that spans generations. Alice Walker describes the power of such communities in her poem "In These Dissenting Times":

> To acknowledge our ancestors means
> we are aware that we did not make
> ourselves, that the line stretches
> all the way back, perhaps, to God; or
> to Gods. We remember them because it
> is an easy thing to forget: that we
> are not the first to suffer, rebel,
> fight, love and die. The grace with
> which we embrace life, in spite of
> the pain, the sorrows, is always a
> measure of what has gone before.[22]

This affiliation with past, present, and future generations is often fluid, expressed in family ties; in many, if not all, churches; in schools; and in friendships. The solidarity with those who work for justice in the present is enhanced by learning from those who have lived before and working for the ability of children and youth to continue the struggle in the future in new, unimaginable ways.

The wisdom of African-American women is also marked by strategic risk-taking. Martyrdom is not encouraged, yet the willingness to risk physical harm, and even death, is acknowledged as sometimes necessary. The measure of an action's worth is not, however, the willingness of someone to risk their life but the contribution such an action will make to the imagination and courage of the resisting community. Mildred Taylor depicts such risk-taking in the many decisions of the Logan family to defy the oppressive power of whites, thereby risking physical retaliation, without acting in a way that would ensure such retaliation (i.e., responding in kind by killing whites and destroying their property.)

The aims of an ethic of risk may appear modest, yet it offers the potential of sustained resistance against overwhelming odds. The aim is simple—given that we cannot guarantee an end to racism nor the prevention of all war, we can prevent our own capitulation to structural evil. We can participate in a long heritage of resistance, standing with those who have worked for change in the past. We can also take risks, trying to create the conditions that will evoke and sustain further resistance. We can help create the conditions necessary for peace and justice, realizing that the choices of others can only be influenced and responded to, never controlled. Even if we stop war in our lifetime, the challenge of preventing such destruction will also be faced by another generation. We cannot make their choices; we can only provide a heritage of persistence, imagination, and solidarity. As June Jordan has written:

> And for ourselves, the intrinsic
> "Purpose" is to reach, and to remember,
> and to declare our commitment to all
> the living, without deceit, and without
> fear, and without reservation. We do
> what we can. And by doing it, we keep
> ourselves trusting, which is to say,
> vulnerable, and more than that,
> what can anyone ask?[23]

3

Memory and Accountability

———— ■ ————

I have identified several elements of an ethic of control as it operates in our public life and values, and in the reigning assumptions behind our national security policy. It not only stands behind many of the large-scale societal problems that threaten our world but also behind the frustrations and despair of those who seek to redress those same problems.

Yet we who are middle class cannot easily move from an ethic of control to an ethic of risk. The transition from middle-class cultured despair and cynicism to joyful resistance requires painful lessons in memory and accountability, lessons richly illustrated in Paule Marshall's novel, *The Chosen Place, The Timeless People.*[1] These lessons, full of promise and uncompromising in their demands, pave the way into an ethic of risk.

Memory, accountability, and healing are inseparable in the work of Paule Marshall. She claims that "two themes [are] basic to her work: the encounter with the past and the need to reverse the present social order."[2] The complex relationship of memory and political, personal, and spiritual transformation is central in *The Chosen Place, The Timeless People* and in her recent novel *Praisesong for the Widow*. In *Praisesong for the Widow,* Marshall explores the connections between African-American and African and Caribbean peoples. In *The Chosen Place, The Timeless People,* she addresses Euro-Americans and Europeans as well. The work begins with a West African proverb:

> Once a great wrong has been done, it never dies. People speak the words of peace, but their hearts do not forgive. Generations perform ceremonies of reconciliation but there is no end.[3]

Paule Marshall calls those of us who are Euro-American and European to remember the great wrong done by our ancestors in colonialism and in the slave trade. She also calls us to accountability for the continuing legacy of that great wrong. Barbara Christian describes the political and spiritual challenge of Marshall's work.

> Whenever there are those wealthy enough to plan projects for those from whom their wealth is derived, we will find the same elements of arrogance and tenacity, obtuseness and revelation. What Marshall does is to analyze the contour of this relationship so we may perceive more intensely why a great wrong cannot be righted by goodwill, money, new ideas—by ceremonies of reconciliation.[4]

In my analysis of *The Chosen Place, The Timeless People,* I focus on only one aspect of this complex work, Marshall's indictment of Western constructions of virtue. I do not explore other equally central themes such as the complex interaction between Merle Kimbona, the "spokesperson for her people" and the community that sustains and impels her. I also leave unexplored the disturbing treatment of sexism and of gay and lesbian life in the novel.[5] These themes are examined by other critics of Marshall's work. My analysis complements the studies of Marshall by Barbara Christian and Eugenia Collier, explicitly addressing the ethical and political challenge Marshall's work poses to my own community.

LEGACY OF OPPRESSION

Marshall's novel tells the story of a struggle between liberal white reformers and the black people who resist their attempts to address superficial problems, leaving intact the sources of poverty and inequality—the imbalance of power between whites and blacks. Marshall's critique of Euro-American culture is wide-ranging, drawing connections between the exploitation of developing nations and the nuclear arms race.

Marshall describes the ongoing consequences of capitalism and the slave trade, consequences ranging from the persistence of a diet of salt cod (instituted as a part of the slave trade) to the continued physical degradation of the people who work as cane cutters on large plantations. Men and women are no longer legally slaves, but they are still bound to physically dangerous, poorly paid, brutal work on the land of a white Englishman.

Marshall extolls the wisdom of those who realize that change will not occur until whites recognize the evil done in the past and its ubiquitous legacy. The poison of racism and exploitation mars any attempts to end poverty among those who have been, and are still, its victims. Marshall challenges whites to look at themselves and the consequences of their abuse of power, not evading either the extensive damage it still causes nor their accountability for this suffering.

Marshall also offers the prospect of hope. Her work reflects a deep love of life and of people, a love that motivates resistance to merely cosmetic changes. The deep love within the black community punctures the complacency of whites and those who seek easy solutions, making uncomfortable those who want to change things without going through the necessary stages of repentance and conversion. While uncompromising in its call for repentance, the mood of the novel is also one of affirmation and celebration, a paean to the dignity of those who are not satisfied with partial answers, an indictment of white power yet a celebration of what is possible once evil is acknowledged and restitution made.

Marshall depicts the fundamental immorality of Euro-American ethics. She demonstrates three important aspects of the twist at the heart of Western concepts of virtue: the way too much power poisons virtue; the evil caused by whites refusing to see the consequences of their actions; and the passionate destruction by whites of anything that cannot be controlled. Marshall relates this destructive power to the slave trade, to the exploitation of modern capitalism, and to the development of nuclear weapons.

Marshall helps whites see that we do have the power to act alone and decisively. Yet such decisive action is intrinsically immoral. We do have the power to act alone to repress, to exploit, to blow up the world. We do not, however, have the power to make the world peaceful and just. That is a qualitatively different task and requires a qualitatively different exercise of power. Justice cannot be created for the poor by the rich, for it requires the transfer of power from the oppressors to the oppressed, the elimination of charity, and the enactment of justice.[2]

Marshall depicts the consequences of constructions of responsible action as acting alone. She names the seemingly innocuous assumptions of the powerful: that it is responsible to act for others, that one can be certain of one's moral intent and strategic and practical wisdom. These assumptions prevent powerful groups from seeing the destructive consequences of their well-intentioned projects.

Marshall not only names this distortion in Western ethics, she traces its origins to a fundamental disrespect for others, especially those who are the ostensible beneficiaries of one's help. The fundamental disrespect of the powerful for the marginalized is manifest in the assumption that the elite can solve the problems of others, an assumption that masks disdain for the capabilities and perceptions of the victims of oppression. Attempts to resolve basic social problems are also marred by the maintenance of social distance, an atomization in which change is sought without a redefinition of social roles and power relationships. Marshall depicts the tragic costs of an unwitting, unconscious atomism and an equally unconscious lack of respect for other people.

Marshall's novel centers around the efforts of people from the United States to design a development project for the poorest part of a Caribbean island. Bourne Island as a whole is poor, and yet there is one portion of it, Bournehills, that is even poorer than the rest. The people own only small plots of land, and they work for a large sugarcane plantation. There is a long history of failed development projects in Bournehills, and the resistance of the people of Bournehills to accept "modern" ways is a source of frustration to outside reformers and an embarrassment to the island's middle class. The development team consists of Saul, his wife Harriet Shippen, and his assistant Allan. Saul has been involved in anthropological research for decades and is a pioneer in the attempt to use the research gained in field work for the benefit of those studied. He plans an extensive study of Bournehills, wary of attempts to impose diagnoses, much less solutions, from the outside. The money funding the project is given by Harriet Shippen's family, a Philadelphia family whose fortunes originally were made in the slave trade. Harriet's fortune, now used for charity, was made from the suffering she now seeks to relieve. The source of this money and the meaning of its use in Bournehills is, significantly, unacknowledged by Harriet. In fact, Harriet actively denies the significance of this legacy. The protagonist of the novel is Merle Kimbona, a woman committed to Bournehills, to the memory of exploitation, and to change that not only redresses wrongs but eliminates the power imbalance that originally caused them. She is the host for the research team during their stay in Bournehills.

The people of Bournehills teach an invaluable lesson to both whites and blacks, to oppressors and oppressed: unless evil is acknowledged, unless the imbalance of power that causes exploitation is addressed, further change is impossible. The land, the sea, and the people of Bournehills all voice unremitting sorrow—a sorrow that cannot be forgotten or erased by time or good intentions. Even the sea speaks of the evil of slavery, of the millions of deaths in the passage from Africa to the United States and the Caribbean, and of the horror of the conditions that awaited those who survived the brutal passage:

> It was the Atlantic this side of the island, a wild-eyed, marauding sea the color of slate, deep, full of dangerous currents, lined with row upon row of barrier reefs, and with a sound like that of the combined voices of the drowned raised in a loud unceasing lament—all those, the nine million and more it is said, who in their enforced exile, their Diaspora, had gone down between this point and the homeland lying out of sight to the east. This sea mourned them. Aggrieved, outraged, unappeased, it hurled itself upon each of the reefs in turn and then upon the single beach, sending up the spume in an angry froth which the wind took and drove in like smoke over the land. Great boulders that had roared down from Westminster centuries ago stood scattered in the surf; these, sculpted into fantastical shapes by the wind and water, might have been gravestones placed there to commemorate those millions of the drowned. (106)

The sea expresses the unappeased sorrow that marks the dignity of the people of Bournehills. They continue to mourn the unredressed evil of the past and the similar evils of the present. They are the current victims of the same exploitation, the same forced labor. The means of servitude have changed, financial bondage now replaces the chains of slavery, yet the bondage and degradation are real and ever present. Most of the land is still owned by a single white man, and the people of Bournehills are forced to work for him, risking their lives and their health to produce and maintain the wealth first derived from the slave labor of their ancestors.

Marshall describes the physical brutality of the work of cutting cane, a brutality exacerbated by the fact that it is work for someone else. The profits will go to another, and the workers will remain poorly compensated, as dependent as ever. It is this combination of physical threat and economic servitude that makes the work so bitter. Marshall describes the researcher's, Saul's, perception of a cane worker, his work, and its devastation:

> And still Stinger pressed the assault. . . . But although his pace did not slacken, Saul saw him undergo as the noon hour passed a transformation that left him shaken and set in motion his own collapse. For one, Stinger's essentially slight, small-built body, which was further reduced by the canes towering above him, appeared to be gradually shrinking, becoming smaller and painfully bent, old. By early afternoon all that was left of him it appeared were the shriveled bones and muscles within the drawn sac of skin and the one arm flailing away with a mind and will of its own. . . . But most telling of all was that the low private grunt of triumph which Stinger uttered whenever he sent one of the cane plants toppling had ceased and the only sound issuing from him was a labored wheeze which came in short desperate gasps—and which, in the klieg-light intensity of the afternoon sun, called to mind a winded wrestler being slowly borne down in defeat by an opponent who had proved his superior. (162)

The people of Bournehills bear witness to the continued brutality of oppression, its physical and psychological degradation. They bear its brunt, and they resist development schemes that merely mask the continued power differential that produces such oppression.

The people of Bournehills maintain a unique perspective—a clear recognition of the lack of fundamental change in ostensible schemes for change. Merle Kimbona embodies this wisdom and sharply attacks the plan of the middle-class blacks on the island to attract outside capital by allowing development without the developers paying local taxes, without even reinvesting the money made in the island. She correctly names this as another form of slavery, only this time the people are giving themselves away.

Lyle, an affluent lawyer, describes the plan to concentrate on small industry and tourism. He rejects Saul's alternative plan for development—land reform and a drive to attain self-sufficiency in agriculture. While agreeing that land reform should be studied, Lyle maintains that the plan now in operation is better:

> . . . the tax-free period for new businesses was being extended from five to fifteen years, and all customs duties for them were also being waived for the same period. In addition, the Bourne Island government was planning to build at its own expense a huge industrial park, so that when an investor arrived he would find a plant awaiting him—and this for only the most nominal rent. ("How much? Give us a figure," Merle said in the dangerously still voice. "Oh, just a token amount, no more than ten or fifteen dollars a year." . . .) Finally, under the new plan, anyone from abroad setting up a business on Bourne Island would not only be allowed to send all of his profits out of the country, but could repatriate his capital in full should the business fail. (206–7)

Merle listens calmly to the plan and then quietly and clearly assesses the fundamental meaning of the whole scheme: "Signed, sealed and delivered. The whole bloody place. And to the lowest bidder. Who says the auction block isn't still with us?" (209)

Lyle acknowledges the injustice of the scheme he has put in place but insists that nothing else is possible. He has given up on the idea of fundamental equality, of economic development that would benefit everyone on the island. While he identifies his diminished expectations with maturity, deriding what he calls Merle's "bogus youthful idealism" (211), she names the luxury and comfort that allows him to forget about fundamental change. She names the ideological despair of the middle class, the luxury of cynicism about extensive change common to those who are already the beneficiaries of partial change. Lyle attempts to silence her, and Merle then responds fiercely:

". . . But hear me, all your big ideals are quite out of order in the present discussion, as is your emotionalism—which has always been your worst fault, and I see that I shall have to remind you as I did the doctor of the realities of our situation. . . ." "The reality, blast you"— her cry jarred the air and caused the lamplight within its enclosure of glass to waver—"is that you and others like you have got yours: the big house, the motorcars, the fat jobs, the lot, and it's to hell with the other fellow. You don't even see him. Do you realize that? . . . Instead of us pulling together when we need each other so much, it's every man for his damn self. That's the reality—and the tragedy of us on this island. (211–12)

Merle names the dis-ease, the guilt, of the politically aware middle class: the awareness of the redistribution of power required for social change, yet the fear of risking what privilege has been gained personally (the affluence of middle-class life) to work for economic and social justice for all. She names that bad faith and its personal and social costs: the cost to the individual of the loss of dignity, the derision of the desire for change and the derision of even the ability to imagine a better world as "bogus youthful idealism." Merle sees the death of the imagination and the death of compassion that characterize the lives of people like Lyle. She also sees the social and political costs of such capitulation, schemes that perpetuate the economic and social dynamics of slavery. White people are enriched at the expense of the exploited labor of black people. Unless this disparity in power and the divisions among black people are recognized, slavery is only masked, not eliminated.

THE TWIST IN WESTERN
CONSTRUCTIONS OF VIRTUE

Marshall explores the dangerous oblivion of liberal whites to the nature of their exploitation of black people. Since the exploitation of the past is not acknowledged, whites are bound to repeat it in the present. There is no repentance for slavery and therefore no possibility of conversion. Conversion means turning away from sin. Such turning away requires seeing the sin, knowing what constitutes it, and knowing what creates its power. Without understanding the mechanisms of sin and its hold on themselves, conversion, the turn away from exploitative habits of action and thought, is impossible.

Oblivion to the evil of the past mars the entire development project. Although the money funding the research was initially made in the slave trade, this connection is not acknowledged by either the governing board of the foundation or by Harriet Shippen. Harriet is the heir to "a questionable legacy" that she fiercely denies. Harriet refuses to talk about her family with her husband Saul, denying her difference from other families because of the foundation of her fortune in the slave trade. While she asserts that her family is no different than other families, she is also aware of the difference, denying that she should be held accountable for her family's actions. In that denial, she manifests her awareness of the exploitation that was intrinsic to the history of the family business:

> "But what's there to say about them?" she cried with the laugh. "They're no better or worse than most people's families, I suppose. . . ."
> Then, with a sudden despairing cry that seemed less directed at Saul than at some other presence, visible only to her, seated in silent judgment in the room, "Must I really be held liable for them?" she cried. "For all those Harbins and Shippens and what they did and didn't do. . . . Well, I refuse. They're too dull." She had recovered and was laughing again. (46–47)

Harriet is aware of a blot in her past, yet she refuses liability for the wrongs of her ancestors, assuming that she is unaffected by their legacy. She is unaware of the mechanism of oppression, the way solid citizens, people who love their families, men and women who are educated and well-mannered, can sell other human beings into slavery. She is unaware of the patterns of action and thought that lead people to become oppressors and of the structures of ethics and economics that mask this oppression from others and especially from themselves. Unaware of the complexity of this oppressive legacy, she is bound to repeat it. Harriet carries the same patterns of feeling, action, and thought; the same inability to hear the rage of others; the same inability to imagine that she could possibly be the agent of exploitation; and the same inability to see those who are oppressed as equal to her in dignity. Harriet is a creation of the legacy of oppression—blind to the voices of the oppressed, blind to her own capacity for evil, blind to the dignity of those who are the victims of her class. Harriet does not see that what are to her natural behaviors are in fact socially effective means of maintaining oppression. She does not realize that personal values and social mores have a political function and a political genesis.

Harriet's rejection of the anger of others is a strong case in point. Repeatedly in the novel, Marshall recounts Harriet's ability to stop listening to another as soon as she detects a note of anger in his or her voice. She is present when Saul and Merle criticize Lyle and the blatantly unfair "development scheme," yet she hears none of the debate, is oblivious to the discussion:

> Harriet, gazing thoughtfully down at her unfinished letter . . . might have heard none of what had transpired from her expression. And in a way she hadn't. Because the moment Merle's voice had struck the first angry note, a door in her mind had automatically slammed shut, closing out the sound. (214)

Marshall depicts in the character of Harriet one of the most effective defense mechanisms of the upper class and of all those in power: an inability to tolerate the rage of those they have oppressed and an inability to hear what is being expressed through that rage—the fact that they have violated something deep and valuable, the dignity of another human being. The self-righteous rejection of rage as a legitimate form of expression is itself a perpetuation of the cause of the rage. It is a way of denying the dignity of the peoples they have violated. Those who are victimized by their oppressors are dismissed with contempt as being overly emotional, childish, or immature.

Harriet also embodies the certainty of rightness, of legitimate control and privilege (23). This upper-class certainty of her right to control others distorts her well-meaning attempts to respond to the needs of others. When Harriet sees the terrifying hunger of two children, she acts without respect for the children or their parents. Harriet visits the home of Stinger and Gwen, both of whom are away cutting cane. It is past five, and the children have had nothing to eat all day:

> . . . she could sense their hunger, almost see it. It was like something that had detached itself from their potbellied bodies and round quiet eyes, and assumed an awesome form all its own. And this creature (for that's what it seemed to be to her) had none of their silence and restraint, their resignation, but prowled angrily up and down, its footsteps shaking the weak floorboards, its fists pounding the walls, demanding to be appeased.
>
> It had even, it seemed, barred the door behind her as she entered, shutting her in with them. She was suddenly as trapped as the children amid the squalor and the smells of too many bodies crammed into too small a space; she was as much at the mercy of that palpable hunger as they were. And she would not gain her release, she knew, until she had in some way satisfied their mutual jailor. (175–76)

This moment of connection with the suffering of others is marred by Harriet's unwitting arrogance, her assumption of the universal validity of her mores. Seeing a half-dozen eggs, she ignores the resistance of the oldest child and breaks them, making an omelet. She leaves, convinced that despite their protests and lack of gratitude, she has acted responsibly. When Saul tells her what she has done—destroying the eggs that the family sold, one of their few sources of income, leading to the young girl being beaten for allowing her to do it—she is stunned, refusing to understand the way of life she has so cavalierly disregarded, not even imagining that her conception of helping might cause more harm than good.

> "If only you would stop and ask, Harriet, before taking things into your own hands! I'm sure it never even occurred to you to find out if the eggs hadn't been left there for a reason. I don't know," he [Saul] said, slowly shaking his head, "there's this thing in you which makes you want to take over and manage everything and everybody on your own terms. It really worries me. And it's not to say you don't mean well most of the time, but it still makes for complications."
>
> "But they were hungry!" Her voice was sharp and emphatic; she had not permitted herself to hear what he had just said. "Besides, it doesn't make any sense to sell perfectly good, nourishing eggs to buy that awful rice they all eat."
>
> "It might not make sense to you," he said . . . "but it obviously does to Gwen. She's probably discovered she can feed more mouths doing it her way. . . . Everybody doesn't live by your standards. Your values aren't necessarily the world's. Why, the kids didn't even eat the goddamn omelet."
>
> "They didn't eat it?" And she was perhaps more stunned by this than anything else he had said. (180–81)

Harriet becomes increasingly a spectator of life in Bournehills, visiting the women and children, offering them fruit juices and minor first aid, but her attempts to relate and help are all marred by the legacy she unwittingly repeats. Unable to acknowledge the evil of this legacy, unable to ferret out its manifestations in herself, she continues to see the people of Bournehills as somehow different from herself. She interprets their failure to respond to her overtures as a mark of some inferiority in them and does not see this rejection as a challenge for her to rethink her responsibility toward them. In a letter to a family member at home she states that she has to remind Saul that "this place isn't home, after all, or these people, as likable as some of them are, the kind we would normally be associating with, and that once the project's over we'll be returning home to the life and people we know" (235). Harriet is the creation of oppression, a person whose very concept of morality is poisoned by the legacy of oppression, unable to see the oppression that has been the work of whites and unable to accept the seriousness of its damage.

Despite the persistent pressures to remember the past and the opportunity to act in a way redemptive of herself and of those oppressed by her family's greed, Harriet resists, refusing the change that she knows is required. Her response is first isolation, then the destruction of the project. She has her husband, Saul, recalled. Harriet cavalierly destroys the chances of a solid development program in Bournehills, acting to save her own certain identity. Rather than face the challenge of forging a new identity in light of the legacy of oppression, she ends the project.

Harriet's action is a repetition of the evils intrinsic to an imbalance of power and intrinsic to the failure of whites to regard blacks as equal to themselves. The directors of the center easily accede to her request, not realizing its impact on the people of Bournehills. Like Harriet, they embody a disconnected exercise of power, seeking the fulfillment of their aims without an awareness of the consequences of those actions in the lives of others (445).

Saul quickly discovers that Harriet is behind the destruction of the project. He tries to communicate to her a sense of the "terrible thing" she has done to the people of Bournehills. He names the nature of the power that she carries and indicts the power of the white upper classes:

> "*What is it with you and your kind, anyway?*" The question, hurled at her across the intervening space, jarred the room and everything in it, but had no effect on her. "If you can't have things your way, if you can't run the show there's to be no show, is that it?" His voice shook and the face thrust her way across the desk was quivering. "You'd prefer to see everything, including yourselves, come down in ruin rather than 'take down,' rather than not have everything your way, is that it . . . ?" (454)

Although Saul waits for an answer, he knows there will be none. Harriet is unable to see the significance of the lives she has damaged, and knows she would act in the same way again. Saul leaves. The relationship is over. During the long night, Harriet becomes aware of the evil of the power that is her legacy. She remembers the ancestors who "trafficked in moldy flour and human flesh"; she remembers the talk between her father and uncles of "money and mergers and manipulating the market"; she recalls her mother's racism, a woman "whose tone when speaking to the maid Alberta had casually assumed her to be a lesser person" (457–58). She also remembers her first husband, Andrew, the nuclear physicist she divorced, leaving him because she realized that his work in developing nuclear weapons was fundamentally opposed to life, that it poisoned him, and that it poisoned her. She dreams "once again of her hand on top of his on the lever and together the two of them, perversely, as if driven by an excess of power, committing the monstrous act that could only bring about their own end" (458).

The admission of the truth of her life "aged her" (459). After seeing the evil that is her legacy and unable to imagine an alternative, Harriet commits suicide. Her physical death is a culmination of the death of compassion, the death of connection, hope, and imagination that could have sustained her. Unable to connect with those her class has wronged, she is unable to respect their wisdom and courage. Seeing her time with them as an anomaly, thus perpetuating the fundamental lack of connection and lack of respect that is the correlate of oppression, she misses the chance of conversion and the opportunity to learn from the wisdom of those who have confronted genocide and who now resist such annihilation.

Marshall names a crucial bar to conversion—the equation of change with loss. Harriet senses that there is a reason behind "the failure of Gwen, the children and everyone else in the village whom she sought to help, to respond in even the slightest way to her efforts" (408). She realizes that they think that "she was not doing enough and, in their refusal to respond, were holding out for some greater effort on her part. . ." (408). She refuses the request, refuses the task of discerning what those changes might be. Harriet understands change only in terms of loss. She exemplifies the upper-class person so identified with privilege that it has become his or her sole identity. Without privilege, she fears that she would cease to exist. She sees becoming other only as loss, blind to the opportunities for being human in a way that does not require domination:

> *What was it they wanted?* She could not have said. But it was too much, of that she was certain. She could not give it, whatever it was, without being herself deprived, diminished; and worse, without undergoing a profound transformation in which she would be called upon to relinquish some high place she had always occupied and to become other than she had always been.
>
> She would never agree to this; and so, in the face of what she felt to be their unreasonable demand, for the sake of her own self-preservation, her sanity, she had turned from Bournehills, slipping into an indifference which made everything going on around her . . . seem remote, unimportant. . . . (408)

Harriet chooses the death of compassion over a life of challenge and work. The death of compassion follows the death of the imagination. She is unable to envision meeting the people of Bournehills wholly as herself, acknowledging her family's legacy and accepting accountability for the suffering of the people of Bournehills, acknowledging her own accountability for its perpetuation. Unable to imagine change without loss, Harriet withdraws from the people of Bournehills, ceases to care about them, and convinces herself that her life and theirs are fundamentally unrelated.

THE COMMUNAL MATRIX
OF ACCOUNTABILITY

Marshall does more than indict Western constructions of responsible action; she describes the type of communal action that can lead to long-lasting, fundamental social change. At the heart of this alternative ethic is a deep sense of community. This communal ethos is expressed in many ways, one of the most notable, and frustrating to outsiders, is the rejection of development schemes that benefit only a portion of the community.

Saul is aware quite soon after his arrival in Bournehills that the reason for the failure of so many development projects is far from simple. He cites all the usual reasons for failure: "generally poor planning, the condescending attitude of the people in charge, the failure to include the villagers directly in the project from the beginning," yet he is convinced that something more is at work (157). He talks to one of the men in the town who adds another reason to those Saul has already discerned, speaking of an irrigation project that helped only a few of the farmers, not all. Delbert, the local shopkeeper, speaks of the affront this system posed to the people of Bournehills:

> "But there was nothing wrong with the irrigation pipes," Saul said. "They would have helped."
> "Is true," he conceded. "Although only a few of the small farmers got the pipes, which wasn't right. If you give one, you must give all. But as you say they would have helped those that had them. What to say, yes?" he shrugged. His aged massive shoulders were scarcely able to lift. "Maybe Bournehills people just want the old place to stay as is for some reason." (158)

The people of Bournehills embody another necessary ingredient of fundamental social change: they see the oppression of both past and present. They are continuously aware of the horrors of the past and the suffering of the present. They do not forget the soul- and body-destroying effects of exploitation.

In the character of Merle Kimbona we see an acknowledgment of the suffering of the people of the West Indies that is neither naive or sentimental. Merle bears the price of continuing to see the repeated forms that slavery takes. For her the cost is periods of depression and insanity. She realizes that she has "had to pay with my sanity for the right to speak my mind" (11). The responsibility of remembering the past and seeing the horrors of the present is not borne lightly.

Nor is it a responsibility borne alone. The people of Bournehills also carry the memory of slavery and acknowledge the horrors of the present, in spite of the resistance of the other people of Bourne Island. One of the vehicles for this memory is the recounting of a slave revolt. This revolt, led by Cuffee Ned, it discussed at night in the local pub and is the subject of the masque that the people of Bournehills perform every year at Carnival. Their reenactment of the revolt was applauded when first performed, but after several years of its repetition, others are beginning to grow weary of it. Their resistance to seeing the masque is grounded in resistance to remembering the slave past. Many people want to believe that slavery is no longer relevant, that it is no longer a structural factor in all their lives:

> The masque is the same every year, beginning with a silent march, an awesome sound—the measured tread of those countless feet in the dust and the loud report of the bracelets, a somber counterpoint to the gay carnival celebration. It conjured up in the bright afternoon sunshine dark alien images of legions marching bound together over a vast tract, iron fitted into dank stone walls, chains . . . rattling in the deep holds of ships, and . . . an exile bitter and irreversible. (282)

The people themselves seem broken, yet challenging, looking up all at once to "stare out at the crowd," their eyes regarding the people from the "vista of another time." It was a gaze that asked that the crowd "act in some bold, retributive way that would both rescue their memory and indemnify their suffering" (283). The challenge is too great. The crowd refuses to respond:

> "I can't look" . . . "they's too pitiful. Oh, God, what is it with them" . . . "Why must they come dragging into town every year in the same old rags, looking s'bad and embarrassing decent people with some old-time business everybody's done forgot. Who wants to see all that? What's the purpose behind it . . . ?" Then, angrily: "The shameless whelps! The disgraces! I tell you, I's hiding from them with tears in my eyes!" (283)

The attempts to hide fade as the masque moves into the next stage, the actual revolt. The white man, Byram, who owned all the land and people in Bournehills is taken prisoner, and a battle rages against government troops. The people sing of the struggle and capture of the white slave owner, the burning of his house and the hill on which he lived (Pyre Hill), and the shackling of him:

> to the great horizontal ox-driven wheel at Cane Vale's old windmill, which had been used in those days to power the roller when the wind failed. It was punishment Byram was known to have meted out regularly to those whom he had considered no more than oxen, and he had soon collapsed and died at the wheel as many of them had also. (286)

The people then sing "triumphantly," a song not only of this particular event but a song "of people like them everywhere," singing of "a struggle both necessary and inevitable" (286–87). They continue to sing of the three years that the people of Bournehills were able to live "free, at peace, dependent only on themselves" (287), celebrating as "their greatest achievement that they had worked together!" "They had been a People!" "They had trusted one another, had set aside their differences" (287). The voices then drop suddenly and sing of the defeat of Cuffee, killed by white government troops but content because "he had seen his life and deeds . . . pointing the way to what must be" (288).

The masque is continually repeated. By late afternoon the slave march and the revolt diminish until "the only thing retained was the soaring tribute in song and dance to Cuffee, his victory on the hills and life in Bournehills during his reign" (288). At that time all resistance ceases. Onlookers sing with the band, and whole troops come running down side streets to join them (289).

> With that the resistance of the crowd gave way, as it did every Carnival Tuesday when the Bournehills band reached its climax and in so doing seemed to lift the entire town onto its shoulders and take it marching with it. . . . . Even those who had cursed the marchers and declared they should be barred from town found themselves swaying as the Bournehills steelband passed and the music leaping off the surfaces of the drums to describe visible arabesques in the air entered them. (288–89)

Through the masque, the people of Bourne Island relive their past and remember what is required for freedom. They remember a time of overturning the power relations that still imprison them and experience again the joy that comes with freedom, the dignity and well-being, the delight of "being a people," of working together for justice. The Bournehills band, "swollen to almost twice its size by the newcomers" resembles "a river made turbulent by the spring thaw and rising rapidly— a river that if heed wasn't taken and provision made would soon burst the walls and levees built to contain it and rushing forth in one dark powerful wave bring everything in its path crashing down" (289–90).

The people of Bournehills are the bearers of a "dangerous memory"—the memory that it was a people of dignity and self-respect who were violated in slavery, and who are violated in the continued exploitation of capitalist development. And they bear the equally dangerous memory of victory, the three years after the revolt in which they lived as a people without the scourge of white oppression. They bear this memory and the sense that they are worth far more than their white oppressors realize. The people of Bournehills, in spite of the continued brutality of their oppression, remain strong enough to value each other. Valuing each other enough to denounce injustice, they remain alive to hope and to a vision of a world without exploitation.

The people of Bournehills bear a heritage of courage and wisdom, one that can heal the despair of whites who finally see the extent of injustice, one that offers a way to a life of deep satisfaction. The quality of life possible when the memory of suffering and the hope for justice are retained is far deeper than the easy happiness or physical contentment of the affluent. The type of satisfaction is not mere contentment, for it is a joy that carries as its correlate immense pain. Not everyone in the community of Bournehills can sustain this intensity, but the community serves as the matrix of its possibility, the foundation of a life of deep hope, anger, and love.

Marshall offers a vision of hope. She explores the possibility for change as blacks and whites both realize that retribution is required and power must be redistributed. Merle survives her bouts with insanity because of the support of the community. She is able to continue her work of speaking out, planning a run for office as the representative for Bournehills. Her hopes for what she can accomplish are modest, but she knows something can be done, if not all the injustice eradicated at once. She wants to be part of the conditions of possibility for justice, one voice representing people who demand justice (468–69).

Saul is able to imagine a change in his work as well. He has allowed himself to face the consequences of his actions as a scholar. He recognizes the fundamental injustice of development schemes, the failure to redistribute power and wealth, and decides, therefore, to forego such work. He chooses to focus on changing conditions within his own country and training social scientists to do work in their countries, certain that outsiders can never do the work that needs to be done. He imagines his role as aiding the redistribution of knowledge, and thus power, to people so that they can engage in their own research and development plans.

As Saul and Merle make their plans, the people of Bournehills continue to bear witness, "serving in this way as a lasting testimony to all that had gone on then: . . . and as a reminder—painful but necessary—that it was not yet over, only the forms had changed, and the real work was still to be done; and finally, as a memorial . . . to the figures bound to the millwheel . . . and to each other in the packed, airless hold of the ship(s) . . ." (402). This memory can only be justified, can only be redeemed by an "act on the scale of Cuffee's"—a complete redistribution of power (402). Until that happens, Pyre Hill smolders—"the fire that Cuffee had started, which legend would have it had burned for five years, refusing to die. It would flare again, full strength, one day" (472).

Part Two
AN ETHIC OF RISK

■

4

A Heritage of Persistence, Imagination, and Solidarity

━━━━━━ ■ ━━━━━━

The constitutive elements of an ethic of risk come clearly into view in the writings of Toni Morrison and Mildred Taylor. These authors evoke both outrage at social justice and a passionate commitment to social change. Taylor motivates resistance through the story of a family and a community that maintain a socially disruptive dignity in the face of systematic oppression. Morrison challenges the reader through a story of a young girl and a community who have been defeated by racism. In Morrison's work resistance has been stifled, yet she evokes a response of resistance in the reader through the power of her writing. Her description of defeat is itself an expression of courage and risk-taking. As an author she manifests the deep love and outrage that enables resistance. And, as Barbara Christian states, Morrison dares her readers to also acknowledge the significance of all that has been destroyed by the "mythic, political and cultural mutilation of racism."[1]

THE BLUEST EYE

With an ethic of risk, action begins where much middle-class thought stops. Action begins in the face of overwhelming loss and the recognition of the irreparable damage of structural evil. Toni Morrison heralds the truth of this moral lesson as she portrays, passionately and vividly, the dignity of lives that are violated in her novel *The Bluest Eye*. This is a story of sheer pain, of victims of oppression further hurting other victims. There are no victories here, only the condition for later victories—seeing the lives that are violated as worthy of more than cruel neglect and callow exploitation. Her writing evokes horror, outrage, and a passion to end the racism that cruelly destroys the lives of so many people.

Morrison's wisdom and courage in the face of racism offer an escape from self-indulgent cynicism. Through her writing she grieves fundamental, overwhelming evil. Her unabashed grief and rage challenge anyone aware of the complex networks that constitute and sustain racism, ecological destruction, militarism, and sexism.

Within an ethic of risk, actions begin with the recognition that far too much has been lost and there are no clear means of restitution. The fundamental risk constitutive of this ethic is the decision to care and to act although there are no guarantees of success. Such action requires immense daring and enables deep joy. It is an ethos in sharp contrast to the ethos of cynicism that often accompanies a recognition of the depth and persistence of evil.

Morrison's vision of the evil of racism is bleak but never cynical. Her love for the lives ruined by racism is too deep for resignation; it motivates a fierce denunciation of the costs of racism. She describes the horizontal violence that often exists among the oppressed. In *The Bluest Eye,* she describes the self-hatred experienced by blacks in a society in which beauty and goodness are all defined by whites. Seen as ugly by the whites around them, the children in this novel learn to hate themselves and other black children, voicing their own self-disdain in their torment of a young girl, Pecola Breedlove:

> "Black e mo. Black e mo. Yadaddsleepsnekked. Black e mo black e mo ya dadd sleeps nekked. Black e mo. . . ." They had extemporized a verse made up of two insults about matters over which the victim had no control: the color of her skin and speculations on the sleeping habits of an adult, wildly fitting in its incoherence. That they themselves were black, or that their own father had similarly relaxed habits was irrelevant. It was their contempt for their own blackness that gave the first insult its teeth. They seemed to have taken all of their smoothly cultivated ignorance, their exquisitely learned self-hatred, their elaborately designed hopelessness and sucked it all up into a fiery cone of scorn that had burned for ages in the hollows of their minds—cooled—and spilled over lips of outrage, consuming whatever was in its path.[2]

The children's self-hatred emerges from a society in which they and the adults around them face lynching, beatings, and economic deprivation because of their race. They know the horrors of poverty, of being unable to find a job or a place to live. All too often families are forced out of their homes, having no place to go, no relatives to live with, no money to rent another apartment or house, no way of finding a job. Even the children are aware of this threat, what they call being put outdoors:

> If you are put out, you go somewhere else; if you are outdoors, there is no place to go. The distinction was subtle but final. Outdoors was the end of something, an irrevocable, physical fact, defining and complementing our metaphysical condition. Being a minority in both caste and class, we moved about anyway on the hem of life, struggling to consolidate our weaknesses and hang on, or to creep singly up into the major folds of the garment. Our peripheral existence, however, was something we had learned to deal with—probably because it was abstract. But the concreteness of being outdoors was another matter—like the difference between the concept of death and being, in fact, dead. Dead doesn't change, and outdoors is here to stay. (18)

Pecola Breedlove comes from a family that has been put outdoors. They have no place to go, no way to come back, no way to escape the poverty and misery that destroys their lives. The moments of joy they experience are quickly followed by oppression and humiliation. The moments of joy serve merely as a reminder of what has been lost: they are too fleeting and fragile to provide escape. Morrison recounts the lost potential of Pecola's parents—times when they were able to love each other and to love life. "Young, loving, and full of energy, they came to Lorain, Ohio. Cholly found work in the steel mills right away, and Pauline started keeping house" (92). And then the problems start. Pauline is abused by the white woman who employs her and then fires her, unable to understand Pauline's poverty and her dependence on Cholly. Cholly is both victim and victimizer, unable to understand how to be a father. He had been abandoned at birth by his mother and father and then raised by a "dying old woman who felt responsible for him" but who died, leaving him alone when he was thirteen. Never having a "stable connection" with others, he does not know how to have one with his children. He "reacts" to them, "his reactions . . . based on what he felt at the moment" (127).

Cholly's reaction to his daughter, Pecola, is to rape her. She becomes pregnant, and the infant dies soon after birth. Abused by the only possible sources of support in both family and community, Pecola becomes insane:

> The damage done was total. She spent her days, her tendril, sap-green days, walking up and down, up and down, her head jerking to the beat of a drummer so distant only she could hear. Elbows bent, hands on

shoulders, she flailed her arms like a bird in an eternal, grotesquely futile effort to fly. . . . We tried to see her without looking at her, and never, never went near. Not because she was absurd, or repulsive, or because we were frightened, but because we had failed her. (158)

Morrison indicts a racist society by depicting its human costs—the madness of a young girl impregnated by her victimized father. The soil of racism destroys the life that tries to grow there. Morrison expresses the moral wisdom that sees this destruction as tragic waste and refuses to accept it as inevitable or warranted.

This soil is bad for certain kinds of flowers. Certain seeds it will not nurture, certain fruit it will not bear, and when the land kills of its own volition, we acquiesce and say the victim had no right to live. We are wrong, of course, but it doesn't matter. It's too late. At least on the edge of my town, among the garbage and the sunflowers of my town, it's much, much, much too late. (160)

One of the most painful aspects of an ethic of risk is knowing in one's mind and in one's heart that "it's much, much, much too late," and continuing to mourn this loss, continuing to rage against the innumerable onslaughts against life. Inseparable from this grief and rage is a profound, wrenching, far-from-sentimental affirmation of the beauty and wonder of nature, of human life. Morrison's basic "yes" to life, her tribute to Pecola's "tendril, sap-green days," inevitably brings pain in a society so hostile, so destructive of life.

The ethic of risk offers a model of maturity that challenges the equation of maturity with resignation, with an acceptance of the improbability of fundamental social change. Within an ethic of risk, maturity means recognizing that ideals are far from realization and not easily won, that partial change occurs only through the hard work and persistent struggles of generations. Maturity entails the recognition that the language of "causes" and "issues" is profoundly misleading, conveying the notion that work for justice is somehow optional, something of a hobby or a short-term project, a mere tying up of loose ends in an otherwise satisfactory social system. Within an ethic of risk, maturity is gained through the recognition that evil is deep-seated, and that the barriers to fairness will not be removed easily by a single group or by a single generation. Maturity is the acceptance, not that life is unfair, but that the creation of fairness is the task of generations, that work for justice is not incidental to one's life but is an essential aspect of affirming the delight and wonder of being alive.

ROLL OF THUNDER,
HEAR MY CRY

Mildred Taylor conveys the wisdom of an ethic of risk in her children's novels. Here we learn that work for justice cannot be left to a few. Justice is not merely the province of professional activists, but a dimension of the lives of everyone in a particular community. Whatever the occupation—teacher, railroad construction worker, farmer, homemaker—work for justice is intrinsic to what it means to be fully engaged with life, fully responsive to the challenge and support of life in community.

Mildred Taylor's novels *Roll of Thunder, Hear My Cry* and *Let the Circle Be Unbroken* are written for children. She tells the story of a young girl, Cassie Logan, and Cassie's increasing maturity. The story is set in a Southern community during the Depression. In these novels Taylor depicts the courage of men and women who continued to struggle against the evil of racism when it was impossible for them to imagine even its partial eradication. She states that the intent of the novels is to remind us of the heritage of clear-sightedness, of dignity and resistance, that lays the foundation for the civil rights movement. Taylor writes of the "life-guides that have always been mine," and she hopes that recounting these in the story of the Logan family will help children of all colors to recognize the monumental achievement of the generations who struggled before the civil rights movement of the 1950s and 1960s. She hopes that we will learn from their wisdom, that we will understand and cherish the social and political changes they made possible. Taylor states that to "identify with the Logans, who are representative not only of my family but of many black families who faced adversity and survived, and understand the principles by which they lived" may make it possible for "children of today and of the future" to understand their potential strength and may make it possible for them to respect the courage and tenacity that has characterized the lives of those who work for justice.[3]

One of the most striking features of the Logan family is their deep joy: a profound affirmation of life expressed in their connections with, and delight in, family, nature, and the African-American community. She describes the happiness of the children's grandmother, Big Ma, "who enjoyed every season" (76). The children also are at home with nature and find comfort in the forest, feeling at home with the trees, listening to their songs, realizing that they are part of the forest. The central character of these novels, Cassie Logan, describes this belonging:

We grew quiet, and in our silence all the sounds of the day seemed louder. A bee zoomed past trumpeting its presence, and a dragonfly spun in rapid delight above our heads, then flew on in happy celebration. I shaded my eyes with my hands and looked out over the land. The forest, deep greens and shades of brown, the fields looking like a patchwork quilt of growing things, the house, the orchard, the meadowland, were as much a part of me as my arms, my legs, my head. (230)

The Logan family's joyful connection with the community is expressed in Mama's work, in Papa's organizing skills, and in their attempts to help each other survive. Mama is a teacher, and when fired from working at the school, she continues the work she loves by tutoring children after school. It is a work that sustains the dignity of the children and brings her deep satisfaction (76).

The Logans' joy is not superficial or sentimental. It is a mature, costly joy, sustained in a context of the continual threats of racism, threats to their dignity and threats to their very lives. Although the Logans own their own farm, they obtained it only through unusual means: it was sold to an ancestor during Reconstruction. While some of it is mortgage free, a significant part is not, and they face the continual efforts of the white man whose family once owned the farm to take the land from them. The story is set in the Depression, and the Logans, like other farmers, are finding it difficult to make a living. Papa is forced to spend most of the year away, working on the railroad, to earn enough money to pay the taxes and farm mortgage.

Mama is also threatened by the racism of whites. She is a teacher and finds in this work the opportunity to sustain the dignity of the children she instructs. This commitment to their dignity, however, costs her her job. She teaches her students a history different from that contained in her textbooks—a history of the evils of slavery and of the courage and strength of their ancestors—even when she is being observed by the whites who run the local schools. These men are angered by her defiance, and they fire her for teaching this version of history:

Mama seemed startled to see the men, but when Mr. Granger said, "Been hearing 'bout your teaching, Mary, so as members of the school board we thought we'd come by and learn something," she merely nodded and went on with her lesson. . . . Mama was in the middle of history and I knew that was bad. . . . But Mama did not flinch; she always started her history class the first thing in the morning when the students were most alert, and I knew that the hour was not yet up. To make matters worse, her lesson for the day was slavery. She spoke on the cruelty of it; of the rich economic cycle it generated as slaves produced the raw products for the factories of the North and Europe; how the country profited and grew from the free labor of a people still not free. Before she had finished, Mr. Granger picked up a student's book, flipped it open to the pasted-over front cover, and pursed his lips. . . . "I don't see all them things you're teaching in here."

"That's because they're not in there," Mama said.

"Well, if it ain't in here, then you got no right teaching it. This book's approved by the Board of Education and you're expected to teach what's in it."

"I can't do that."

"And why not?"

Mama, her back straight and her eyes fixed on the men, answered, "Because all that's in that book isn't true."

Mr. Granger stood. . . . "You must be some kind of smart, Mary. . . . In fact, . . . you're so smart I expect you'd best just forget about teaching altogether . . . then thataway you'll have plenty of time to write your own book."[4]

In addition to economic insecurity, the hatred and fear of white people leads to continual humiliation and threats of death. Simple trips to the nearest town to buy supplies and sell farm products become occasions of degradation. Degradation cannot be met by direct defiance, for this is a time in which the lynching and murder of black men by white men is not an idle threat. Cassie and her brothers are taken by their mother to see a man who had been burned by the white men who live near them.

"The Wallaces did that, children. They poured kerosene over Mr. Berry and his nephews and lit them afire. One of the nephews died, the other one is just like Mr. Berry." . . . "Everyone knows they did it, and the Wallaces even laugh about it, but nothing was ever done. They're bad people, the Wallaces. That's why I don't want you to ever go to their store again—for any reason. You understand?" We nodded, unable to speak as we thought of the disfigured man lying in the darkness. (12)

The Logans instill in their children a type of maturity that entails understanding racism without accepting it as inevitable. The children are given textbooks only after they have been used by white children for a decade. Mama pastes over the humiliating record contained in them. One of the other teachers disagrees with her, saying that the children need to learn to accept the way things are, that black people receive only the cast-offs of white society.

"Well, I just think you're spoiling those children, Mary. They've got to learn how things are sometime."

"Maybe so," said Mama, "but that doesn't mean they have to accept them . . . and maybe we don't either." (21–22)

This construction of maturity is repeated as the Logans and their community face the continued assaults to life and dignity by the white people around them. It is a way of living that provides courage and honesty in the face of the humiliation of inadequate school facilities and the danger of lynching. Papa repeats this wisdom as the children face the terrible realization that although their friend T. J. has been saved from being lynched, he is now in jail, and it is unlikely that a white jury will acquit him of the murder for which he has been framed. Papa helps them face the reality that T. J. will be killed by the whites, and he also sustains their solid conviction that such a verdict is fundamentally wrong.

> "Papa, could he . . . could he die?" asked Stacey, hardly breathing.
> Papa put a strong hand on each of us and watched us closely. "I ain't never lied to y'all, y'all know that."
> "Yessir."
> He waited, his eyes on us. "Well, I . . . I wish I could lie to y'all now."
> . . . "Oh, P-Papa—d'does it have to be?"
> Papa tilted my chin and gazed softly down at me. "All I can say, Cassie girl . . . is that it shouldn't be." (209–10)

The Logans do not have a sentimental or naive understanding of the challenges they face. Their resistance to racism cannot be called utopian or simplistic. They recognize the costs, the efforts entailed, and the necessity of continuing to work even when complete change is not in sight. They are not at all likely to downplay the evil of whites or the intransigence of racism. Their hope for change rests in an appreciation of the dignity of their lives, not in a sentimental hope that whites will easily change. They repeatedly teach the children to be wary of white people, recognizing that friendship with whites is not possible within a racist society. They respect the lawyer who works for them and the other blacks of the community, and they respect the risks he takes to defend T. J. from lynching and to defend him in his trial, but they realize that it is impossible to trust most whites, that they will easily turn from support of blacks to defending the interests of other white people. The Logans remind their children that a change in the structures of racism will not emerge spontaneously from the benevolence of white people.

RESPONSIBLE ACTION AND THE
COMMUNAL MATRIX OF RESISTANCE

The model of maturity central to an ethic of risk leads to a particular type of action, a construction of responsible action as the creation of a matrix of further resistance. The extent to which an action is an appropriate response to the needs of others is constituted as much by the possibilities it creates as by its immediate results. Responsible action does not mean one individual resolving the problems of others. It is, rather, participation in a communal work, laying the groundwork for the creative response of people in the present and in the future. Responsible action means changing what can be altered in the present even though a problem is not completely resolved. Responsible action provides partial resolutions and the inspiration and conditions for further partial resolutions by others. It is sustained and enabled by participation in a community of resistance.

Although the problems the Logans face are often overwhelming, their connection with nature and with those who have struggled for justice sustains them, and it is this connection that they offer their children. Taylor celebrates this heritage of love and resistance. The Logans are deeply connected with their children and, through the young people of the community, with a struggle for life and for justice that began before them and will continue after them. They know that although they cannot solve the problems of injustice now, they can provide a heritage of resistance.

This connection and commitment sustains the Logans as they attempt to work with others in the community for economic justice and self-respect by shopping at a store in another town, ceasing to trade with the Wallaces, the white men who not only cheat them but who set three black men on fire and flaunt their crime without being held accountable for it. Mr. Jamison, the white lawyer who works with them and agrees to help finance the boycott of the Wallaces, reminds Papa, David Logan, of the probable futility of this action. The resistance of white men in the community, men like the plantation owner Harlan Granger, will be strong. In response, David Logan voices his conviction that in acts of resistance it is as important that the connections be maintained, the heritage of courageous action conveyed, as it is that they completely succeed in the present. He works to support the strength of the children of the community, hoping that one day they will be able to do things their parents cannot.

Mr. Jamison speaks of the dangers of the boycott:

> . . . "you're pointing a finger right at the Wallaces with this boycott business. You're not only accusing them of murder, which in this case would be only a minor consideration because the man killed was black, but you're saying they should be punished for it. That they should be punished just as if they had killed a white man, and punishment of a white man for a wrong done to a black man would denote equality. Now *that* is what Harlan Granger absolutely will not

permit. . . . The sad thing is, you know in the end you can't beat him or the Wallaces."

Papa looked down at the boys and me awaiting his reply, then nodded slightly, as if he agreed. "Still," he said, "I want these children to know we tried, and what we can't do now, maybe one day they will." (124–25)

The type of responsible action celebrated by Mildred Taylor is an ethic of persistence and cooperation. The people whose wisdom she recounts know that action includes far more than merely getting what one wants. They convey a heritage of work for justice. Their work has both immediate and long-term goals: they work for as much change as is possible in the present and realize that an important part of that work is providing a matrix of love and respect that enables further resistance in the future. Although there is no guarantee that work for justice will continue, people can provide the groundwork without which further work would be impossible, the matrix of love and respect that enables others to continue the work for justice they have begun.

One of the basic requirements of further work for justice is the creation and maintenance of self-respect in the face of people and institutions who violate an individual's, a people's, sense of self-worth.

The Logans struggle to maintain their own self-respect and to nurture that of their children. They respect themselves and help their children face the frequent humiliations of racism with the firm conviction that such abuse is not warranted. *Roll of Thunder, Hear My Cry* begins with just such an incident: Mary Logan, Mama, supports the children in their refusal to accept the humiliation of receiving textbooks that are in poor condition. She understands her son's proud refusal to accept a book that has inscribed on the frontispiece the record of its use—from "new" when given to white children to eleven years old and ragged when given to black children. She refuses to punish her children for their resistance to accepting such books and even acts in resistance to this visible manifestation of the lack of respect whites have for blacks by pasting over the record of use in each of the books given to students in her classroom (17–22).

The effectiveness of the Logan's attempts to give their children self-respect is reflected throughout Taylor's novels. The children are obviously loved and have enough confidence in themselves and their value to be outraged by racism. This is demonstrated in Cassie's visit to the town of Strawberry. Taylor recounts Cassie's painful first trip with her grandmother to Strawberry and the humiliation she receives by seeing how black farmers are forced to stay at the far reaches of the farmers' market. She is also angered by having to wait in a store to place an order while the owner ignores her to serve whites. She also bumps into a white girl near her own age and is forced not only to apologize to her but to call her "Miss" (80–87). Cassie tells her mother and uncle about the day's events:

> "That ole Lillian Jean Simms made me so mad I could just spit. I admit that I bumped into her, but that was 'cause I was thinking 'bout that ole Mr. Barnett waiting on everybody else in his ole store 'fore he waited on us—" . . .
>
> "But I told him he shouldn't've been 'round there waiting on everybody else 'fore he got to us—" . . . Stacey made me leave and Mr. Barnett told me I couldn't come back no more and then I bumped into that confounded Lillian Jean and she tried to make me get off the sidewalk and then her daddy came along and he . . . twisted my arm and knocked me off the sidewalk!" . . .
>
> His [Uncle Hammer's] eyes had narrowed to thin, angry slits. He said: "He knocked you off the sidewalk, Cassie? A grown man knocked you off the sidewalk?" . . .
>
> Uncle Hammer grasped my shoulders. "What else he do to you?"
>
> "N-nothin'," I said, frightened by his eyes. "'Cepting he wanted me to apologize to Lillian Jean 'cause I wouldn't get in the road when she told me to." . . .
>
> . . . he stood slowly, . . . and he started toward the door. . . . Big Ma jumped up from her chair, . . . and dashed after him. She grabbed his arm. "Let it be, son!" she cried. "That child ain't hurt!"
>
> "Not hurt! You look into her eyes and tell me she ain't hurt!" (91–92)

Cassie learns much about the danger of racism. Not only is she humiliated by the Simmses, but she realizes that her Uncle's justifiable anger, if it leads to violent action, could cost him his life.

Mama's (Mary Logan's) response to Cassie's pain is thoughtful and supportive. She commends the dignity that led Cassie to challenge the insults of the whites yet teaches her the necessity of choosing how she resists that abuse. Mama tells Cassie that she had to leave the store and apologize to Lillian Jean and even call her Miss to make sure that Lillian Jean's father would not hurt her. She explains the roots of this particular incident in the history of racism and counsels a style of resistance that incorporates both the accommodation necessary to survival and the creative defiance that lays the groundwork for change in the future. Mary Logan's description of how to resist while avoiding being killed by whites is a lesson in maintaining self-respect—the foundation of further resistance:

> . . . "White people may demand our respect, but what we give them is not respect but fear. What we give to our own people is far more important because it's given freely. Now you may have to call Lillian Jean 'Miss' because the white people say so, but you'll also call our

own young ladies at church 'Miss' because you really do respect them." (97)

The strategy practiced by the Logans is neither that of the martyr nor that of the pragmatist. While the consequences of actions are taken into account so that one does not risk death over every offense, the approach is not narrowly pragmatic, acting only when one is sure of the consequences of that action. Risks are taken—both risks of immediate harm and risks that what is done will provide the foundation for victory later on.

The Logans' resistance is far from naive. They know the risks they are taking and the danger of resistance, and they make sure that their children are aware of the possible costs of resisting racism. When the Logans decide to help other farmers boycott the Wallaces by doing the buying and transporting of goods from another town, they know they will anger many of the whites, especially the influential landowner, Harlan Granger (122–25). They are resisting white men who have killed and seriously injured other black men and are flaunting their crime. Mary Logan also teaches the children the consequences of racism, acknowledging that what has happened to their friend T. J.—barely saved from being lynched, now unfairly convicted and likely to be executed for a murder committed by two white men—could happen to them (*Let the Circle Be Unbroken,* 29).

It is in full awareness of these risks that the Logans then act. Their actions are courageous, not foolhardy. They take risks yet try to mitigate further brutality by whites. T. J.'s lynching is stopped, for example, not by directly attacking the white men who are trying to lynch him, but by David Logan setting fire to his own cotton, cotton adjacent to that of Granger, the white man who supports the lynching. The white men are deflected from murder to fight the fire (*Roll of Thunder,* 196–210). The children know that their father has risked their own livelihood by burning part of their crop in order to save T. J. from being murdered. They also know that this act of defiance must remain unnamed, for the whites attribute the fire to lightning, and if they discover the truth, they might kill David Logan. (209).

The Logans are not only fully aware of the risks they face, they are also aware of the different costs faced by others. They respect the stricter limits that others have because they do not share in the relative financial independence of the Logans. Most of the Logans' neighbors are sharecroppers and do not have the freedom to continue the Wallace boycott as do the Logans, who farm their own land. When the boycott ends because of the pressure put on the sharecroppers by the white landowners, David Logan respects that decision.

David Logan hears the decision of Mr. Avery and others to stop the boycott and explains their action to his son, Stacey:

> "But—but that ain't all Mr. Granger said. Said, too, we don't give up this shoppin' in Vicksburg, we can jus' get off his land. . . . Then them Wallaces, they come by my place, Brother Lanier's, and everybody's on this thing that owes them money. Said we can't pay our debts, they gonna have the sheriff out to get us . . . put us on the chain gang to work it off." . . .
> Mr. Lanier said, "I pray to God there was a way we could stay in this thing, but we can't go on no chain gang, David."
> Papa nodded. "Don't expect you to, Silas."
> Mr. Avery laughed softly. "We sure had 'em goin' for a time though, didn't we?"
> . . . When the men had left, Stacey snapped, "They got no right pulling out! Just because them Wallaces threaten them one time they go jumping all over themselves to get out like a bunch of scared jackrabbits—"
> Papa stood suddenly and grabbed Stacey upward. "You, boy, don't you get so grown you go talking 'bout more than you know. Them men, they doing what they've gotta do. You got any idea what a risk they took just to go shopping in Vicksburg in the first place? They go on that chain gang and their families got nothing. They'll get kicked off that plot of land they tend and there'll be no place for them to go. You understand that?"
> . . . "You were born blessed, boy, with land of your own. If you hadn't been, you'd cry out for it while you try to survive. . . . Maybe even do what they doing now. It's hard on a man to give up, but sometimes it seems there just ain't nothing else he can do. (155–56)

The inability to stop oppression weighs heavily on the Logans, even though they do have a measure of independence because they own the land they farm. They are continually aware that to respond to the brutality of whites with forthright anger and defiance would lead to their death. It is this awareness that keeps Uncle Hammer living in the North, supporting the family by sending as much money as he can, knowing that if he stayed in the South his anger would lead him to act in a way that could lead to his murder and possibly the murder of others in his family (104):

> Uncle Hammer . . . motioned languidly at the Wallace store. "Got me a good mind to burn that place out," he said.
> "Hammer, hush that kind of talk!" ordered Big Ma . . . "that kinda talk get you hung and you know it." (104)

Because of the costs and extreme risks of resistance, the Logans teach their children that it is important to choose their battles carefully. Not to resist means death, yet to resist continually would be impossible, also bringing death. They have to learn to resist in such a way that they maintain their self-respect and lay the groundwork for further struggle. As Papa tells Cassie, "there'll be a whole lot of things you ain't gonna wanna do but you'll have to do in this life just so you can survive" (133). He tells her that there are some things that she has to "let be" and others that she must challenge. He tells her that only she can discern the importance of different battles: "But there are other things, Cassie, that if I'd let be, they'd eat away at me and destroy me in the end. And it's the same with you, baby. There are things you can't back down on, things you gotta take a stand on. But it's up to you to decide what them things are" (133–34).

Making this choice, learning to tell the difference between what has to be fought and what can be tolerated, is inescapable for anyone trying to maintain self-respect in the face of oppression, in the face of struggle against deep-seated problems. Papa reminds Cassie of the importance of working for self-respect: "You have to demand respect in this world, ain't nobody just gonna hand it to you. How you carry yourself, what you stand for—that's how you gain respect. But, little one, ain't nobody's respect worth more than your own" (134).

The difference that Cassie is being taught is as real and as important to self-respect as it is intangible. It is the difference between "bending" and "bowing and scraping"—a difference Mary teaches her children by her words and actions (*Let the Circle Be Unbroken,* 176). The Logans bend, but they never bow and scrape. They do what they can, taking risks that bring moments of freedom that lay the framework for further action.

This interaction between risks, failures, and the potential for later victory is manifest in the communal boycott. Although the boycott is broken, it provides a moment of freedom, good in itself and portentous in its impact on the future. Such actions are manifestations of the power people have when they work together. They sustain hope for freedom and encourage further reaches of the imagination, further visions of ways in which black people can work together to resist exploitation by whites. While the risks and the consequences of such actions can never be calculated, neither can the possible benefits. The Logans and the other members of their community act courageously to sustain and extend the freedom they know in relation with each other.

The ability to resist—the continual reminders that it is possible and worthwhile—is sustained by the creation of alternative structures, by a community in which the love that compels and sustains resistance is fully expressed. These communities include the family structure itself, the school, and the church. Here the Logans and their neighbors experience mutual respect and dignity: the respect expressed in calling each other "Miss," the respect expressed in Mary Logan's teaching the children a history not found in the county's textbooks. Within these structures of church, school, and family the Logans and their neighbors experience the mutual respect they seek from white people. Here is what Martin Luther King, Jr., called "the beloved community," the space of justice and joy. While not free of internal tensions, it serves as the matrix of resistance—the source of love and self-respect that sustains the struggle against racism.

5

The Healing Power
of Love

——— ■ ———

Toni Morrison and Mildred Taylor set the context for an understanding of what enables work for justice. Morrison describes the tragic loss caused by oppression; her stark depiction of unnecessary human suffering evokes in her readers outrage and an impassioned search for avenues of overturning and transforming the causes of that suffering. Taylor depicts a history of resistance, the wisdom of elders that offers inspiration and direction for moral action in the present. Toni Cade Bambara, in her novel, *The Salt Eaters,* directly addresses the challenges and opportunities of the present. Angela Jackson claims that Bambara defines our time as one of healing, of intellectual and spiritual challenges. She speaks of the book's "magnetic pull into health" for individuals and for the social order.[1] Gloria Hull highlights the timeliness of Bambara's work, claiming that *The Salt Eaters* "accomplishes even better for the 1980s what *Native Son* did for the 1940s, *Invisible Man* for the 1950s, or *Song of Solomon* for the 1970s: it fixes our present and challenges the way to the future."[2] Bambara examines blocks to social change and passionately celebrates the communal strength that evokes transforming moral and political choices.

INTERLOCKING STRUCTURES
OF OPPRESSION

The Salt-Eaters is both visionary and analytical.[3] It reflects a particular history, the political and spiritual movements within the African-American community in the late 1970s. It is also a call to a less well-known history, that of the "mud-mothers," the bearers of African traditions, of ancient wisdom and enduring dreams. Bambara's analysis of these traditions addresses the extreme difficulty of maintaining a supportive and challenging community of resistance. She describes the costs of such community and the tensions that lead to destructive splits within a once-solid network. Bambara's work does not stop, however, with merely decrying the periodic dissolution of leftist groups. She moves to an analysis of the causes of much dissolution and to a convincing depiction of the forces that can heal the breaks within a community. Bambara sees the causes of repeated dissolution as basically twofold: externally, the overwhelming pressure of structures of oppression; internally, an inability to come to terms with pain. The resolution she depicts is multifaceted, including a reaffirmation of the value and wonder of life, the recovery of "ancient covenants," and an acceptance of the risk of engaging in wholehearted efforts to create and respond to injustice without the comfort of ontological, religious, or historical guarantees.

Bambara describes the formidable achievements of African-American resistance in the United States. The setting of her novel is a strong African-American community in the South. The black people in the town of Claybourne have developed a community of healing and resistance, incorporating the traditions of their struggle in the United States and the wisdom they have retained from their African heritage. The novel centers on the activities of two related institutions, the Southwest Community Infirmary and the Academy of the 7 Arts. The infirmary was built in 1871 by "the Free Coloreds of Claybourne" (120). The infirmary is now a center of traditional and Western medicine. The academy is the site of teaching in "the performing arts, the martial arts, the medical arts, the scientific arts, and the arts and humanities," all taught without credit to "workers, dropouts, students, housewives, ex-cons, vets, church folk, professionals, an alarming number of change agents, as they insisted on calling themselves" (120).

The substantial institutional achievements of the African-American community in Claybourne are accompanied by wide-ranging political and social analysis. There is a commonly recognized and understood awareness of the connections between various political problems. The connections between racism and the threat of war, between both of these and the dangers of nuclear power, are clearly seen, as are the roots of all these evils in the drive for power of Europeans and Euro-Americans.

Bambara provides a concise, clear discussion of the connections between racism, sexism, and the dangers of war and of nuclear power. Two activists are discussing the range of concerns appropriate for a newly formed political coalition of women. Ruby explains why she voted down a proposal to work on the dangers of nuclear power and the threat of nuclear war, stating that she wants to keep the group focused on its original purpose, ensuring "input" in local politics, "an interim tactical something or other until the people quit fooling around and decide on united Black political action" (243). She wants to work on local issues and does not see the point of "taking on everything" (243). Janice reminds her of the artificiality of a division between local issues and the threat of nuclear disaster. She cites the blatant conjunction of racism and the dangers of nuclear power and nuclear weapons, a conjunction manifest in the location of uranium mines in Native American lands, and in the predominance of African-American workers in the most dangerous jobs at nuclear power plants:

> "All this doomsday mushroom-cloud end-of-the-planet numbah is past my brain. Just give me the good ole-fashioned honky-nigger shit. I think all this ecology stuff is a diversion." "They're connected. Whose community do you think they ship radioactive waste through, or dig up waste burial grounds near? Who do you think they hire for the dangerous dirty work at those plants? What parts of the world do they test-blast in? And all them illegal uranium mines dug up on Navajo turf—the crops dying, the sheep dying, the horses, water, cancer, Ruby, cancer. And the plant on the Harlem River and—Ruby, don't get stupid on me." (242)

The blatant conjunction of racism and the nuclear threat—people of color bearing the brunt of the dangers of producing nuclear power and nuclear weapons—is grounded in larger "power configurations," the imbalance of power between African-Americans and Euro-Americans, and the character of Euro-American political power, a power used to dominate and exploit nature and other peoples. Janice's persistent reiteration of these connections convinces Ruby:

> "You think there's no connection between the power plant and Trans-chemical and the power configurations in this city and the quality of life in this city, region, country, world?"
> "Sold. But can't I specialize just a wee bit longer in the local primitive stuff—labor with the ordinary home-grown variety crackers and your everyday macho pain in the ass from the block?" (242)

The women are clearly aware of the causes of all these dangers. Their analysis includes a critique of the construction of power that propels the use of military force. They are critical of constructions of power as omnipotence, the ability to act alone, without impediment and without threat. They see how the attempt to attain that level of security leads to its opposite—absolute insecurity. The arms race has resulted in total insecurity: everything, not just the political power of a certain group, not just the solidity of a particular economic system, is now threatened with destruction: "'The drive for invulnerability usually leaves one totally vulnerable.' Jan mumbled. 'Take U.S. policy on nuclear armament for a case in point'" (216).

Neither the threat of nuclear war nor the danger of nuclear power are seen as mysterious, as inexplicable aberrations in an otherwise healthy system. They are the apotheosis of what it means to be Euro-American, the logical outcomes of a definition of living that involves conquering other nations, other peoples, other forces. These women name the parasitical nature of Euro-American society and realize that, once the host has been exhausted, this parasite refuses to die alone, but tries to take everything else with it. This wisdom is conveyed to the children of Claybourne "by more than one community sage": "Their world-wide program, their destiny, youngblood, is to drain the juices and to put out the lights. And don't you forget it" (121).

TRANSFORMING POWER

The analysis achieved by the people of Claybourne and the 7 Arts Academy is accompanied by a creative view of the future. Their work is more than merely critical. Critique is grounded in a vision of social change, a vision that includes not only specific rearrangements in the balance of power but a redefinition of power. The vision also encompasses more than the social relationship between people. Its roots include a different relationship with nature.

The remembrance of a different sort of power is intrinsic to healing. As one of the central characters in the novel, Velma Henry, moves toward wholeness, she remembers the lesson she has learned from her Navajo friends about alternative ways of hunting. They have taught her a way of expressing power that is diametrically opposed to the power of Western technological society, the power that destroys or diminishes that which it needs for survival. The native wisdom does include drawing from the resources of others, but the drawing is grounded in respect for the other. Even if the hunting is literally that of killing an animal for food, the taking of life is limited by need and characterized by a recognition of dependence on the animal that is killed, not by an assertion of independence from it or superiority over it. The metaphor of hunting is also extended to include finding resources for living, a finding that welcomes and saves rather than destroys.

> And hadn't Nilda and Inez told her about hunting? Hadn't Maazda explained what it was to stalk, to take over the hunted, but not with arrows or bullets but with the eye of the mind? And hadn't she observed the difference, watched the different brands of hunting? The pulling of the bow, the pulling of the truck alongside the prey and mowing it down, taking it over. . . Taking over a life. That was not hunting as the sisters explained it, sang it, acted it out. To have dominion was not to knock out, downpress, bruise, but to understand, to love, make at home. . . . The hunt for balance and kinship was the thing. A mutual courtesy. She would run to the park and hunt for self. (266–67)

Velma and her sisters approach their political work with the same reverence for balance and kinship. To be political is to be fully alive, responding with integrity and care to the fractures in the fabric of life, seeking ways to mend the rifts of racism and sexism, of political exploitation and the despoiling of the environment. Bambara celebrates the persistence of men and women who stay with the struggle for transformation despite the many opportunities to care a little less and work on ostensibly "personal" issues alone. This temptation, and the strength required to resist it, is described in terms of an encounter between Velma—the long-term, steady activist, and her friend, Barbara, a veteran of civil rights work, now tired and angry, no longer active in political work, and thankful that "I got out of here in time" (261). Velma, too honest about the difficulty of the work and her own frustrations to be self-righteous, expresses the basic wisdom that sustains long-term political work—a social commitment inseparable from her sense of personal integrity.

> "You seem the same, Velma. Crazy as ever." Looking at the tables tumbled down with leaflets and pamphlets, the boxes of rolled-up posters, the mimeo machine in the middle of the living room. "Same o same o, hunh?" . . . She [Velma] didn't know what the sister wanted, sitting there smoking one after another, describing her latest march down the butt- and spit-spattered aisle of City Hall, talking on and on, bits and snatches of jailhouse anecdotes and back-road remembrances, as if all that had happened a century ago and the war were over. Asking after everyone but not listening to Velma's answers. And that smile that was anything but a smile. "We're all still here," was all Velma could think to say. "And still into the same idealistic nonsense, I gather," sounding edgy, irritable. "You honestly think you can change anything in this country?" Her anger flaring now, bewildering. "I try to live," Velma said, surprised at her evenness, "so it doesn't change me too much." "You'll learn," she snapped back. (260–61)

FRAGMENTATION

Although Velma has tried to keep oppression "from changing her too much," she is far from unscathed by the pressures of being healthy, female, and black in a racist, misogynist, life-denying society. The struggle for fundamental social change is taking its toll on her, on her community of activists, and on the wider social fabric. Bambara concentrates in Velma's breakdown the trauma of contemporary society. Overwhelmed by external threats (ecological damage, sexism, racism, and the threat of nuclear war) and drained by the damage those threats wreak in the internal workings of the 7 Arts Academy, Velma tries to kill herself, suicide her only way of withdrawing from a suicidal society.

The matrix of Bambara's work is our contemporary suicidal society. Her protagonists are the men and women who see the damage and courageously resist it. Far from stopping with the gains of the civil rights movement, the men and women Bambara describes continue to work against racism and find themselves seeing even more manifestations of the sickness that leads to racism and discovering ever more problems requiring denunciation and healing. The list of problems is increasing, and their horror is compounded by their interrelation. The pressure of this danger is expressed by Ruby: "Women for Action is taking on entirely too much: drugs, prisons, alcohol, the schools, rape, battered women, abused children. And now Velma's talked the group into tackling the nuclear power issue. . ." (198).

The list of causes addressed by Women for Action is not superficial but organic. All express immediate threats to the lives of people. These threats are also compounded by the health dangers of the nearby plant, Transchemical. The precise nature of the plant's operation is not described by Bambara, but its threat to the environment and to its workers is inescapably clear. Ruby and Janice raise this concern in discussing Velma's sickness, a sickness that has increased since she has been working at Transchemical: "She's probably sick. And no wonder. The plant is not a healthy place to work, even in the office wing. Do you know that all the workers have to report for a medical once a month to the company infirmary, plus they can't see their own records?" (201).

While many women and men try to maintain clarity and courage in the face of these interrelated dangers, the costs are becoming ever greater, leading to fragmentation and frustration within the black community of Claybourne. The tensions experienced within the 7 Arts Academy are the tensions experienced periodically by many activists: "It was starting up again, the factions, the intrigue." The academy is torn by internal struggles, by debates over which group bears the key perspective, is grounded in the one social location productive of both the central diagnosis of the present and the vision for the future. The "old ideological splits" are "threatening to tear the Academy apart": "the street youth as vanguard, the workers as vanguard; self-determination in the Black Belt, Black rule of U.S.A.; strategic coalitions, independent political action" (90).

The two poles of the academy, the "spiritual" and "political," have become two camps, each blaming the other for the lack of progress and vision of the movement as a whole, seeing the other as incapable of the needed analysis and action: "Causes and issues. They're vibrating at the mundane level." "Spirit this and psychic that. Escapism. Irresponsible, given the objective conditions" (293). Velma had held the two groups together, "urging each to teach the other its language." Now each wants the other to accept its language and analysis as definitive (92).

> The one argued relentlessly now for the Academy to change its name from 7 Arts to Spirithood Arts and to revamp the program, strip it of material and mundane concerns like race, class and struggle. The other wanted "the flowing ones" thrown out and more posters of Lenin, Malcolm, Bessie Smith and Coltrane put up. (92–93)

There is also resistance by the men within the academy to work with Women for Action, although the members overlap and they share the same work: "to develop, to de-mystify, to build, to consolidate and escalate" (93).

The common agenda and analysis cannot nullify the different understandings of what it means to be "change agents." The women in Women for Action are opposed to the institutional concerns of the men, claiming that the men focus on the organization as an end in itself. They seem to lack the necessary freedom toward institutions, the ability to work with them and through them but not for them, the ability to use them as necessary and discard or modify them when appropriate. "It was like Mrs. Heywood said: Keep the focus on the action not the institution; don't confuse the vehicle with the objective; all cocoons are temporary and disappear" (99).

In addition to describing internal debates over leadership and organizational style, Bambara describes the process by which "cadres become cargo cults," the process in which illusory gains are welcomed to the detriment of more fundamental change. This occurs as activists become satisfied with individual success, forgetting the larger issues, and as organizations become excited by the appearance of their own growth and forget what they are working for and how it can be gained. When a cadre becomes a cargo cult, workers are coopted, believing

the congratulations received by those in power, not seeing that
the gains are illusory and that thinking those are real gains vitiates
further work. Bambara's description illumines the enervation of the
women's movement and the civil rights movement—seeing the gains
of middle-class women and men as success and forgetting the structural change still required. Her analysis is quite appropriate for a
so-called "postfeminist" society, for people who think the work of
civil rights and of women's liberation has been completed. She points
to the further tasks, the importance of turning the success of a few—
their inclusion in formerly all-white, male, middle-class worlds such
as business, politics, and higher education—into the basis for more
radical change. She addresses the dangers of tokenism that leaves
given power relationships intact:

> Thought she knew how to build immunity to the sting of the serpent
> that turned would-be cells, could-be cadres into cargo cults. Thought
> she knew how to build resistance, . . . not be available to madness,
> not become intoxicated by the heady brew of degrees and career and
> congratulations for nothing done. . . . (258–59)

Another significant tension is that between women and men. Bambara recounts the possibilities for resistance as members of movements heed the wisdom of women, and she depicts the resistance by
men to that wisdom in an account of the formation of Women for
Action. In the past the women activists were consulted after decisions
had been made. Then they were expected to do the mundane tasks
necessary to accomplish grand political objectives. Ultimately they
found themselves and their work taken for granted:

> Like going to jail and being forgotten, forgotten, or at least depriori-
> tized cause bail was not as pressing as the printer's bill. Like raising
> funds and selling some fool to the community with his heart set on
> running for public office. Like being called in on five-minute notice
> after all the interesting decisions had been made, called in out of per-
> sonal loyalty and expected to break her hump pulling off what the men
> had decided was crucial for the community good. (25)

This time when the men are trying to get the women to support a
man running for public office, they rebel. Once more they listen to
a man speaking in grand terms of the labor movement, of "new al-
liances," and they think of the concrete tasks required to give shape to
his vision of African-American people working together for change:

> . . . receptions to cater, tickets to print, chickens to fry, cakes to box,
> posters to press, so many gifts to extort from downtown merchants for

raffles and Bingo, ads to place, billboards to commandeer, a hot-plate demo at the auto show, bands to book, a crafts-and-books booth at the school bazaar, a rummage sale, an auction of whatever first edition Old Reilly might still have on his shelves, and what home boy or home-girl-made-good-in-show-biz could be counted on for a benefit show. (22)

Velma and the other women rebel because the men are insensitive and arrogant; they do not understand the work involved in giving concrete shape to their goals, and they lack appreciation of the women and their work. One woman describes her husband's blindness to the mundane tasks essential to survival. He is as blind to what it takes for him to survive as he is to the work required for the movement:

"Not a clue, my friends, as to how the eggs, bacon and biscuits come to appear before him every morning. He makes up lists, see, of all the things he wants done and posts this list on the refrigerator door just like there were little kitchen fairies and yard elves and other magic creatures to get all these things done." (31)

This oblivion to the work required to live is not innocuous. Bambara relates it to the oblivion of men to the costs of their wars, their willingness to fight for a grand political end without knowing and without feeling the human damage that war causes. She has Velma name the "habit, the unmindful gap between want and done, demand and get" as "abstractionist"—"And abstractionists make good bombardiers, good military beasts" (31).

The men are not only unaware of the work required in political organization, but they confuse their own personal competition with significant political work, the thrill of internal political intrigue substituting for cooperative work on external problems. The women decide to form their own organization, inviting the men to work with them if they want to work. They are tired of the men's oblivion, tired of watching "still another organization sacrificed on the altar of male ego" (26). This separation is momentous—a significant challenge to the men, an opportunity for them to learn from the concrete wisdom of women. Yet the learning from and with women does not come easy. It is hard for men so accustomed to having women as helpers see them as teachers. As the healer Minnie Ransom states, "Something's up in a fiercesome way between the men and the women" (62).

The tensions within the Academy are not isolated but are manifestations of a wider social breakdown—a more subtle form of the violence that characterizes the relationships of parents and children, family, and friends. The healer, Minnie Ransom, is deeply troubled by the African-American community's internalization of the suicidal society around them. She expresses her frustration and concern to her spirit guide, Old Wife:

> "It's these children, Old Wife. I can handle the dry-bone folks all right. And them generations of rust around still don't wear me any. But these new people? And the children on the way in this last quarter? They gonno really be a blip. But the ones pouring into the Infirmary are blip enough. Soon's they old enough to start smelling theyselves, they commence to looking for blood among the blood. Cutting and stabbing and facing off and daring and dividing up and suiciding. You know as well as I, Old Wife, that we have not been scuffling in this waste-howling wilderness for the right to be stupid. . . ." (45–46)

Minnie is as sensitive to the more subtle violence, the political infighting, as she is to the physical stabbing, the charges of "you ain't correct, well you ain't cute, and he ain't right and they ain't scientific" (46). She's distressed by the pain of the women, their inability to "draw up the powers from the deep" and grapple with the challenges of life: "What is wrong with the women? . . . What is happening to the daughters of the yam? Seem like they just don't know how to draw up the powers from the deep like before" (43–44).

PAIN AND HEALING

Bambara analyzes carefully the causes of this dissolution of creative resistance in her description of Velma Henry's breakdown. The novel begins with Minnie Ransom trying to heal Velma after she has attempted suicide. Velma was involved in all the struggles, understanding the different factions, and trying to help them work together and learn from each other. Somehow, Velma kept them arguing with each other in a way that led to work together:

> . . . things had seemed more pulled together when Velma had been there, in the house and at the Academy. Not that her talents ran in the peace-making vein. But there'd been fewer opportunities for splinterings with her around, popping up anywhere at any time to raise a question, audit a class, monitor a meeting, confront or cooperate. It was all of a piece with Velma around. (92)

Velma's breakdown itself is also "all of a piece," integrally related to the momentous choices being faced by activists: how to continue to work in the face of escalating threats and how to work together without demanding that one faction become the sole voice of the movement. While Velma has been at home with both groups of community workers, those who regard themselves as "political" and those who regard themselves as "psychically adept," this "home" has not been maintained easily. Velma has broken from the strain: "she'd fallen into the chasm that divided the two camps" (147).

Yet even Velma's falling has seeds of new growth. The wise women of the community know this and are trying to help Velma find the possibilities contained in the chasm, knowing that her healing makes it possible for a larger healing to occur as well. The lessons that Velma must learn in order to remain "at home" and well are the lessons that all activists must learn.

One of the most salient lessons is discovering how to learn from pain without trying either to conquer it or to become immune to it. Minnie Ransom sees avoidance of pain as one of the most striking follies of the children of the "last quarter," wanting to feel good all the time, not knowing that at times "you're supposed to feel bad." Minnie Ransom sees such an avoidance of pain frequently in her work at the infirmary. She tells of an incident in which a woman came to the infirmary "clawing at her hair, wailing to beat the band, asking for some pills. Wanted a pill cause she was in pain, felt bad, wanted to feel good" (8). The woman was overcome with pain because her mother had died. Minnie is appalled: "Her mama died, she's *supposed* to feel bad. . . . Bless her heart, just a babe of the times. Wants to be smiling and feeling good all the time. Smooth sailing as they lower the mama into the ground" (8–9).

Minnie sees "wanting to feel good all the time" as a symptom of amnesia: the "children" have forgotten their history; they have forgotten the wisdom gained through the work of their elders: "And looks like we clean forgot what we come to do, what we been learning through all them trials and tribulations to do and it's now. Come in here after abusing themselves and want to be well and don't even know what they want to be healthy for. Lord, the children" (46–47).

A fundamental point of Velma's healing, and the healing possible for all of us, collectively and individually, lies in the recognition that although there is a way through, there is no way out. The first sentence of the book raises this challenge: "Are you sure, sweetheart, that you want to be well?" (3). Minnie's question to Velma is far from idle. It gets at the heart of the matter: Does Velma want to be well? Do we want to be well? This seemingly obvious question is actually a serious one. Wellness does not mean conquering pain or having happiness unshaded by terror, struggle, anger, or disappointment. Minnie's work involves more than healing the sickness of these "children of the last quarter," for they require a transformation of their conception of what it means to be well. She diagnoses a central

danger in the current social situation, an inability to respond courageously and defiantly to pain. People want to feel good all the time,
thus denying or evading pain. When they do hurt, many people do not
know what to do with their pain and cling to it as a mark of special
identity. The lesson Minnie carries is a memory of how to learn from
pain and how to shoulder the responsibilities that health brings. Minnie Ransom is the voice of old wisdom, the recognition that health
does not mean undifferentiated bliss, but the ability to face challenges, the ability to dance with nonbeing, not conquering it, but
learning with it. As she tells Velma, ". . . wholeness is no trifling
matter. A lot of weight when you're well" (10).

One of Minnie Ransom's clearest lessons—and the easiest to
grasp—is that it is all right to feel pain and anger and that it is necessary to withdraw for a time. Faced with humiliation, with the devastation of racism, with ecological destruction, with sexism, it is healthy
to notice that something is wrong; it is healthy to grieve and rage over
the violation of life. Minnie affirms Velma's need to withdraw for a
time, telling her, "you want to stomp around a little more in the mud
puddle, I see, like a little kid 'fore you come into the warm and be
done with mud. Nothin' wrong with that. . . . I can wait" (36).

The damage caused by continuous pain takes many forms, however,
not all of them avoidance and denial. Far from denying pain, Velma is
holding on to her suffering in a way that prevents growth. The challenge is to experience pain without denial—"when you hurt, hurt"—
and yet know when to go on, learning from past pain without either
trivializing it or clinging to it. Velma is paying the price of "hanging on
to old pains." She recounts incidents from the past—times of betrayal,
failure, and humiliation—reliving them each time (22). She reaches
the point where she is unable to relax: "Walking jags, talking jags,
grabbing his arm suddenly and swirling her eyes around the room, or
collapsing in the big chair, her head bent over." Her lover grows
"afraid for her" and then "afraid of her" (162).

The challenge facing Velma and many others is knowing when to
accept the risk of facing new causes of rage and anguish, letting go of
old pain and being open to more. Minnie knows the danger of becoming defined by sickness—"holding on to sickness with a fiercesome-
ness that took twenty hard-praying folk to loosen" (107). Minnie
understands this ferocious identification with past pain and knows its
costs. She works with those who cling to their hurt and anguish,
wearing it

> like a badge of honor, as though it meant they'd been singled out for
> some special punishment, were special. Or as though it meant they'd

paid some heavy dues and knew, then, what there was to know, and therefore had a right to certain privileges, or were exempt from certain charges. . . . But way down under knowing "special" was a lie, knowing better all along and feeling the cost of the lie, of the self-betrayal in the joints, in the lungs, in the eyes. Knew, felt the cost, but were too proud and too scared to get downright familiar with . . . their bodies, minds, spirits to just sing, "Blues, how do you do? Sit down, let's work it out." Took heart to flat out decide to be well and stride into the future sane and whole. And it took time. (107–8)

Minnie is working with Velma, waiting for her to express her pain and then release it. Only then can she go on "into the future sane and whole." Velma does release the pain, but her expression does not come out as something "intelligible and calm and hip and funny so the work could take precedence again." The words are "caught in the grind of her back teeth," in a "rip and a shriek," and she releases her anger in a fierce expression of outrage and defiance, what Minnie calls "a good ole deep kneebend from-the-source growl" (41).

LIFE-GIVING LOVE

In Velma's healing Bambara encapsulates the process that leads to the healing of community. She describes three aspects of persistent, joyful communal resistance to structural evil: an abiding love for other people, an acceptance of the need for taking risks in political action, and an active commitment to "ancient covenants" with life.

As she is healed, Velma experiences once again the deep love that leads both to sanity-threatening rage and to joyful resistance. Both rage and joy are grounded in a life-giving love for other people, a love essential for all members of the community. Bambara tells us that Velma's rage, hope, and energy are intricately, inseparably intertwined. She is angry and hurt because she knows how much is lost through the exploitation of workers, through the continual limitations of human lives through racism. She knows how precious are the lives ruined by being forced to work in jobs that destroy the spirit and the creativity of the workers as well as destroying the body and causing cancer and sterility.

Velma experiences deep rage because she knows the power and value of transformation. She has defied the limitations of racism and sexism, has "sported power for others," has found what oppressors say we no longer have. Velma could "simply slip into the power, into the powerful power hanging unrecognized in the back-hall closet" (265). She wants to be well again so she can be part of finding that power for others, helping them realize what they already have:

Get up and go seeking again, knock on all the doors in Claybourne and quick too. . . . Knock and be welcomed in and free to roam the back hall on the hunt for that particular closet with the particular hanging robe, coat, mantle, veil or whatever it was. And get into it. Sport it. Parade around the district in it so folks would remember themselves. Would hunt for their lost selves. (266)

Velma demonstrates a further dimension of the basic commitments and attitudes necessary to sustain community. Empowered and emboldened by love, she is once again ready to take risks for justice although there are no guarantees of success. Velma's daring is intrinsically communal, motivated by her love for others, encouraged by the defiance and creativity of others. She is healed as she finds herself ready to join again in the celebration of all those who have defied limitation and oppression. She is ready to join the singers, the musicians, and the activists who have spoken the truth of their lives, who have revealed their genius and insight, and have, despite oppression, gone forward on "sheer holy boldness":

She could dance right off the stool, . . . celebrating all those giants she had worshiped in their terrible musicalness. Giant teachers teaching through tone and courage and inventiveness but scorned, rebuked, beleaguered, trivialized, commercialized, copied, plundered, goofed on . . . till they didn't know, didn't trust, wouldn't move on the wonderful gift given and were mute, crazy and beat-up. But standing up in their genius anyhow ready to speak the unpronounceable. On the stand with no luggage and no maps and ready to go anywhere in the universe together on just sheer holy boldness. (265)

Velma recovers the wisdom of working without a clear vision of how to solve immense problems, simply knowing that to live is to see the problems and to find a way forward, boldly living although you're not sure how to stop the forces of oppression. Bambara sees great courage expressed in the giants of jazz and blues, their passionate musical creativity akin to the political daring she celebrates. Bambara challenges activists to relish a free-wheeling proliferation of analyses and strategies for social change. Drawing from an abundance of local initiatives and strategies is more enlivening than fostering competition between them. Just as there is no one right improvisation, there is no one right political strategy.

Bambara's analogy also holds for the courage required to resist injustice when there are no blueprints for either effective resistance or a just alternative society. Bambara claims that it is possible to work without guarantees. She gives as her model jazz musicians and the creation of a fleeting world with only a rudimentary chart, years of practice, sensitivity to other players, and daring. She challenges activists to work creatively with analogous resources—rudimentary analyses of causes of oppression and types of resistance, years of working for social change, openness to the wisdom of other people, and the bold invention of fitting, evocative strategies.

Bambara adds yet another dimension to her portrayal of the resources that sustain community—the renewal of ancient covenants. Velma intuits that the strength to go on, to continue facing the pain intrinsic to loving life enough to struggle against all that diminishes it, is to be found in ancient wisdom as well as in the wisdom of her immediate predecessors. She is haunted by images of "mud-mothers," the bearers of ancient wisdom, of the covenant with nature, that characterized African societies. She discerns that what has been missing from the "political / economic / social cultural / aesthetic / military / psychosocial / psychosexual mix" of the movement is the wisdom of ancient traditions (259). She finds the ancient mothers trying to "talk to her, tell[ing] her what must be done all over again" (255). Velma intuits that in ancient traditions she will find what must be rekindled—the "covenants remembered in fragments," the ability to "remember the whole in time and make things whole again" (247–48). Velma knows that it is possible for humans to become so committed to the earth, to life, that work against its violation will have power and direction. She senses that there is a healing way to resist the denial of life expressed in the exploitation of women, workers, and the earth.

Bambara's depiction of "ancient covenants" is challenging as well as comforting. Although the recognition of the mud-mothers and their commitment "to remember the whole . . . and make things whole again" offers a foundation for communal activism, it does not include any guarantees. The wisdom of the mud-mothers signifies both the reality of a foundation for action outside oneself and one's community and the dependence of that foundation on one's actions. Remembering the mud-mothers and their commitment to make things whole again gives Velma and her community the courage that comes from knowing that one is not the first to love life, not the first to struggle against oppression. Communal resistance in the present is a construction and an affirmation of what has gone before.

Bambara conveys the imperative of action in two ways. First, she reminds us that adherence to ancient wisdom does not mean the achievement of a utopian order or even an individual peace. Velma's acceptance of the wisdom of the mud-mothers is her acceptance of the need to resist continued threats to her sanity and continued threats to life. Velma's healing occurs as she is ready to face the ongoing onslaught of pain and anger, grounded in her love of life and in the wisdom of ancient communities of people who also loved and raged. She moves out of old pain, knowing that deeper pain and deeper joy are ahead.

> Velma would remember it as the moment she started back toward life, the moment when the healer's hand had touched some vital spot and she was still trying to resist, still trying to think what good did wild do you, since there was always some low-life gruesome gang bang raping lawless careless pesty last straw nasty thing ready to pounce, put your total shit under arrest and crack your back—but couldn't. And years hence she would laugh remembering she'd thought *that* was an ordeal. She didn't know the half of it. Of what awaited her in years to come. (278)

Velma's healing occurs at a time of choice, a time in which individuals and social movements face the possibilities of destruction and fragmentation or struggle and growth. Bambara signals this irruption of choice with an ominous storm. Bambara uses this cataclysmic storm as the sign of the irruption of possibility.

While it is not clear if the rumbling is merely thunder or an explosion at the plant, it is clear that it represents the beginning of something new. It is the beginning of new political awareness and new activism. While the increase in activism is definite, the degree of catastrophe required to initiate such activism is indeterminate. Bambara explores various possibilities: the new activism follows a disastrous explosion at a nuclear power plant, "the very threat of rain . . . reviv[ing] the terror" of radiation poisoning; or resistance becomes revivified after the use of nuclear weapons (274–76).

It is also possible that the rumbling is the irruption of decisiveness, a decisiveness born of facing the reality of the threat of nuclear war and the threat of ecological disaster if there were a major accident at a nuclear power plant. The range of political activity includes such concrete forms as one man understanding "that industrial arrogance and heedless technology was first and foremost a medical issue, a health issue, his domain" (281). It encompasses Velma's healing, the widespread beginning of more intense, sustained resistance and rebuilding. Bambara names this time, our time, as one in which choices and decisions have to be made: "It was clear the downpour was no spring shower. . . . Choices were being tossed into the street like dice, like shells, like kola nuts, like jackstones" (294).

By describing the present as the time of choice, Bambara imagines the alternative futures—none determined yet all highly probable, some devastating, others promising. The high probability of both destruction and renewal makes it a time of risk and opportunity. The choices are momentous; daring and courage are imperative.

Bambara evokes a very particular vision of the future. She rejoices in the decision to resist, not in the final victory over evil. She celebrates the joy of a communal covenant with life, with all its attendant costs and risks, not an idyllic utopian state in which all problems have been solved. She affirms the power and wisdom of struggle without guarantees of success.

Part Three

A THEOLOGY
FOR THE BEARERS
OF DANGEROUS MEMORY

———— ■ ————

6

The Ideology of Cultured Despair

———— ■ ————

The power and wisdom celebrated in the novels of African-American women are both compelling and startlingly foreign to many members of the Euro-American middle class. The combination of hope and a sober assessment of the difficulties of political change is challenging and unsettling. In Part Three I examine the theological correlates of both an ethic of risk and an ethic of control. In chapter six I analyze the relationship between liberal theology and an ethic of control. In chapter seven I describe the methodological implications of an ethic of risk, and I conclude in chapter eight with a discussion of a theology that can sustain an ethic of risk.

The search for guarantees and for single comprehensive solutions is often paralyzing. Taking as the norm of power the ability of the political and economic establishment to meet its goals, middle-class activists often become trapped in cultured despair. We are well aware of the costs of systems of injustice but find it impossible to act against them, because no definitive solutions are in sight. The memories of the middle class are deceptive and enervating: deceptive in their accounts of economic and military victory without victims, enervating in their emphasis on the failure of "utopian ideals."

The memories of the Euro-American middle class often hinder the move from critique to action. Shaped by memories of conquest in the name of the common good (the settling of the West, the growth of technology and economic affluence, the strengthening of U.S. military power during and after World War II), many middle-class people are paralyzed when we see that our work against the dangerous costs of this legacy of conquest does not have as much success as did campaigns for military and economic control. Given this disparity, the lack of control and precision in work for justice seems almost irresponsible. If control is the norm, then responsible action for justice is a contradiction in terms. American culture relegates such concerns to the young and the terminally idealistic. Responsibility is equated with action that is more likely to succeed, thus identifying responsibility with action that is, by definition, supportive of the status quo.

Alternative interpretations of the nature of responsible action, hope and the scope of human limitations can be found in the work of liberation theologians. These theologians offer a much-needed critical perspective on the ethic of control and its inflated expectations for complete and final victories. In the work of feminist, African-American and Latin American liberation theologians I find a strong criticism of the ethic of cultured despair, and in feminist theology, a critique of the theology of transcendence that accompanies this ethic of despair and resignation.

The ethic of cultured despair is marked by two distinct features: (1) the despair is cultured in the sense of its erudite awareness of the extent and complexity of many forms of injustice; and (2) the knowledge of the extent of injustice is accompanied by despair, in the sense of being unable to act in defiance of that injustice. Such despair is manifest in the incomprehension by many Americans of the resilient faith and persistent struggles of the people of El Salvador, Nicaragua, and Guatemala.[1]

The ability to hope in the face of continued defeat is grounded in both the method and the content of liberation theology. Attention to each poses a decisive challenge to the tradition of liberal theology.

A CRITICAL THEOLOGICAL METHOD

Theologians of liberation (African-American, third world, and feminist) bring a methodological challenge to liberal theology. These theologians develop critical interpretations of traditional doctrines and symbols and articulate a deep awareness of structural manifestations of sinfulness.[2] They bring far more, however, to theological work than additional information. They also call for repentance and conversion. The response of liberal Euro-American theologians to these voices must be more than polite acknowledgment, for they call us to a recognition of the ways in which the Christian tradition and the liberal political and theological traditions of the first world have served to perpetuate various forms of oppression.

The challenge of liberation theologians is not the only formidable critique of liberal theology. More conservative theologians, such as George Lindbeck, criticize liberal theology's turn to experience and argue that theology should be more solidly grounded in particular religious traditions.[3] Given these critiques from the left and the right, I begin my critique of liberal theology by acknowledging a foundational characteristic of liberal theology that both impels further critique and offers a resource for a constructive response to Lindbeck's criticism.

The hallmark of liberal theology at its best is its intellectual honesty. From Friedrich Schleiermacher on, liberal theologians have forthrightly acknowledged and explored the disparity between the limitations of their categories of knowing and the richness of their subject. They have delineated the various ways in which the categories of human knowledge are incommensurate with the realm of faith. They have maintained healthy skepticism about their own claims about God and have delighted in exposing the bad faith of those theologians who claim identity between certain interpretations of the divine (in Scripture, doctrine, and tradition) and the divine itself.[4]

Liberal theologians are also responsive to human suffering. Edward Farley, for example, criticizes insensitive assumptions of divine beneficence, assumptions undaunted by the horrors of history.[5] David Tracy advocates turning attention from "the crisis of cognitive claims" to "the social-ethical crisis of massive suffering and widespread oppression and alienation in an emerging global culture."[6] One of the central criteria in Gordon Kaufman's theological work is that of humanization, and in his most recent work he criticizes notions of the sovereignty of God in light of their function in perpetuating the nuclear arms race.[7]

While many liberal theologians are responsive to human suffering, this attention to the political matrix of their work has not yet fully radicalized liberal theological method. A critical theological method would be as self-critical of its anthropology as it is of its Christology, as modest in its claims about the human as it is in its claims about the divine.

Liberal theologians have been criticized by Lindbeck for turning to human experience as a primary source, relying on what he calls a "logically and empirically vacuous," unspecified and unspecifiable common religious experience.[8] Others criticize liberal theology's characterization of human experience as being unwittingly exclusive, describing as universal the experience of a small, powerful segment of humankind.[9] While I agree with these critiques, the solution I advocate is quite different from those proposed by Lindbeck and others. Rather than assuming that it is possible to find a more secure foundation for theological work than the turn to experience, the turn to human experience can be radicalized, including a rigorous specification of the range of human experiences addressed and the particular social location within class, race, and gender divisions that shape both resources offered and problems investigated.

I disagree, therefore, with Lindbeck's call for a "grammar of faith," a theology founded on a cultural-linguistic approach to religion. Lindbeck's reliance on the cultural-linguistic approach evades two fundamental problems: (1) the determinative effect in theological work of the theologian's own social and political location within this cultural-linguistic matrix and (2) the possibility that the "grammar of faith" is itself oppressive.[10]

A critical theological method requires examining the failures as well as the resources of liberal theology and liberal ethics. The promise of liberalism can best be served by honestly examining the barriers to social transformation found within the liberal tradition. In the next section I will argue that a common liberal interpretation of eschatology functions as a support for cynicism, despair, and resignation, thus thwarting sustained participation in work for justice.

THE ESCHATOLOGICAL RESERVATION

While a denial of the fragility of our political strategies and structures is undoubtedly dangerous, the evasion of the resiliency of our work for justice is equally devastating. Sole attention to the failures in history can blind us to the partial successes; the realization that more is yet to be done masks the fact that some good has been attained. Secular critics as well as theologians are prone to an equation of self-critique and despair. One practitioner of deconstruction argues, for example, that the political import of deconstruction is "the reminder of the fact that any really 'loving' political practice must fall a prey to its own critique."[11] The negative valuation of critique, interpreting it as "falling prey," is crippling to middle-class activists. For many of us, a negative interpretation of critique is based on the idea of the eschatological reservation.

Theologians have examined the relationship between continued human fault and the power of divine presence in terms of the concept of eschatology and the eschatological reservation.[12] The eschatological reservation is the reminder that all of our good works are partial. Though inspired and guided by God, they cannot be directly identified as the work of God nor identified as the kingdom of God. Liberal and conservative theologians alike criticize liberation theologians for our failure to abide by the eschatological reservation.[13] We are criticized for too easily identifying human political projects for social change with the work of God or with the creation of the kingdom of God in history.

Johann Baptist Metz, for example, while concerned with a religiously-based political critique, is wary of the identification of alternative political structures with the kingdom of God. Metz defines the "eschatological proviso" as the recognition that the "eschatological promises of the scriptural tradition—freedom, peace, justice, reconciliation—cannot . . . be identified with any social situation that has been achieved."[14] He argues that the eschatological proviso serves as a corrective to an idolatrous commitment to particular political programs and parties: "it serves to check any form of political absolutism."[15] Such a critique supposedly frees the church to function as an "institution of social criticism."[16]

Despite the persuasiveness of Metz's argument, the political logic of this system of ideas is the opposite of its conceptual logic. Metz's work is faulted by the liberation theologian Juan Luis Segundo for its reactionary impact. Too concerned with absolute purity of intent, actualization, and consequences, some political theologians avoid activism, and their theological position legitimates that avoidance in others. As Segundo states, the critical value of the "relativization of any and every political system, in the name of God," is lost when the "eschatological reservation" is "generalized":

> Even before some new regime is worked out, it is criticized in the name of some new hope. At the same time, the opposed regime is being criticized under the same head but for opposite reasons. And even the search itself is relativized because there is no element in history that can be related causally to the construction of God's eschatological kingdom.[17]

A search for only absolute victory leads to "faith and hope in something metahistorical and a disgusted turning away from real-life history."[18]

> Hope is paradoxically translated into a radically pessimistic view of the whole process of change, even when the latter is not violent, precisely because any and every change prompted by man cannot help but lose out to world-dominating sin. The kingdom of God can only be fashioned by someone who is free from sin, and that comes down to God alone.[19]

Metz and others are right to identify the ways in which human action falls short of perfection. Our intent is certainly mixed; we often act out of accountability and love, yet this genuine openness may be tainted by unacknowledged ideological blinders—the influence of class, race, or gender privilege. Our vision is always perspectival. The problems we see and the solutions we envision cannot be separated from our social location. Interest is always operative and does need to be checked.

The Christian notion of the eschatological reservation is also intended to remind us of the disparity between political aims and the actual consequences of implemented programs and policies. We cannot imagine in advance all the consequences of any action. The environmental costs of agricultural and energy policies are a case in point. Attempts to produce social goods have had disastrous consequences. Rachel Carson, for example, describes the destruction of birds, animals, and insects through the use of pesticides.[20] Ecologists now are warning of the dangerously high levels of extinction of plant, animal, and insect species due to agricultural expansion and unchecked deforestation.[21] Scientists working on genetic alteration of plants and bacteria have yet to heed the lessons available from the destructive consequences of the intended goods of the use of pesticides and nuclear power.[22] It is possible that the fatal flaw of the human species is the lack of commensuration between our ability to act and our ability to imagine the consequences of our actions.

This dangerous, possibly fatal, lack of commensuration might seem sufficient evidence for the necessity of the eschatological reservation. Insofar as the eschatological reservation points to these limits, its functions are positive, yet these positive functions are negated by the complete discourse within which the notion is framed. It is a social imperative that this disparity between intent and consequence be acknowledged, yet it makes all the difference in the world if the source of such knowledge is a contrast between human power and absolute power or a positive recognition of the complex structure of the web of life. From the latter perspective, people come to see their inability to imagine consequences from a positive *appreciation* of the dependence of humans on nature and in *appreciation* of the complexity of the natural world. That is, we do not exist *outside* nature, manipulating it for our own ends. We *are* nature, our intelligence itself material—dependent on physical health and the operations of the natural world, dependent on political and economic structures, dependent on access to education and influence.[23]

Human intelligence is limited, and our understanding of the complex interconnection of the natural world is ever growing. The result of such a perspective is the expectation of partial success and partial defeat. Social policies and environmental policies require continual monitoring and reevaluation. The need for correctives and revision is not, however, a sign of the failure of action; it is a manifestation of the nature of human action. The ability to be self-critical, to remain open in a systematic structural manner to revision, is a sign of maturity. As Jürgen Habermas has reminded us, rather than revisions occurring only because of crises—environmental catastrophe, social insurrection—a mature institution or social system would have as a sign of its strength the operation of structures to *elicit* critique and note negative consequences.[24]

Within a framework of valued interdependence, the work of revision and self-critique is grounded in strength, not weakness. The revision of social systems and the critique of programs for political change are positive responses to a community's increased awareness of the consequences of its actions.

The notion of the eschatological reservation cannot provide such resiliency if grounded in a contrast between human actions and divine power. If political programs are faulted for not bringing about the kingdom of God, and if failure is seen as evidence of the folly of all human actions, the will for political action is destroyed.

The notion of the eschatological reservation is used to explain both the limits of human action and the horizon of human hope. The latter dimension of the eschatological reservation is highlighted in Dennis McCann's critique of liberation theology from the perspective of Christian realism.

McCann argues that the perspective of Christian realism developed by Reinhold Niebuhr is more Christian than is the perspective of liberation theology and also provides a more adequate basis for political action. McCann contrasts "religious disinterestedness" with "solidarity with the oppressed."[25] McCann, like Niebuhr before him, wants to develop an interpretation of faith than can sustain critical (that is, nonfanatical), and transformative political activity. McCann and Niebuhr are also aware of the dangers of cynicism and apathy, and they argue that "religious disinterestedness" provides an effective check against these ills of inaction. McCann contrasts "religious disinterestedness" with "revolutionary enthusiasm." He argues that liberation theology cannot make a distinction between "genuine limit-situations and illusory ones" and cannot offer, therefore, "criteria for distinguishing limits that summon people to worshipful contemplation rather than political action."[26] McCann contrasts the unbounded hope of the liberation theologian with the qualified hope of the Christian realist. He claims that there are some limits that cannot be removed, and he faults liberation theologians for supporting a naive hope: "Genuine limit-situations must be accepted in faith, a response that leads, it is hoped, to repentance and a measure of serenity in social conflict."[27]

According to McCann, liberation theologians are naively utopian, seeing no limits to human possibilities.

In McCann's interpretation of the choice between "religious disinterestedness" and "solidarity with the oppressed," the profound challenge of liberation theology is lost. For liberation theologians the foundation of action is not a particular view of what is possible in history but is rather a perspective from which one determines the current boundaries of human hope. The foundation of analysis and action is a passionate love for the oppressed.[28] When I fully love myself, my people, and others who are oppressed, my hope for our lives is expanded. I begin to question whether previously accepted limits are actually necessary. What emerges is not the naive denial of any genuine limits but a sophisticated questioning of what a social system has set as "genuine limits." Women of all races are questioning "natural" physical and social limits, that is, women "naturally" being defined socially and rewarded economically primarily through their relationships with men. Men and women of color question the worldwide distribution of wealth and political power, and their questioning is grounded in a vital self-love. June Jordan describes a worldwide movement of women and men challenging the necessity and legitimacy of existing political systems, a phenomenon she describes as grounded in love: ". . . the movement into self-love, self-respect, and self-determination is the movement now galvanizing the majority of human beings everywhere."[29]

Liberation theologians do offer "criteria for distinguishing limit-situations that summon people to worshipful contemplation rather than political action."[30] The criteria are primarily those of loyalty and action. The genuineness of the limits facing a people can best be assessed from the point of view of love for people and from the perspective of those involved in concrete struggles to live with joy and integrity.

From such involvement some limits formerly seen as genuine are criticized as socially imposed, and some described as removable are reinstated. Examples of the former abound in the work of liberation theologians—landless Latin Americans asserting social and political equality with formerly feared landowners and demanding a more equitable distribution of land ownership and political power.[31] Feminist theologians challenge the assumption that love for others limits self-love and self-concern. Rosemary Ruether, Judith Plaskow, and Mary Daly, for example, all criticize definitions of love as self-sacrifice.[32]

Feminist theologians, especially those reaffirming earth-based spiritual traditions, argue that the limits of finitude and death, seen as transitory in Western cultural and religious traditions, are, in fact, irremovable. Loving the earth, nature, and humanity as part of nature does lead to the recognition of "limits" and does provide a principle of self-critique, a check against the idolatrous reification of any particular human project.

The deep, resilient love for humanity and for the earth that motivates societal critique and self-critique is missing in the work of many liberal theologians. Even when an overemphasis on divine transcendence is criticized, vestiges remain in skepticism about the value of the finite in and of itself. It is instructive to find a dangerous equation of divinity and control and a correlated depreciation of all that is finite (humanity itself, efforts to establish justice, nature) in the work of liberal theologians.

THE EROTICS OF DOMINATION

A theology that valorizes absolute power through its concept of an omnipotent God is dangerous for middle-class people. While the conceptual logic of the notion of God's absolute power points to establishing a critical principle in regard to human domination, I find the political logic of such doctrines to be the glorification of domination.[33] Doctrines of the sovereignty and omnipotence of God are meant to relativize human claims to power. Theologians argue that the value of such doctrines lies in their reminder of our lack of power and our dependence on God. The idea of an omnipotent and sovereign God, however, assumes that absolute power can be a good. In the Christian tradition, one does not attribute demonic or destructive traits to Deity. And yet absolute power *is* a destructive trait. It assumes that the ability to act regardless of the response of others is a good rather than a sign of alienation from others. Alfred North Whitehead described the phenomenon well:

> When the Western world accepted Christianity, Caesar conquered; and the received text of Western theology was edited by his lawyers. . . . The brief Galilean vision of humility flickered throughout the ages, uncertainly. . . . But the deeper idolatry, of the fashioning of God in the image of the Egyptian, Persian, and Roman imperial rulers, was retained. The Church gave unto God the attributes which belonged exclusively to Caesar.[34]

Although rituals and doctrines that affirm the absolute power of God also claim that such power is had only by God, they also reinforce a human desire for absolute power, a dangerous desire for those who have political and economic power. The distinction between divine and human, masks, but does not eliminate, the valorization of absolute power. In fact, the claim of relativization, of submission to the greatest power, legitimates the domination of others. This phenomenon can be described in terms of the erotics of domination.[35] A powerful group claims that its primary, essential activity is submission and obedience to a higher power. Members of the ruling class experience intense satisfaction in the abdication of power and responsibility and in the willing acquiescence to the directives of another. The result of willed abdication is not passivity, however, but the legitimation of total power. A group or individual exercises power indirectly, their actions now legitimated as the fulfillment of commands. Critique and accountability are displaced: the powerful regard themselves as merely the agents of a higher power. Augustine's legitimation of the coercive power of the state is a case in point. Elaine Pagels has described the astonishing success of Augustine's views of human freedom as "free slavery": "Since man has been so naturally created that it is advantageous for him to be submissive, but disastrous to follow his own will, and not the will of his creator" (De civ. Dei, 14. 12).[36] This view is sharply divergent from the orthodox concepts held by many in the first four centuries of Christianity, for whom "the moral freedom to rule oneself" was "virtually synonymous with the gospel."[37] Pagels traces the changes that led to the Christian acceptance of the necessity of imperial rule even for Christians. She claims that such acceptance of coercive power follows from a belief that even a Christian government is corrupt and that such government is nonetheless necessary because even the redeemed remain captive to a divided and unruly will: "Augustine . . . draws so drastic a picture of the effects of Adam's sin that he embraces human government, even when tyrannical, as the indispensable defense against the forces sin has unleashed in human nature."[38] What Pagels describes as "a theology of politics far more complex and compelling than any of its rivals," I see as the erotics of domination.[39] I agree with Pagels that Augustine's definition of liberty is "far more agreeable to the powerful and influential men with whom he himself wholeheartedly identifies."[40] Augustine's views of "our true good [as] free slavery"[41] is "compelling" and "agreeable" because it justifies and legitimates the brutal exercise of power in the interest of total control. Those who exercise power are not held accountable for that exercise by themselves or others, for they are also "slaves" to the Lord. The claim of complete obedience to a higher power justifies total control of others. "Later in his life Augustine came to endorse, for the Church as well as the state, the whole arsenal of secular government that Chrysostom had repudiated—commands, threats, coercion, penalties, and even physical force.[42]

Claiming to be as sinful as all of humanity, Augustine became a tyrant, using coercive power against non-Catholic Christians. "First came laws denying civil rights to non-Catholic Christians; then the imposition of penalties, fines, eviction from public office; and finally, denial of free discussion, exile of Donatist bishops, and the use of physical coercion."[43] In Augustine's work as a bishop we see clearly the political effects of the valorization of absolute power. Augustine defines himself and all humanity as free only when submissive to the absolute power of God. His view of unremitting human weakness and the goodness and necessity of divine control legitimates his exercise of coercive power as a bishop. "Many Christians as well as pagans, he noted regretfully, respond only to fear."[44]

Augustine's understanding of human bondage, while denounced as heretical by many of his contemporaries, became definitive of Christian orthodoxy. It is a view of human weakness and divine power that has had disastrous effects in Western history. If humans are regarded as incapable of self-government—saved only through obedience to an absolutely powerful God—the church and the state, far from being relativized and limited, become the agents of the necessary control of sinful human beings.

The results of the valorization of absolute power are indeed dangerous: either domination of others in the name of the common good or despair at not being able to readily attain the essential goals of peace, freedom, and justice. A theology that emphasizes the absolute power of God holds as an ideal a type of power not possible for those working for justice. The expectation of certain victory leads middle-class activists to disillusionment in the face of defeat, to cynicism in the face of partial remedies to overwhelming problems, or to acquiescence to the efficient, triumphal workings of even unjust power.

Dietrich Bonhoeffer describes this latter phenomenon in any essay written in 1943. Writing in prison, he explores the theological and ethical significance of Hitler's rise to power. Bonhoeffer decries both the power of fascism and the weakness of resistance. He points to a feature of the Third Reich often forgotten in the light of hindsight: this rule of monstrous cruelty wore the garb of moral purpose and human fulfillment:

> The great masquerade of evil has played havoc with all our ethical concepts. For evil to appear disguised as light, charity, historical necessity or social justice is quite bewildering to anyone brought up on our

traditional ethical concepts, while for the Christian who bases his life on the Bible it merely confirms the fundamental wickedness of evil.[45]

Bonhoeffer was tormented by the failure of "moral" and "reasonable" people to persistently work against fascism:

> The "*reasonable*" people's failure is obvious. With the best intentions and a naive lack of realism, they think that with a little reason they can bend back into position the framework that has got out of joint. In their lack of vision they want to do justice to all sides, and so the conflicting forces wear them down with nothing achieved. Disappointed by the world's unreasonableness, they see themselves condemned to ineffectiveness; they step aside in resignation or collapse before the stronger party.[46]

Bonhoeffer explores this resignation thoroughly and describes it as folly. He argues that supporters of Hitler cannot be swayed by reason, for their support has as its ground "a moral rather than intellectual defect."[47] Support for the forces of oppression is grounded in folly—capitulation in the face of overwhelming power:

> . . . we see that any violent display of power, whether political or religious, produces an outburst of folly in a large part of mankind [sic]; indeed, this seems actually to be a psychological and sociological law: the power of some needs the folly of the others. It is not that certain human capacities, intellectual capacities for instance, become stunted or destroyed, but rather that men are deprived of their independent judgment, and—more or less unconsciously—give up trying to assess the new state of affairs for themselves. . . . Having thus become a passive instrument, the fool will be capable of any evil and at the same time incapable of seeing that it is evil. Here lies the danger of a diabolical exploitation that can do irreparable damage to human beings.[48]

What Bonhoeffer sees in the Third Reich is present elsewhere in the Western tradition. He describes what I call the erotics of domination, a typical pattern in which oppressive power gains much of its force through the claim of submission to a greater moral purpose. The claim of moral purpose blinds both oppressor and those who acquiesce to oppression. The valorization of absolute power is constitutive of the dreams of the oppressors and the capitulation to force on the part of others. Without the valorization of absolute power, it would not make sense "that the upsurge of power makes such an overwhelming impression that men are deprived of their independent judgment."[49]

The exercise of folly is not limited to Germany under the sway of fascism. Its presence can be traced throughout the Western tradition, a dangerous corollary to the construction of virtue in imperial societies.

When absolute power is valorized and is not seen as inimical to the pursuit of social goods, a people becomes susceptible to the propaganda of those in power. The attraction of power overrides critical judgment. Media and congressional capitulation to the power claims of the Reagan administration are a case in point. In a recent article in *The Atlantic,* Thomas Ferguson and Joel Rogers analyze the myth of America's turn to the right.[50] They argue that popular support for the Reagan presidency was neither solid nor widespread. Ferguson's and Roger's arguments are based on two sets of information, measures of agreement with Reagan on particular issues and indicators of Reagan's popularity.

The first case is more well known. Most people in the United States disagreed with Reagan on a wide range of issues, from social welfare policies to foreign policy. Ferguson and Rogers demonstrate that "the central claim made by revisionist Democrats and Republicans alike— that a majority of the public has reached a stable, well-informed consensus on the desirability of right, or center-right, policies . . ." is not true.[51]

> On virtually all the important issues identified with the "Reagan revolution" in public policy, public opinion ran against the President. Moreover, of those voting for Reagan only six percent (as compared with an already low 11 percent in 1980) directly identified his conservatism as one of the things that mattered to them, and only five percent offered agreement with his views as their chief reason for support.[52]

Ferguson and Rogers also dispute the widely held reason for Congressional acquiescence to Reagan's policy initiatives, that despite disagreements on specific issues, he was "the most popular President in modern times or . . . he has a magical hold over the electorate."[53] While Reagan did receive an unusually large share of the two-party vote (59.2 percent in 1984), his share of the *potential* electorate, in both 1980 and 1984, was remarkably low, 27.6 percent in 1980, and only 32.3 percent in 1984.

> As a percentage of the potential electorate, voter turnout was stagnant, rising only 0.7 percent from its 1980 level to run at 55 percent. Some 77 million eligible Americans—24 million more than voted for Reagan—abstained. In 1984 Reagan garnered 32.3 percent, or a smaller share than that gained by Eisenhower in both his elections, by either Kennedy *or* Nixon in 1960, by Johnson in 1964, or by Nixon in 1972.[54]

What is most revealing about Ferguson's and Rogers' analysis is their demonstration that Reagan was not "the most popular President of the postwar period." When they compared his approved ratings with those of other presidents, they found that his public support was not measurably greater than that of Eisenhower, Nixon, or Kennedy.[55] What can account, then, for the reelection of Reagan and the powerful myth of his popularity? Ferguson and Rogers claim that Reagan was reelected for the simple reason that any incumbent president has been reelected, the perception of economic recovery.[56] They do not analyze, however, the resiliency of the myth of Reagan's personal popularity and the effects of that myth in curbing Congressional challenges to Reagan's policy initiatives. These latter factors have roots deeper than a concern with economic growth. They were an expression of folly, the acquiescence of people in Congress and the media to the appearance of overwhelming power. Such capitulation, a truly remarkable abandonment of independent thinking, is a natural outcome of the valorization of absolute power in the Western philosophical and religious traditions. While Reagan was not extremely popular, the myth of his personal appeal had effects of truth, as seen in his reelection and in Congress's capitulation to his domestic and foreign policies. This support was a manifestation of an economic and religious expression of the erotics of domination.

THE VALORIZATION
OF ABSOLUTE POWER

In the Western religious traditions the greatness of deity is often construed in terms of absolute power. This construal has several dimensions. First is the principle of exclusivity. That which is worthy of worship is categorically unique. The interpretations of this uniqueness may vary, but an emphasis on the singularity of divine eminence is a constant in the Western tradition since Augustine. Anselm, for example, defines God as "that than which nothing greater can be conceived."[57] H. Richard Niebuhr gives a modern rendition of this principle in his definition of radical monotheism: "Radical monotheism dethrones all absolutes short of the principle of being."[58] While other beings are valued, they are not valued in themselves but are respected as holy "because of their relations to the holy One."[59] Only God is "deserving of . . . unqualified reverence."[60] Karl Barth gives an exceedingly clear and consistent exploration of the singularity of divine power.

> The stone wall we first ran up against was that the theme of the Bible is the deity of *God,* more exactly God's *deity*—God's independence and particular character, not only in relation to the natural but also to the

spiritual cosmos; God's absolutely unique existence, might, and initiative, above all in his relation to man.[61]

The concept of the singularity of divine power is accompanied by a definition of power as the ability of a single actor to control other actors or a course of events. Paul Tillich, for example, defines power as "the possibility a being has to actualize itself against the resistance of other beings,"[62] and he sees the power of God as the absolute manifestation of such control: "The Divine Life is the eternal conquest of the negative; this is its blessedness."[63] The Divine Life is the absolute defeat of nonbeing. Tillich claims that the negative is not forgotten, for that entails a moment of remembering, but "is present in the eternal memory as that which is conquered and thrown out into its naked nothingness. . . ."[64] Barth is here in accord with Tillich, with his definition of the power of God as the choice to be with and for humanity but in such a way that there is no dependence on human response. "*He* is the initiator, founder, preserver, and fulfiller of the covenant."[65]

The result of the theological valorization of the absolute power is the erotics of domination, the glorification of submission to the greatest power. Tillich and Barth both emphasize the self-sacrifice of Jesus, Tillich naming this sacrifice as constitutive of Jesus' power:

> Jesus of Nazareth is the medium of the final revelation because he sacrifices himself completely to Jesus as the Christ. He not only sacrifices his life, as many martyrs and many ordinary people have done, but he also sacrifices everything in him and of him which could bring people to him as an "overwhelming personality" instead of bringing them to that in him which is greater than he and they. This is the meaning of the symbol "Son of God." . . .[66]

The return for total sacrifice is absolute cosmic and historical power. Jesus as the Christ is not only the bearer of the final revelation in human history but the bearer of truth for the entire cosmos:

> The final revelation, the revelation in Jesus as the Christ, is universally valid, because it includes the criterion of every revelation and is the *finis* or *telos* (intrinsic aim) of all of them. . . . It is the criterion of every religion and of every culture. . . . It is valid for the social existence of every human group and for the personal existence of every human individual. It is valid for mankind [*sic*] as such, and, in an indescribable way, it has meaning for the universe also. . . . Christian theology affirms that he is all this because he stands the double test of finality: uninterrupted unity with the ground of his being and the continuous sacrifice of himself as Jesus to himself as the Christ.[67]

While intended to relativize all human claims to power, the valorization of domination and submission leads to the legitimation of imperial power. Such legitimation is clear in Tillich's work. While critical of some claims to domination (the fascism of the Nazis), he is not critical of the will to power present in fascism but only of its "distorted" form: "the need for a vocational self-understanding is so strong that the absurdities of Nazi-racism were accepted because they filled a vacuum."[68]

For Tillich, "vocational self-understanding" is, by definition, universalist and requires coercive power. Tillich claims that a great people or nation assumes, by definition, that their version of the good, of the just, of the most appropriate form of political organization, should be accepted by all peoples and nations. According to Tillich, such acceptance also entails the unification of all peoples and nations into one nation. He dismisses alternative, nonuniversal formations of national identity as merely reactive:

> Is it justifiable to speak of *one* aim? . . . not all tribes and nations have striven or are striving toward all-inclusiveness, that not every conquest has the ambiguity of empire-building, and that even those in whom the drive toward universal integration has been effective have often made it ineffective by withdrawing to a limited tribal or national centeredness. These facts show that there is in history-bearing groups a tendency against the universalistic element in the dynamics of history. . . . But one can show that in all important cases of this kind the isolationist movement was and is not a genuine action but a reaction, a withdrawal from involvement in universalist movements. Historical existence stands under the "star" of historical time and runs ahead against every particularist resistance.[69]

For Tillich, striving toward the "universal integration" of all peoples into one political system has more than historical significance; it expresses the religious meaning of history as well. It is this element of global integration that is meant by the symbol of the kingdom of God.

> It is significant that the symbol in which the Bible expresses the meaning of history is political: "kingdom of God," and not "life of the Spirit" or "economic abundance." The element of centeredness which characterizes the political realm makes it an adequate symbol of the ultimate aim of history.[70]

Tillich's valorization of empire is not naive. He is aware of the coercion inevitably entailed in "universal integration." Yet the "ultimate aim of history" is still represented in the search for empire despite the violence and coercion that accompany "universal integration" and that may lead to the destruction of humanity through nuclear war:

No imagination can grasp the amount of suffering and destruction of structure, life, and meaning that is inevitably connected with the growth of empires. . . . The tragic consequences of their conflict (the United States and the Soviet Union) are noticeable in every historical group and every individual human being, and they may become destructive for mankind itself.[71]

Despite the possibility of ultimate destruction attending the pursuit of empire, Tillich affirms this effort and rejects a particularistic or pacifist option. His reasons for rejection are explicitly theological. Though possibly destructive, the power of empire is akin to the power of God: both are affirmations of being against the forces of nonbeing. "The depreciation of power in most pacifist pronouncements is unbiblical as well as unrealistic. Power is the eternal possibility of resisting non-being. God and the Kingdom of God 'exercise' this power eternally."[72]

Tillich does qualify the affirmation of power by stating that wherever the kingdom of God is victorious in history, the element of compulsion essential to empire is mitigated by the democratic idea, which can be present in aristocratic and monarchic constitutions as well as explicitly democratic ones. Yet in his description of the way in which coercion is limited, Tillich evokes what I have called the erotics of domination: the rulers are themselves ruled, thus legitimately controlling others. "Under the impact of the Spiritual Presence, the members of the ruling group (including the ruler) are able to sacrifice their subjectivity in part by becoming objects of their own rule along with all other objects and by transferring the sacrificed part of their subjectivity to the ruled."[73]

While coercion may be limited, the aim of universal integration and universal rule mystifies relations of domination.

. . . the community must create centeredness, . . . by a ruling group which itself is represented by an individual (king, president, and so on). . . . The ambiguities of justice which follow from this character of communal centeredness are rooted in the unavoidable fact that the ruler and the ruling group actualize their own power of being when they actualize the power of being of the whole community they represent.[74]

Like Augustine, Tillich sees humans as fundamentally incapable of self-rule. He claims that the attempts to avoid necessary forms of coercion lead to "unrestricted tyranny": "The other consequence, resulting from opposition to the implications of power, is a powerless liberalism or anarchism, which is usually soon succeeded by a conscious and unrestricted tyranny."[75]

Tillich, Barth, and H. Richard Niebuhr are explicitly opposed to all forms of tyranny, human or divine. They try to describe a divine power that fulfills essential human possibilities and criticizes human pretensions to absolute power. Their work fails, however, on both counts. Human coercive power is legitimated, and work for the transformation of human life is undercut. The cause of the failure is the valorization of absolute power present in their works. In their works we can see the inexorable logic of absolute power—the only type of power that is guaranteed to be successful is destructive power. One can ensure the death of an enemy, but one cannot ensure the cooperation of another in mutually fulfilling and transforming work. The pursuit of guaranteed total fulfillment produces the destruction of life.

Tillich's valorization of a power that is ultimately destructive of finite human life is not an anomaly in Christian theology. H. R. Niebuhr makes the same claim. The power of the logic of destruction can be seen in its operation in the thought of men who want to affirm human life. Niebuhr, for example, repeatedly states that "whatever is, is good."[76] His affirmation of life is decisively undercut, however, by the valorization of absolute power. The fact that our power is not absolute (we are conditioned by time, place, and the ongoing process of life) is regarded as a tragedy, not celebrated as the source of the richness, diversity, and novelty of life:

> The tragedy of our religious life is not only that it divides us within ourselves and from each other. There is a greater tragedy—the twilight of the gods. None of these beings on which we rely to give content and meaning to our lives is able to supply continuous meaning and value. The causes for which we live all die. The great social movements pass and are supplanted by others. The ideas we fashion are revealed by time to be relative. The empires and cities to which we are devoted all decay. At the end nothing is left to defend us against the void of meaninglessness.[77]

Niebuhr's thought is decisively shaped by the valorization of absolute power. What I also worship, naming it the web of life or the dance of life, he values as the source and "slayer of all." Assuming as a positive norm the ability to exercise absolute power and avoid the changes attending interdependence, he claims that the force that leads to such change is both creative and destructive:

> What is it that is responsible for this passing, that dooms our human faith to frustration? . . . Against it there is no defense. This reality, this nature of things, abides when all else passes. It is the source of all

things and the end of all. . . . our faith has been attached to that great void, to that enemy of all our causes, to that opponent of all our gods. . . . We have been enabled to say of this reality, . . . "though it slay us yet will we trust it." We have been allowed to attach our confidence to it, and put our reliance in it which is the one reality beyond all the many, which is the last power, the infinite source of all particular beings as well as their end. And insofar as our faith, our reliance for meaning and worth, has been attached to this source and enemy of all our gods, we have been enabled to call this reality God.[78]

The search for absolute power, for a final fulfillment, leads Niebuhr to worship that which is "source and slayer" with more emphasis on the slaying than the source. His ability to criticize unjust human structures is undercut by his fear of change. He makes the dangerous equation of finitude and wrong and loses a principle of critique that would allow him to unreservedly value structures and relationships of justice.

To attach faith, hope and love to this last being, this source of all things and this slayer of all, is to have confidence which is not subject to time, for this is the eternal reality, this is the last power. . . . "It is a consoling idea," wrote Kierkegaard, "that before God we are always in the wrong." All the relative judgments of worth are equalized in the presence of this One who loves all and hates all, but whose love like whose hatred is without emotion, without favoritism.[79]

Unable to imagine the eternal value of any human projects, Niebuhr is consoled by a power that can guarantee the defeat of all human projects. This choice of security, even the security of always being wrong, undercuts efforts toward justice. Tillich gives a clear statement of this logic in his critique of any hope that the kingdom of God can be manifest in history. He claims that the "popular imagination" hopes for merely "an idealized reduplication of life as experienced within history." These hopes reflect a limited imagination; they "are projections of all the ambiguous materials of temporal life" and "far exceed the limits of essentially justified hope."[80]

If one valorizes empire, as does Tillich, the establishment of a modicum of justice within one's own borders is of little account. The hope of reformers and revolutionaries reflects both too little and too much: too little, merely a modification of the conditions of finitude and not conquering the finite; too much, audaciously expecting that sinful humans can substantially alter the conditions of their existence by doing more than replacing one form of domination with another.

In chapters seven and eight I explore the audacity of those activists and theologians who unreservedly value the finite and consistently acknowledge both the limits and the value of our attempts to establish justice. Feminist theologians and feminist ethicists challenge the motivating hopes and aspirations of much of Western theology. We offer alternative ethical sensibilities and a radically different religious imagination. In the next chapters I present my construction of an ethic and a theology that values finitude, interdependence, change, and particularity.

7

An Ethic of
Solidarity and Difference

————— ■ —————

Once a community has decided what is "caring," "right," or "just,"
what blocks the implementation of those choices? What enables a
community to work with integrity and persistence for a just society?
Working for justice entails far more than the determination of what is
just. Strategies must be developed and refined; persistence and imagination must be fostered and nurtured. In this chapter I present a
reorientation for ethical theory that begins from the vantage point of
the disjunction between a principled analysis of injustice and sustained work to transform conditions of injustice. In addition to examining the process by which a community chooses particular norms
(such as justice or peace) or particular ends (eliminating racism or
the threat of war), I examine the blocks that prevent the transla-
tion of communally chosen norms and ends into sustained political action.

My analysis in this chapter has, therefore, a dual focus. On the
one hand, I describe the interaction between Euro-Americans and
African-Americans that has led me to a critique of Western understandings of responsible action as an instance of communicative
ethics. On the other hand, I explore the implications of communicative ethics for the development of criteria for both moral norms and
political strategies.

My defense of a feminist ethic of risk and my critique of liberal ethics
and politics emerge from the practice of communicative ethics. Communicative ethics are an alternative to the communal ethics of Alistair
MacIntyre and Stanley Hauerwas. Unlike theorists who argue that the
prerequisite of solid moral reasoning is a cohesive community with a

shared set of principles, norms, and mores, I argue that material inter-action between multiple communities with divergent principles, norms, and mores is essential for foundational moral critique. I argue that a cohesive community, such as the Aristotelian polis, lacks the means to criticize constitutive forms of injustice, forms of exclusion and limitation (like the Athenian institutions of slavery and the sup-pression of women) central to the operation of a given social system. The moral critique of structural forms of injustice emerges, rather, from the material interaction of different communities. In contrast to Jürgen Habermas, I argue that morally transformative interaction requires far more than conversation between different groups and peo-ples and that "genuine" conversation presupposes prior material inter-action, either political conflict or coalition, or joint involvement in life-sustaining work. In this chapter I discuss the relationship between epistemology and political practice by examining the stance of the interpreter, the inherent and desirable partiality of understanding, and the political prerequisites of self-critical moral reasoning.

COMMUNICATIVE ETHICS

Many theologians, like scholars in other fields, are currently involved in debates over the best means of including fundamentally different perspectives in academic work. Stephen Fowl, for example, contrasts two schemes for acknowledging the significance of different per-spectives in biblical studies, the pluralist view and the social respon-sibility view. Pluralists claim that different prerogatives (both those of different methods and different definitions of the subject to be studied) should be taken seriously because "plurality . . . [is] a wor-thy end in and of itself."[1] According to pluralists, the criterion for pursuing a particular type of textual interpretation (e.g., Marxist or feminist) "is that it is interesting to sufficient numbers of interpreters to enable a conversation to take place."[2] The "social responsibility view" brings to the fore a question impossible for the pluralist com-munity: "whether its members should pursue one [interpretive] inter-est over another," as demanded by the criteria of social justice and well-being.[3]

Fowl goes on to claim that the social responsibility view requires "a Rawlsian view of justice as an ahistorical, transcultural virtue recognizable by all rational people." He assumes that without such a criterion it would be impossible to adjudicate the claims of differ-ent interpretive practices to better "serve the pursuit of justice."[4] In contrast to either position, Fowl advocates the adoption of

Alistair MacIntyre's communal position, in which the criteria for choosing among interpretive interests lie in the "shared convictions" of particular communities as to the "goods and ends they are to pursue."[5]

While I agree with Fowl's rejection of the pluralist point of view, seeing in it the inability to make principled distinctions between various interests, I find MacIntyre's conception of the communal position equally inadequate. MacIntyre argues that we should pursue historical and anthropological investigation of systems of morality, learning about a wide range of "moral practices, beliefs and conceptual schemes."[6] MacIntyre sees in one such community, the cohesive Aristotelian polis, the solution to the "moral calamity" of our day— the impossibility of appealing to shared moral criteria.[7] In contrast to MacIntyre, I argue that the "moral calamity" of our day lies not in the lack of shared moral criteria but in the inability of most communities to engender or accept a thorough critique of their "own purposes" and their "terms" of implementing those purposes. From this perspective, the Aristotelian polis appears to be fundamentally flawed in the same way that many contemporary communities are flawed—unable to see as unjust the inequality crucial to its functioning.

The ethic of the Aristotelian polis was intrinsically one of exclusion, limited to the relationships of free men. In Michel Foucault's detailed description of the ethical categories through which classical Greek culture (fourth century B.C.E.) understood the use and limits of sexuality, I find a clear connection between what a particular society considered normative and the maintenance of oppression. Foucault states that the ethical systems developed by Plato and Aristotle were not meant to be universally applicable but were, quite self-consciously, an ethics for free men.[8] Within this ethical system, freedom did not mean independence "of any exterior or interior constraint; in its full positive form it was a power that one brought to bear on oneself in the power that one exercised over others."[9] Foucault states that "virtue was not conceived as a state of integrity, but as a relationship of domination, a relation of mastery."[10] For Aristotle and for Plato, "self-mastery and the mastery of others were regarded as having the same form; . . . one was expected to govern oneself in the same manner as one governed one's household [women and slaves] and played one's role in the city. . . ."[11]

Far from leading to a critique of the harsh treatment of women and slaves, the ethical system of classical Greek culture found an intrinsic harmony between virtue and the domination of women, slaves, and the "low-born populace."[12] Foucault finds in Xenophon's *Oeconomicus,* for example, a clear description of "the continuity and isomorphism of these three 'arts':"[13] Xenophon claimed that "governing oneself, managing one's estate [which included slaves and women], and participating in the administration of the city were three practices of the same type."[14] Within this ethical system, the problematic area for sexual ethics was not that of relationships to women (who were by definition subject to men) or to slaves (who were "properly" the "sexual objects" of their masters) but the sexual relationships between freeborn, elite males and freeborn, elite boys, a relationship in which the domination proper to sexual relationships between free, elite males and women and slaves became ethically questionable.[15]

In his defense of Aristotelian ethics, MacIntyre, in sharp contrast to Foucault, notes only the exclusion of slaves and ignores the exclusion of women. While he argues that Aristotle's justification of slavery is "indefensible," he claims that it is unrelated to the adequacy of his ethics, that it "need not carry any large implications for our attitudes to his overall theory."[16]

I argue in a quite different fashion that what led to Aristotle's defense of slavery is what is most dangerous in our own society: the assumption that one's own community and social class possesses the prerequisites for moral judgment and that other groups are devoid of those same prerequisites. As MacIntyre states, Aristotle dismisses non-Greeks, barbarians, and slaves as "incapable" of political relationships and thus incapable of participating in political forms that are necessary for the existence of virtue:[17] "He [Aristotle] seeks to be the rational voice of the best citizens of the best city-state; for he holds that the city-state is the *unique political form in which alone the virtues of human life can be genuinely and fully exhausted.*"[18]

The confidence in the superiority of the Aristotelian polis precludes being challenged by either the political systems and ethical standards of other communities or by the ethical standards and experiences of other groups (e.g., women and slaves) within the same community. Communicative ethics, on the other hand, avoids the dangers of isolation and self-justifying ethical systems by its involvement in political coalitions and its openness to political conflict. Foundational ethical critique requires difference. Michel Foucault has argued that we can see a system of logic as partial and not as reason itself only because we participate in alternative systems of making and validating truth claims. The same is true of ethics. We can see foundational flaws in systems of ethics only from the outside, from the perspective of another system of defining and implementing that which is valued. In order to determine which interests or positions are more just, pluralism is required, not for its own sake, but for the sake of enlarging our moral vision.

Communicative ethics combines, therefore, pluralism and social responsibility. From this perspective, Euro-American feminists are justified in criticizing the oppression of women in other cultures, for example, Indian suttee and African genital mutilation. We must remember, however, that critique goes both ways. Genuine communication has not occurred until we become aware of the flaws in our culture that appear quite clearly from the vantage point of Indian and African societies, taking seriously an Indian critique of the Western treatment of children, and a traditional African critique of our extreme individuality and valorization of symmetry and order.[19] From the perspective of communicative ethics, we cannot be moral alone. The discernment of both norms and strategies requires the interaction of different communities.

The concept of communicative ethics that I advocate is being developed by feminist theorists in conversation with the work of Habermas and Foucault. Seyla Benhabib, for example, argues for the importance of acknowledging different perspectives and communities. She criticizes as elitist and exclusive liberal understandings of who should be involved in the determination of what is just. She defines the liberal view as the positing of a "generalized other." Within liberalism, the "generalized other," the partners in moral dialogue or the persons affected by decision-making, are assumed to be fundamentally the same; each individual is seen as "a rational being entitled to the same rights and duties we would want to ascribe to ourselves." There is no need to take into account "the individuality and concrete identity of the other" for "our relation to the other is governed by the norms of *formal equality* and *reciprocity:* each is entitled to expect and to assume from us what we can expect and assume from him or her."[20]

Benhabib questions the validity of this notion of the generalized other (found in Lawrence Kohlberg, John Rawls, and others) because it ignores determinative differences in both access to political power and in the definition of norms and strategies. She argues for an identification of the partners in moral dialogue that is keenly attuned to "specific [and socially constituted] needs, talents and capacities," and finds this identification in Carol Gilligan's focus on the "concrete other":

> The standpoint of the concrete other, by contrast, requires us to view each and every rational being as an individual with a concrete history, identity and affective-emotional constitution. In assuming this standpoint, we abstract from what constitutes our commonality. We seek to comprehend the needs of the other, his or her motivations, what she or he searches for, and what she or he desires. Our relation to the other is governed by the norms of *equality* and *complementary reciprocity:* each is entitled to expect and to assume from the other forms of behavior

through which the other feels recognized and confirmed as a concrete, individual being with specific needs, talents and capacities. . . . The norms of our interactions are . . . friendship, love and care. . . . The corresponding moral feelings are those of love, care and sympathy and solidarity.[21]

A communicative ethic takes as its standpoint the interaction between "concrete others." The ideal situation for moral discernment is thus a collective, historical process. Moral reasoning cannot be carried out by any one theorist but requires dialogue with actual members of different communities. Beverly Harrison makes a similar claim, arguing that "objectivity" or freedom from subjective bias in moral decision-making, requires conversation with people from different groups. "'Objectivity' here means openness to others' history and to the critical claims that history bears and also the ability to learn from others' historical experience."[22]

Harrison reminds us of another significant aspect of taking the standpoint of the concrete other. For not only are we members of different groups, but our groups are related to each other within networks of hierarchy and exploitation. The perspective of Euro-American women or the perspective of African-American women and men cannot be simply added to that of privileged Euro-American males. Even the feminist imperative to tell our own stories requires telling the stories of Euro-American women's participation in the systemic oppression of women of color. Harrison advocates, therefore, a *critical* history. The collective telling of stories is the foundation for seeing and then challenging patterns of systemic injustice:

"Official" history suppresses the stories of resistance and dissent against the status quo and presents the past either as the triumph of the deserving or as inevitable. Critical history breaks open the past, in its full complexity, and re-presents that past as bearing a story of human struggle against domination. Even failed resistance bears powerful evidence of human dignity and courage that informs our contemporary vocations.[23]

From the standpoint of such a critical history, there is an epistemological privilege of the oppressed. Those of us who are oppressed, while not having an ontologically given primacy, do have a point of view essential to moral critique. Sandra Harding describes the preference for the viewpoint of the oppressed as a "standpoint epistemology":

The logic of the standpoint epistemologies depends on the understanding that the "master's position" in any set of dominating social relations tends to produce distorted visions of the real regularities and underlying causal tendencies in social relations—including human interactions with nature.[24]

As Harding points out, since men are in a master position in regard to women, the knowledge of women is particularly valuable. Harding criticizes what I criticize as well, the tendency among some feminists and social critics to reify a particular standpoint as the only standpoint productive of significant social critique. She argues that the logic of standpoint epistemologies entails greater attention to the knowledge of those who are oppressed at many levels—by reason of gender, sexual orientation (gays and lesbians), race, class, nationality, and degree of physical limitations.

In this book I have listened to the voices of African-American women, not because theirs is the only "true" voice (replacing the vantage point of the proletariat in the nineteenth century), but because these voices disclose a knowledge of gender and race oppression, of ethical responses and strategies, that is critical of my social location and thus of the visions that I and other Euro-American women and men have of the possibilities for social change.

The goal of communicative ethics is not merely consensus but mutual critique leading to more adequate understandings of what is just and how particular forms of justice may be achieved. When such critique occurs we may well find that more than our definitions of what is just are challenged; the prerequisites of acting justly may be challenged as well.

THE MATERIAL BASIS OF TRANSFORMATIVE COMMUNICATION

In the exercise of communicative ethics, I find myself both dependent upon and departing from the work of Jürgen Habermas. As feminists search for a form of individuation outside the categories of abstract individualism, the work of Habermas offers many possibilities for critical reflection and political action. Within his theoretical perspective one can imagine interaction between different groups, and his work is an exploration of the grounds for that interaction within the nature of speech itself. He also claims, in contrast to Michel Foucault, that there is the possibility of significant social transformation and emancipation:

> Forms of life are totalities which always emerge in the plural. Their coexistence may cause friction, but this *difference* does not automatically

result in their *incompatibility*. . . . Convictions can contradict one other [*sic*] only when those who are concerned with problems define them in a similar way, believe them to need resolution, and want to decide issues on the basis of good reasons.[25]

Habermas has tried to explain and ground the emancipatory potential of social analysis. He describes a type of social interaction— communicative action—in which the goal is to reach, without force, a mutually acceptable understanding: "The goal of coming to an understanding is to bring about an agreement that terminates in the intersubjective mutuality of reciprocal understanding, mutual trust, and accord with one another."[26] Habermas's exploration of communicative competence leads him in directions similar to that of many postmodern critiques of objective reason. He criticizes the modern reduction of rationality to the "cognitive-instrumental rationality" of a technocratic society and finds three levels of rationality relevant to social analysis.[27] The critique of logocentrism is found not only in postmodern philosophers such as Jacques Derrida; Habermas, too, writes that "logocentrism means neglecting the complexity of reason effectively operating in the life-world, and restricting reason to its cognitive-instrumental dimension (a dimension, we might add, that has been noticeably privileged and selectively utilized in processes of capitalist modernization)."[28]

Habermas's vision of the self is complex. As Anthony Giddens states, Habermas "does not posit a self-sufficient subject, confronting an object-world, but instead begins from the notion of a symbolically structured life-world, in which human reflexivity is constituted."[29]

Habermas tries to ground noncoercive dialogue in the nature of speech itself, arguing that in each sentence we claim that our words are understandable, that they are accurate in their descriptions of reality, that they are appropriate to a particular situation, and that we intend to speak without deception:

> In action oriented to reaching understanding validity claims are "always already" implicitly raised. These universal claims (to the comprehensibility of the symbolic expression, the truth of the prepositional content, the truthfulness of the intentional expression, and the rightness of the speech act with respect to existing norms and values) are set in the general structures of possible communication. In these validity claims communication theory can locate a gentle, but obstinate, a never silent although seldom redeemed claim to reason, a claim that must be recognized de facto whenever and wherever there is to be consensual action.[30]

Although Habermas is most noted for this "linguistic turn," his work also includes attention to the material dimensions of consensus and emancipatory dialogue. In *Knowledge and Human Interests* he recognized the necessity of first instituting the social conditions that allow mutual communication, and he has continued to acknowledge the psychological and institutional matrix of actually living out the decisions reached through "the force of the better argument."[31]

> The cognitive capacity to justify moral action norms has to be supple-mented if it is to become effective in the context of ethical life. . . . Without the capacity for judgment and motivation, the psychological conditions for translating morality into ethical life are missing; without the corresponding patterns of socialization and institutions, i.e., with-out "fitting" forms of life to embodied moral principles, the social conditions for their concrete existence are missing.[32]

Habermas's recognition and affirmation of interactions between groups in which power can be redistributed and social barriers re-moved is valuable. I am interested, however, in searching for more adequate models of the structures of thought and action that enable the breaking of class barriers and race and gender hierarchies. In this regard, I find Habermas's use of conversation as the mode of mutually transformative, socially emancipatory relation problematic.

Habermas's goal of consensus is shared by liberal feminists, who have argued that the political and philosophical task of feminism is to extend to women the basic rights articulated by male liberal theo-rists. But to focus on the ideal of conversation and the extension of that ideal to include women as participants, elides a material reality that prevents such inclusion. If the inclusion of women and minori-ties is simply a matter of extension, why has it been so long in com-ing? This query has immediate relevance for the work of Habermas. He is faulted by Giddens for his failure to extend the bounds of con-versation to include cultural traditions that are in clear opposition to, or highly different from, that of the Western intellectual and eco-nomic elite.[33] Giddens poses the question sharply:

> I was somewhat surprised to see that the section of your book con-cerned with myth in oral culture amounts to only a few pages. If you are going to demonstrate that oral cultures—and agrarian civiliza-tions—operate at a lower stage of rationality to Western or modernized culture, surely a more detailed treatment is called for?[34]

While Habermas may be right to fault the reliance on tradition in some oral cultures, he fails to recognize the possibility of mutual cri-tique. While the West may offer one way of producing social change, some oral cultures offer models of the social self that Habermas him-self values, and, while not providing, as Habermas does, a critique of the autonomous, isolated self, they do exhibit *practices* that constitute a collective, larger self.

In his two-volume work, *Theory of Communicative Action,* Habermas engages in a thorough and carefully nuanced conversation with other theorists. The insights of oral cultures are, however, summarily dismissed. He dismisses the Zande tribe for its cognitive inadequacy, its closed world view and lack of means of testing validity claims that enable change and modification. According to Giddens, Habermas fails to recognize that gaining education as a condition of conversation in itself precludes genuine conversation. The attainment of literacy destroys the fabric of an oral culture. The condition, then, of conversation, is conquest. Habermas has not imagined the search for alternative modes of conversation and interaction in which not only the validity claims but the substantive proposals of each culture could be fairly explained.

The work of Richard Katz serves as a helpful alternative.[35] In his examination of an oral culture, the Kalahari Kung, he describes the aspects of that culture that challenge Western notions of agency and subjectivity. He describes a process of psychological and physical healing. All members of the tribe participate in a collective dance in which the healing power, or "boiling energy," is raised. While some people circulate among the group as "healers," actually being filled with "boiling energy" and touching the people who are afflicted, they are not viewed as the only healers. The dancers, drummers, and all the other participants in the ritual are fully seen as healers, for their activities are necessary to raise the energy that the "healers" then direct. Katz sees here a recognition of a collective self, and he sees the creation of power that he describes as a serious challenge to Western notions of the autonomous individual actor.

Genuine conversation with other cultural traditions leads to a further fundamental challenge to Habermas. If other cultures are to be included, an assessment of the criteria for successful conversation must be made. While Habermas poses the norm of the force of the better argument, I turn to the more richly textured narrative as a criterion of description, and, as a criterion of strategies, those projects that create the most possibilities for further emancipatory responses. These criteria may have a ground in human experience as basic as that of consensus. Giddens poses a thought-provoking alternative to Habermas: "'Our first sentence,' you once wrote, 'expresses unequivocally the intention of universal and unconstrained consensus.' Why not say that our first gesture of recognition of another person promises a universal solidarity of human beings?"[36]

The intention of solidarity is potentially more inclusive and more transformative than is the goal of consensus. Many liberation ethicists argue that the search for consensus is a continuation of the dream of domination. Taking as an example the interaction of groups from different strata in an unjust social system, what is the meaning of the goal of consensus? Imagine a conversation between Euro-American feminists, African-American womanists, African-American men, and Euro-American upper-class men. What would consensus mean in such a situation? It would be transformative if the Euro-American men and women could be convinced by the African-American men and women of the pervasiveness of racism and become convinced that its costs are intolerable. Similarly, the women involved would want the men to recognize the myriad manifestations of sexual oppression and become actively involved in trying to eradicate this form of injustice. The group identified as the oppressor in each case will work for a recognition of their good intentions and sensitivity to the difficulties entailed in their own transformation.

Even if we accept an understanding of consensus that means a common recognition of social ills and the need for the rectification of those ills, solidarity is presupposed as a prior step. In order for conversations of this depth to occur, there must be the presupposition of solidarity. Solidarity has two aspects in this case: (1) granting each group sufficient respect to listen to their ideas and to be challenged by them and (2) recognizing that the lives of the various groups are so intertwined that each is accountable to the other. These forms of recognition assume working together to bring about changes in social practice.

I agree with Habermas that conversation is valuable, but claim that transformative dialogue occurs only as the fruition of more foundational interchanges. I want to examine the material base of consensus and the materiality of the movement of emancipatory conversation. From the point of view of the women's movement, I will argue that Habermas's model of communicative action requires the inclusion of materiality at two points.

First, the goal of a conversation in which the only force is that of the better argument presupposes material transformation. Let me take as my example the entry of women into the mainstream of theological education. Women can be part of shaping the theological tradition most fully if certain material conditions are met. There is, for instance, the simple matter of numbers. The differences posited by women are apt to be taken more seriously when they are asserted by many women, and the women attempting to bring a different point of view into dialogue are able to do that with more facility if there are many women in the conversation. Many women with differing perspectives can create a fuller explanation of the feminist claim that self-sacrifice is a dangerously inadequate model of love. Also, transformations in understandings of basic values can be entertained and evaluated more easily if one is not the only spokesperson of one's group but has the actual physical presence of women who can also assess the extent to which one is being coopted or challenged to a more adequate understanding of basic values.

Secondly, I am concerned with the distribution of power in dialogue. What enables the acceptance of those formerly oppressed or ignored into conversation? The work of some postmodern social theorists is quite problematic here, focusing primarily on the role of conflict in producing such exchanges. Habermas's insistence that there is another possibility, a dynamic operative within experience that leads to groups and individuals wanting to listen to the voices of others, is important to consider. Given that there are substantial power imbalances between different groups and given that there are substantial conflicts in terms of values and political strategies as well, what leads to mutually challenging conversation between these groups? While I agree with Habermas that such conversation is possible, I find that he fails to note the material changes required for such conversation to occur.

As is evident in Habermas's dismissal of oral cultures, we are not merely rational actors. The imperatives present in speech do not ensure that all others will be included as participants in conversation. It is essential that we examine the ways in which excluded groups are not seen as fully human, or the exclusion itself is not seen, or the pain of exclusion is not heard.

In the work of African-American women I find richly textured narratives of the processes of exclusion. Paule Marshall's work *The Chosen Place, The Timeless People* is an excellent case in point.[37] As we saw, she depicts the racism of well-meaning whites and the way in which material factors, that is, structural imbalances in power, poison even genuine attempts to provide material help to oppressed people. She describes the cultural mechanisms by which efforts at emancipation are thwarted by the inability of those in power, despite their willingness to help, to admit the extent of the damage done by racism. She describes the ways in which those in power inure themselves to the actual costs of oppression by shutting down and not hearing what is said when it is said in an angry tone. Conversation is stopped when deep pain or rage is expressed. Efforts at reform inevitably fall short, for the extent of the wound is not seen. Also, a material power imbalance is maintained in that those who come to help hold on to the privilege of leaving the fray. They choose to help those who are oppressed but hold on to the possibility of leaving the island, of going back to life as usual. As long as some people think they can leave, the trust necessary for genuine conversation is impossible. Those who are being helped cannot trust either that they will be heard or that, if they speak honestly, the group that has more privilege will stay in the conversation.

Another way in which an unacknowledged power differential thwarts transformative interaction is the extent to which the changes sought by those who have been victimized are seen to entail only loss for the more privileged. For some, sharing power seems like death, a loss of self rather than the invitation to explore an alternative construction of selfhood. For some, explorations of alternative structures of persuasion and self-critique seem like the abandonment of reason rather than the entry into a larger conversation in which the nature of rigorous thought is carefully assessed.

An adequate model of transformative relation includes far more than "the force of the better argument." Giddens's alternative goal of solidarity is more inclusive of the complexity of transformative relationships: "Our first gesture of recognition of another person promises a universal solidarity of human beings."[38] When mutual transformation occurs, there is the power of empathy and compassion, of delight in otherness, and strength in the solidarity of listening to others, bearing together stories of pain and resistance. As we saw, Paule Marshall provides a rich depiction of this process in the same novel. She describes the transformation in action, thought, and empathy of another liberal reformer who enters a mutually transformative relationship with those he is helping. Transformation occurs as the reformer feels the pain of the people who are oppressed. He is open to examining different standards of justice, thus understanding why certain development projects were rejected by the oppressed group. Also, listening to the pain of others requires that the oppressor acknowledge his or her own pain, no longer accepting it as a necessary cost of a civilized social order, but evaluating again its necessity and its implications for a cultural and political system. And finally, there is the dimension of the enlargement of the self. Genuine conversation occurs as one finds joy in listening to others and even as previous and present worlds of meaning are challenged, experiences delight in the complexity of what emerges.

Habermas acknowledges that the claims to reason of the ideal speech situation are rarely met. There is a political reason for such frequent failures. Conversation alone is not enough. Emancipatory conversations are the fruit of work together, the result of alterations in relationships between groups. In work we create as much as we affirm the rational principle of shared humanity. We share our humanity in work and then can move to the conversations that explore the nature of this humanity and the political imperatives it entails.

By work I mean material interaction at the most basic level. For those whose differences are great, work together is often possible at only the most basic level: preparing food together, cleaning, building houses, making clothing. In working together, the alienation of class is challenged: One can see the physical effort required for sustenance and, one then has the option of a different sort of conversation, recognizing the wisdom of the use of the body and the humor that often accompanies such material effort. The travesty of the collectivization of labor is as much the isolation of workers from each other in the factory (isolated by the sheer level of noise and by the division of labor) as in the appropriation of the value created by that labor.

For those with more areas of commonality, a different sort of work enables genuine conversation to occur. A genuine conversation between those who are privileged by way of class, gender, or race and those who have experienced oppression or discrimination on the basis of those characteristics is possible when the privileged work to end the oppression or discrimination they denounce. As we do more than vote for those opposed to racism, challenging racism directly in our workplaces, in our families, and in our own lives, we can be trusted in a way that enables those oppressed because of race to speak with us more honestly. In our work we then see more clearly the costs of racism and the intransigence of structures of oppression. Men who work against rape or domestic violence, who are involved in challenging the value systems that lead to such violence, are able to hear the voices of women, and women are able to trust them in a way that would be impossible if the only form of relation is that of dialogue.

Communicative ethics presupposes and sustains political transformation. The process of dialogue, mutual critique, and political action is dynamic, a spiraling movement in which rudimentary forms of political action enable further critique and evoke more adequate forms of political practice. These qualities, so evident in the literature of African-American women, are characteristic of transformative social action and are the central elements in a feminist ethic of risk.

KNOWLEDGE AND DIFFERENCE

Many feminists are engaged in a lively debate, criticizing what Sandra Harding calls "modernist tendencies in feminism toward a politics [and epistemology] based on identities."[39] The vision of these writers is based on a way of interpreting the world and developing strategies that avoid universalism in favor of an epistemology of solidarity (Harding) and a politics of solidarity and difference. This emerging epistemology represents a revaluation and reinterpretation of the ways of knowing and judging exhibited by many contemporary women. Seyla Benhabib summarizes Carol Gilligan's characterization of the moral judgment of contemporary women, finding the partiality of this reasoning central to its strength and seeing the "contextuality, narrativity and specificity of women's moral judgment" as a sign of the "moral maturity" of a self constituted by a "network of relationship with others."[40]

An epistemology of solidarity posits the determination of judgment by concrete, specific relations. To paraphrase Benhabib, we are not generalized knowers but concrete knowers, our knowledge of ourselves, other people, and the world socially shaped and historically determined. Sandra Harding and Donna Haraway ask us "to explore the new possibilities opened up by the recognition of the permanent partiality of the feminist point of view."[41] They argue that the claim of impartiality as "the hallmark of moral reason" is illusory, that it reflects a naive expectation that one can "stand apart from interests and desires" and "see the whole."[42]

An epistemology of solidarity posits the permanent partiality not only of the feminist point of view but of *all* points of view. This view of reason is sharply divergent from that found in the ethics of the Enlightenment. Iris Young describes the Enlightenment understanding of impartial reason and claims that it is predicated on a counterfactual hypothesis, that of a human being without constitutive relationships:

> From the ideal observer to the original position to a spaceship on another planet, moral and political philosophers begin reasoning from a point of view they claim is impartial. This point of view is usually a counterfactual construct, a situation of reasoning that removes people from their actual contacts of living moral decisions, to a situation in which they could not exist. As Michael Sandel argues, the ideal of impartiality requires constructing the ideal of a self abstracted from the context of any real persons: the deontological self is not connected to any particular ends, has no particular history, is a member of no communities, has no body.[43]

Young argues that the impartial observer of normative rationality is led, by necessity, to the exercise of thinking that is reductive or exclusive of difference:

> Why should normative rationality require the construction of a fictional self in a fictional situation of reasoning? Because this reason, like the scientific reason from which deontology claims to distinguish itself, is impelled by what Theodor Adorno calls the logic of identity. In

this logic of identity reason does not merely mean having reasons or an account. . . . For the logic of identity reason is *ratio,* the principled reduction of the objects of thought to a common measure, to universal laws. The problem with the logic of identity is that through it thought seeks to have everything under control, to eliminate all uncertainty and unpredictability, to idealize the bodily fact of sensuous immersion in a world that outruns the subject, to eliminate otherness.[44]

An epistemology of solidarity is partial because of its immersion in a particular historical and cultural milieu. It is self-critical because of the recognition that while we are shaped by particular histories, there are other communities affected by us both for good and for ill. Learning from and with those shaped by other equally partial traditions helps avoid sectarianism and totalitarianism.

The reasons for the partiality of all points of view are not completely negative. Central to many liberation theologies and recoveries of earth-based religious traditions is an attempt to name the particular, partial religious and cultural traditions constitutive of a people's identity. Thus we have the resurgence of attention to Native American traditions by Native Americans, the rejection of cultural assimilation by many Hispanics in the United States, and the recovery of woman-centered earth religions, all signifying an attempt to base one's identity as an individual and as a people in conversation with particular cultural traditions. What is especially exciting about many of these attempts is the effort to recover the past and to be guided by it without the "codes of conservatism."[45] Traditions are valued; they are not authoritative. Feminist spirituality, for example, in its many variants (pagan, Jewish, and Christian) moves from given religious traditions, using them, as Mary Daly states, as a springboard for creative interpretation and invention.

I agree with Harding, Haraway, and Daly that we learn most from the voices of women as we avoid the assumption of a monolithic female experience and explore our varied constitutions of self and other, valuing our diverse resistances to the attempts of others to impose upon us a singular feminine identity.[46] The feminist standpoint is, therefore, intrinsically multiple and fluid. Our efforts at recovering and creating identities other than those imposed by patriarchal cultures are far from finished. As Harding states, the feminist standpoint "emerges from the political struggles of 'oppositional consciousnesses'—oppositional precisely to the longing for 'one true story' that has been the psychic motor for Western science."[47]

I would like to add to Harding's analysis by describing further reasons for the value of permanently partial perspectives. One value is the ability to see and analyze oppression in its many guises and forms. One

group is not the bearer of all forms of social control, all forms of nor-
malization and marginalization. From the perspectives of our multiple
identities—people of color, gay, lesbian, physically challenged, unemployed—we can create a fuller awareness of the subtleties and
forms of social systems of control. Furthermore, we are more than the
identities created by oppression, and this "more" takes many forms.[48]
The function of telling particular stories of oppression and resistance
is not to find the "one true story" of subjugation and revolt but is to
elicit other stories of suffering and courage, of defeat, of tragedy and
resilient creativity. Anne Cameron, for example, in her recounting of
the traditions of Native American women ends with a request that is far
from the Western longing for the "one true story." She asks that her
story not be retold by those from other traditions, that it not be cited,
sung, or danced, but that it serve as the impetus for all of us to recover,
create, and tell our own stories.[49]

The affirmation of particularity tends to a type of universality, universal accountability, that precludes universally true interpretations
of the human condition or final strategies for social change. Particular
stories call us to accountability. As dangerous memories of conflict,
oppression, and exclusion, they call those of us who are, often un-
knowingly, complicit in structures of control to join in resistance and
transformation. For those of us who are members of the Western elite
by reason of race, gender, education, or economic status are challenged by the stories of the marginalized and oppressed to grasp the
limits of our ethical and political wisdom—the limited appeal of our
capitalist economic system, our limited appreciation of the vitality
and determination of other peoples to shape their own identities.

Listening to the stories of other peoples, seeing how these challenge colonial definitions of the "other," the "African," the "peasant,"
or the "worker," leads, according to Barbara Harlow, to a redefinition
of responsibility. We in the first world are not responsible "for 'the
other,' the 'Third World,' the 'Oriental,' or however [we choose] to
designate the unfamiliar, but for the limitations of its [our] own perspective."[50] We in the first world are not responsible for others; we
are responsible for ourselves—for seeing the limits of our own vision
and for rectifying the damages caused by the arrogant violation of
those limits. Nadine Gordimer describes the limits of the white Western perspective concisely and eloquently: "We whites in South Africa
present an updated version of the tale of the emperor's clothes; we
are not aware of our nakedness—ethical, moral and fatal—clothed as
we are in our own skin."[51]

Our stories, as whites and as elites, still need to be told, but from a
new, chastened perspective. The white Western male narrative is

an imposed "master narrative": the story of that imposition and a reinterpretation of this "master narrative," now shaped by the recognition of its partiality, is yet to be recounted.[52] Many of us have complex identities; Euro-American academic women, for example, are shaped by illusory narratives of the triumph of Enlightenment reason and by fractured recognitions of our identities as women in relation to that narrative.

An epistemology of solidarity is partial for yet another positive reason. As we become accountable for the limits of our vision and the damage caused by the violation of those limits, we become a different community. The public that emerges from mutually accountable work and dialogue is mutually transformative. We do not emerge as the same people, but we all become different, our traditions are reformed, as we begin to be liberated or begin to dismantle systems of oppression. Iris Young describes such a new public and the continued role of particularity and difference in it:

> This public is expressed in the idea of a "Rainbow Coalition." Realized to some degree only for sporadic months during the 1983 Mel King campaign in Boston and the 1984 Jesse Jackson campaign in certain cities, this is an idea of a political public which goes beyond the idea of civic friendship in which persons unite for a common purpose on terms of equality and mutual respect. While it includes commitment to equality and mutual respect among participants, the idea of the Rainbow Coalition specifically *preserves and institutionalizes in its form of organizational discussion the heterogeneous groups that make it up.* In this way it is quite unlike the Enlightenment ideal of the civil public.[53]

Young argues that the unity of the Enlightenment ideal of the civil public was approximated only through the exclusion of "bodily and affective particularity, as well as the concrete histories of individuals that make groups able to understand one another."[54] An emancipatory politics emerges from an epistemology of solidarity, a politic in which "consensus and sharing may not always be the goal, but the recognition and appreciation of difference in the context of confrontation with power."[55]

READING RESISTANCE LITERATURE

A communicative ethic emerges from dialogue and work with people from communities other than one's own primary community. I have found the literature of African-American women to be an invaluable resource in my attempt to learn from the histories of other people. It is valuable at this initial stage of engagement with other communities to read in a way that takes our criteria from within the literature of marginalized communities. While a deconstructionist or structuralist reading of the novels of African-American women may be valuable, I find it important to approach this literature first on its own terms. I have, therefore, interpreted the novels of African-American women in terms of the criteria posed by those who write resistance literature and by African-American critics of resistance literature.[56]

Barbara Harlow provides an account of resistance literature (novels, poetry, and prison autobiographies) that has emerged from marginalized communities in the twentieth century. She and other critics argue that literature plays a crucial role in movements for political change by challenging the taken-for-granted identity of social elites and redefining the identity of those in opposition.[57] Resistance literature is explicitly political in content and form. The content of these novels and this poetry challenges imposed identities and works toward alternative communal descriptions of political and cultural identity. The form calls into question Western theories of the production and criticism of literature.

In my reading of the novels of African-American women, I have followed the codes of interpretation implicit in resistance literature. One of the codes described by Harlow is the experimentation with "structures of chronology and temporal continuity."[58] Unlike similar experiments by Western postmodern novelists, such experimentation has an explicitly political aim, the rewriting of history from the vantage point of the oppressed. The "Western calendar of events" is challenged in several ways.[59] Conquest is shown to be partial, and seeds of resistance are found in past struggles against domination. The description of the present also changes valence. The present is described not so much as a series of inevitable facts but as the impetus for defiance and transformation. The source of artistic technique is also political and historical; it does not emerge primarily from individual creativity but is shaped by a writer's identification with a communal struggle to claim "a role on the historical stage" and to develop a "self-critical historicity."[60] We find here not a loss of temporal continuity per se but the presentation of a new continuity, one shaped by oppression and resistance.

Ernesto Cardenal, for example, the Nicaraguan poet and government official, describes his poetry as providing a new chronology, "a documentary account of the daily historical and historic details, events, and actors in the revolutionary struggle."[61] Resistance writers are engaged in a self-conscious "transformation of the historical record," writing history from the point of view of the colonized and describing the way the ostensible "victims" of colonization and technological change are resisting and have resisted cultural genocide. The "victims" of history are seen here as having a complex identity, partially formed and deformed by colonization, partially formed by the retention and invention of other memories, mores, strategies, and visions.[62]

In resistance literature there is an explicit attempt to recover the past, but in terms that implicitly diverge from the codes of conservatism. There is a sharp critique of nostalgia, of tendencies to see the past romantically, or as "a single unchanging entity."[63] Resistance narratives "[analyze] the past, including the symbolic heritage, in order to open up the possibilities of the future."[64] Depending upon what futures are envisioned and created, the past changes—the events that are highlighted and recounted, the actors noted and memorialized. For resistance movements, the past is not static; it is "a constantly changing succession of events and processes."[65]

While the meaning of the past changes, there is a repeated emphasis on historical specificity. Resistance writers try to "anchor theoretical constructions of generalized problems in the historical specificity which informs a given experience."[66] Resistance literature expresses attention to a critical history on the part of the author and demands such knowledge on the part of the reader, whether it be the "Soweto riots of 1976, the Lebanese civil war, the Arab-Israeli war of 1948, El Salvador's death squads, or Nicaragua's liberation struggle of fifty years."[67] Harlow contrasts the emphasis on historicity with the tenets of the New Criticism, in which texts are read without attention to their historical and social matrix.[68] The analyses of resistance literature are historical in a further sense. They are examinations of power structures that emerged in history through social and contingent causes rather than being the product of inevitable social or natural factors.

Resistance narratives criticize the "master narratives" of Western literature, with their conventions of causality and closure. Resistance literature is postmodern in its rejection of a self-referential closure. Like the deconstructionists, resistance writers see their work as endlessly "textual," or better, referential, understandable only as embedded in a play of historical references and having as its function the evocation of political action. Such action reconstitutes the context and thus the meaning of the text.

Harlow demonstrates the politically motivated avoidance of closure in resistance literature through an interpretation of a short story, the "Apocalypse at Solentiname," written by the Argentinean writer Julio Cortazar. The story was written after Cortazar's visit to the community of Solentiname.[69] Cortazar describes attending mass at Solentiname: ". . . the Solentiname mass in which the peasants and Ernesto and the visiting friends comment together on a chapter of Scripture which that day was Jesus' arrest in the garden, a theme that the people of Solentiname treated as if they were talking about themselves."[70]

Cortazar describes in his story taking photographs of the paintings done by the people of Solentiname. When he views the slides at home alone, he is shocked by what appears:

> You think what you think, it always gets ahead of you and leaves you so far behind, I stupidly told myself that they must have made a mistake at the camera place and given me some other customer's pictures, but the mass then, the children playing on the grass, how then. Nor did my hand obey when I pushed the button and it was an endless sand flat at noon with two or three rusty-roofed sheds, people gathered on the left looking at the bodies laid out face up, their arms open to a naked, grey sky; you had to look closely to make out a uniformed group in the background with their backs turned away, the Jeep waiting at the top of a rise.[71]

Cortazar also sees scenes of arrest, torture, and assassination in Argentina and El Salvador. His story evokes in the reader an encounter with the political context of his work and provides the conditions for subsequent mourning, rage, and resistance.

> According to that [Cortazar's] story, neither authorial intention nor limits and definitions of a formal nature are capable of containing the meanings of artistic work and production. The narrative . . . is embedded in a historical process and ideological development. With that implication of the literary text in the historical process, both as recorder of and influence on that process, the *question of closure* takes on different consequences.[72]

Cortazar's writing, like that of many resistance novelists and poets, embodies "novelistic concerns beyond the formal limitations of the work itself and imposes historical demands and responsibilities on a reader."[73]

> The resistance novels seek different historical endings. . . . Cortazar's storied document of the "apocalypse at Solentiname" thus presents in its reading of the images from Solentiname the necessary conditions for subsequent resistance to the situation of repression and terror exercised by the hegemonic powers of the First World and its collaborators in the Third World. The story is in the end less apocalypse than history, a history, however, which must be taken, seized, appropriated on radically altered terms.[74]

Cortazar challenges us to appropriate history in acts of resistance and defiance. Given the agony that motivates such defiance, the power of resistance literature cannot easily be understood in terms of "the pleasure of the text." There is joy in these texts but not pleasure. Joy emerges from a celebration of resistance and an "emphasis . . . on the political as the power to change the world."[75] Joy is tempered, however, by the memory of how much has been lost to repression and by an awareness of how much remains unchanged.

The style of writing in resistance literature is often stark and uncompromising—the starkness mirroring the harshness of its political context and the urgency of that context's demands for redress and for transformation. The brutality and starkness of the text and its political matrix is illuminated by the conviction in resistance movements that people are worth the effort of political struggle and that political change is possible. Although one finds sharp indictments of the corruption and suppression of dissent in some postcolonial nations, there is rarely found what critic and novelist Ngugi wa Thiong'o describes as the European sense of despair: ". . . some European writers' mania for men without history—solitary and free—with unexplainable despair and anguish and death as the ultimate truth about the human condition."[76] Despair is avoided by an embrace of community. Sahar Khalifeh, a Palestinian novelist, describes his move from existentialism to Marxism as a move from inaction and despair.

> You see, being a Marxist you have to sacrifice certain things; as a privileged individual related to the privileged class, the luxury of having thoughts and not having to carry them into reality. A characteristic of the individualists, of the existentialists, is that when trying to solve problems, they go ahead and then when they face a very, very big problem, which needs . . . communal effort, they stop and cannot continue. They make instead this spiritual leap: . . . going back to religion . . . or find it absurd.[77]

Communal effort, although difficult, is buoyed by loving those who resist and being loved in return. Such love is described by Gioconda Belli, a Nicaraguan poet, in "Until we're free." The context of the poem is the struggle against Somoza.

> let's all brandish our heart
> never fearing that it will burst
> for a heart the size of ours
> resists the cruelest tortures
> and nothing can placate its devastating love
> which grows
> beat by beat
> stronger,
> stronger,
> stronger.[78]

One of the challenges facing liberation movements is the maintenance of love and solidarity in a form that enhances differences. Resistance literature recounts the dangerous tendencies toward what Iris Young calls a "politics of identity."[79] Harlow describes the self-criticism within resistance literature, the many attempts to explain and criticize corruption and the suppression of political dissent. Difference can be perceived as threat when outside pressures remain intense. Yet the struggle continues to maintain a definition and construction of community that cultivates difference.

FEMINISM AND
POSTMODERN CRITICISM

Many activists and intellectuals are developing forms of theoretical critique and political work in which difference does not automatically entail opposition. Much of the theoretical debate is couched in terms of the distinction between modern and postmodern understandings of the self, truth, reason, and beauty. E. Ann Kaplan, for example, claims that the concepts of postmodernism "arise in the wake of theories and debates about race, class, sex, and gender during the past twenty years."[80] Given the political matrix of the concern with the postmodern, it is not surprising that many feminists are evaluating its adequacy as a means of understanding and describing the differences intrinsic to our identities as women.

Yet this exploration of postmodern thought is complicated by the contradictory forces identified as representative of postmodernism. It is not easy to define either modernity or postmodernism. The terms indicate a realm of cultural, political, and philosophical ferment in which redefinitions of truth, beauty, responsible action, and the nature of language are expressed in architecture, art, and divergent types of political activism as well as in the work of philosophers and literary critics. "Postmodern" is primarily a term that refers to a chronological relation rather than to a specific content. "Postmodern" is used to describe a range of activities that are unified by their historical location while radically divergent in terms of method and content. The "postmodern" is a rejection of modernity, and its various forms are, therefore, closely correlated with the type of modernity rejected.

In the current debate within critical theory over the political and conceptual superiority of either a critical modernity or some of the variants of postmodernism, the assessment of the significance of the political activities of the women's movement and the critical contribution of feminist theory is uneven. Some of the leading figures in the debate, Jean-François Lyotard, for example, ignore feminism.[81] Many of those who describe or criticize postmodernism do so without examining whether or not the work of feminists and other marginalized people is part of the postmodern voice. Others have mixed opinions. Foucault ignores the experience of women in most of his work, yet he states that the women's liberation movement is one of the few genuinely transformative forms of political expression.[82] Terry Eagleton makes the most audacious claim, placing the women's movement at the heart of contemporary political and philosophical ferment and arguing that the choice we are now facing is that of "feminism or fascism":

> If modernism's underminings of a traditional humanism are at once anguished and exhilarated, it is in part because there are few more intractable problems in the modern epoch than of distinguishing between those critiques of classical rationality which are potentially progressive and those which are irrationalist in the worst sense. It is the choice, so to speak, between feminism and fascism; and in any particular juncture the question of what counts as a revolutionary rather than barbarous break with the dominant Western ideologies of reason and humanity is sometimes undecidable.[83]

Several feminist theorists also point to a positive conjunction between feminism and postmodern, or poststructural, theory. Joan Scott, for example, argues that poststructuralist theory, despite the lack of attention to women's experience by many of its male proponents, may still help feminists in developing one of the central aims of feminist theory, the development of "alternative ways of thinking about (and thus acting upon) gender without either simply reversing the old hierarchies or confirming them."[84] Scott finds valuable the poststructural analysis of "constructions of meaning and relationships of power that called unitary, universal categories into question and historicized concepts otherwise treated as natural (such as man/woman) or absolute (such as equality or justice)."[85]

The convergence of interest between feminist theorists and postmodern critics is worthy of attention yet difficult to assess because of the many variants of postmodernism. One type of rejected modernity is the modern as the "tradition of the new." In contrast to the "tradition of the new," postmodern culture is an attempt "to break with a program that makes a value of crisis (modernism)," an attempt to move "beyond the era of Progress," and also an attempt to "transgress the ideology of the transgressive."[86] Contrary to the prevalent image of postmodernism, this variant is constructive and affirmative of traditions; it is an attempt to live from traditions without the codes of conservatism. A salient example of this variant of postmodernity can be found in architecture: the rejection of the functional glass box skyscraper in favor of the construction of buildings that reflect the combination of architectural models from a wide range of historical periods.[87] The significance of these developments in architecture is unclear. The result may be an acknowledgment of chaos and whimsy as conducive to human well-being. The impact may also be more reactionary. Not only is the functionalism of modern architecture left behind, but the utopianism of modern architecture, the idea that the human condition can be significantly improved through rationalization and social control, is rejected as well. While I would certainly agree with the rejection of functionalism and rationalization as a means to social reform, I find the rejection of the aim of social transformation deeply problematic. Mike Davis, for example, argues that the currents in postmodern architecture manifest a reactionary defense of privilege, and the new style is primarily that of an elaborate fortress, a bastion against the chaos and threat of the permanently excluded urban underclass.[88]

Any attempt to understand postmodern culture is made exceedingly difficult by the existence of a "postmodernism of reaction," a repudiation of modernity and a celebration of the status quo, and a postmodernism of resistance that criticizes both modernity and the status quo.[89] Frederic Jameson and Terry Eagleton are critical of "the postmodernism of reaction," a culture that is compatible with the imperatives of a consumer society. Eagleton cites as an example Lyotard's positive description of cultural eclecticism: "Eclecticism is the degree zero of contemporary general culture. One listens to reggae, eats McDonald's food for lunch and local cuisine for dinner, wears Paris perfume in Tokyo and 'retro' clothes in Hong Kong; knowledge is a matter of TV games."[90]

Another aspect of the contemporary debate centers on the nature of reason. Many criticize the Weberian project: the attempt "to develop the spheres of science, morality and art 'according to their inner logic.'"[91] The postmodern reaction is a critique of the separation of these spheres as well as a reevaluation of the "inner logic" of each.

The "modern" side of the modern-postmodern debate is equally complex. The primary proponent of the continuation of the project of the Enlightenment, Jürgen Habermas, is himself a critic of modernity and its understanding of rationality. While modernity's role in enabling "liberation from traditional ways of thinking, believing, and acting— and later from tradition itself" is valued, other aspects of modernity are criticized: the roots of modernity introduced valuable new ideas into the repertoire of humankind, yet it is rooted "in underlying dichotomous abstractions such as social versus individual, traditional versus novel, fact versus value, conventional versus original."[92] Habermas tries to develop a critical modernity, or as Richard J. Bernstein states:

> a *new* Dialectic of Enlightenment which does full justice to the dark side of the Enlightenment legacy, explains its causes but nevertheless redeems and justifies the hope of freedom, justice, and happiness. . . . The project of modernity, the hope of Enlightenment thinkers, is not a bitter illusion, not a naive ideology that turns into violence and terror, but a practical task which has *not yet* been realized and which can still orient and guide our actions.[93]

Within the worlds of feminist theory and political action, there are feminists working with both strands of critical theory.[94] Both a critical modernity and some variants of postmodernism offer valuable insights for theory and action. There is the possibility of coalitions with those in both camps that are productive of theoretical clarifications in theory and politically transformative work. From the standpoint of feminist theory and activism, however, neither stand is adequate as a conceptualization of feminist anthropology, feminist political practice, or feminist constructions of value and truth.

It is easy to see why many feminists and many male political activists are skeptical about the transformative potential of postmodern thought. The work of Lyotard, for example, is clearly problematic. The fluidity he extols is that of the "perfect consumer," moving easily through the world but only relating to its different peoples and cultures as the components of an ephemeral personal style.

Lyotard is keenly sensitive, however, to the differences among cultural groups and language games and is wary of Habermas's attempts to attain consensus. He is certain that the search for consensus leads to the domination and exclusion of certain groups.[95] While his caution is applauded by many who are aware of the dangers of a too-hasty search for consensus, his alternative concept of justice without consensus is as troubling as the "terror" he seeks to avoid. Lyotard concludes that the recognition of difference entails a recognition of the incommensurabilty of language games and that in such a radically pluralistic world, justice requires keeping language games separate. "Here the idea of justice will consist in preserving the purity of each game."[96] Lyotard's goal of separation elides the often negative effect that these separate groups have on each other (think of the function of the principle of "separate but equal" in the American South). He also denies the possibility of mutually transformative interaction between radically different groups. His program cannot account, therefore, for the type of political and moral transformation in American society occurring through the civil rights movement.

While Lyotard has yet to provide an account of the means by which the voices of the oppressed can be heard, the poststructuralist theory of Michel Foucault is fruitful in this area. Foucault analyzes the "insurrection of subjugated knowledges" and draws attention to the constitutive role of exclusion in claims to truth.[97]

Despite his concern with the insurrection of subjugated knowledges, the work of Foucault is also problematic for feminists. Like Lyotard, Foucault fails to acknowledge women as being as central as men in the creation of culture. Lyotard classes women with other objects of exchange, and Foucault describes the constitution of the self and sexuality solely from a male point of view.[98] He also utilizes the work of the Marquis de Sade as an exemplar of critical consciousness without reflection on the impact for women of an epistemological and moral transgression, seen as fundamentally and positively subversive, that operates through the sexual domination and murder of women.[99] And, as is the case with Lyotard, the exclusion of women as subjects and full objects of analysis is evident in many dimensions of his works, specifically in his discussion of the death of the author and the end of man.

One of the most quoted statements by Foucault is found at the conclusion of *The Order of Things:* "Is this not the sign that man is in the process of perishing as the being of language continues to shine ever brighter upon our horizon?"[100] Foucault is here speaking of the end, not of humanity or even of individuality per se, but of the end of the Enlightenment man, the construction of a unitary self who has a particular voice that can be given expression in philosophy, art, and politics. He is critical of the idea of the ontological givenness of a unified and rational self, able to express himself clearly in thought and action. He sees this self disappearing in the recognition of the historicity of our ways of thinking, feeling, and acting, and finds the clearest note of its disappearance in the late nineteenth- and early twentieth-century explorations of the nature of language, specifically, the assertion of our lack of control over the operations of language.

Foucault claims that the fundamental ethical principle of contemporary writing is indifference to who is speaking. Writing is no longer understood as expression but as an interplay of signs, and it is regulated more by the nature of language than by the content to which it refers. The creativity of writing is primarily an interplay with the codes of signification and a transgression of an order it accepts and manipulates.[101]

Foucault links writing and death, contrasting the contemporary text with the Greek narrative in which the immortality of the hero was guaranteed: ". . . now writing is linked to sacrifice and to the sacrifice of life itself; it is a voluntary obliteration of the self that does not require representation in books because it takes place in the everyday existence of the writer."[102] Foucault cites as examples the work of Flaubert, Proust, and Kafka in which there is the total efface-ment of the individual character of the writer.

Foucault's analysis is both troubling and productive. Other femi-nists, as well as myself, find Foucault's new questions about the role of the writer and the text fruitful, while we reject his answers to these questions.[103] Foucault's questions are suggestive: "What are the modes of existence of this discourse? Where does it come from? How is it circulated? Who controls it? What placements are deter-mined for possible subjects? Who can fulfill these diverse functions of the subject?"[104] He claims that "behind these questions we can hear little more than the murmur of indifference—What matter who's speaking?"[105]

Behind these questions I hear rumblings, the roar of conflict and occasional new harmonies, all produced by the proliferation of art, writing, and activism by marginalized peoples throughout the world. In contrast to Foucault, I would argue that what matters is precisely who is speaking. The last thirty years have witnessed an explosion of new speakers and writers, an emerging literary and political sensibil-ity. What is dead is not the author per se but the author who can assume the mantle of universality, claiming to represent humanity rather than the human experience as grounded in a particular social location, accountable to other groups of people, accountable as well to embeddedness in nature.[106]

Many feminists find the proponents of a critical modernity more receptive to the recognition of the emergence of different voices and the significance of our participation in the world of literature and art. Some feminists have chosen, therefore, to work within the philo-sophical debate framed by Habermas over against that of Foucault, Derrida, or Lyotard.[107] We are now entering the conversations cons-titutive of culture and politics, reclaiming our identity as fully hu-man, asserting our voice. It is ironic to find Foucault's declaration of the death of the author and the self just as women and other marginal-ized people begin to write and assert their identity politically and culturally.

Despite the limitations in the work of postmodern social theory, it can be valuable for at least two reasons. First, we can find in the post-modern critique of Enlightenment reason and "grand narratives" sup-port for feminist critiques of unwarranted claims of universally valid interpretation of human experience and the nature of critical think-ing. Second, we can find in the thinking of Foucault compelling rea-sons for an epistemology of solidarity and a communicative ethic.

I concur with Habermas's conclusion that there is an imperative to enter into dialogue with others, but for Foucault's reasons. Habermas grounds dialogue and the search for consensus in the imperatives of the speech act itself. I find Foucault's reasons for dialogue more compelling. Foucault argues that we can see a system of logic as a particular system and not as truth itself only when we are partially constituted by different systems of producing truth. We can transcend the blinders of our own social location, not through becoming objective, but by recognizing the differences by which we ourselves are constituted and, I would add to Foucault, by actively seeking to be partially constituted by work with different groups. Thus the condition of overcoming ideology is difference, a mutually challenging and mutually transformative pluralism.

Joan Scott, building on Martha Minow's discussion of "the difference dilemma," elaborates a further dimension of the reasons for working with postmodern social theory: the need to uncover specific power dynamics at work in the formation of culturally significant differences.[108]

> The resolution of the "difference dilemma" comes neither from ignoring nor embracing difference as it is normatively constituted. Instead, it seems to me that the critical feminist position must always involve two moves. The first is the systematic criticism of the operation of categorical difference, the exposure of the kinds of exclusions and inclusions—the hierarchies—it constructs, and a refusal of their ultimate "truth." A refusal, however, not in the name of an equality that implies sameness or identity, but rather (and this is the second move) in the name of an equality that rests on differences—differences that confound, disrupt, and render ambiguous the meaning of any fixed binary opposition. To do anything else is to buy into the political argument that sameness is a requirement for equality, an untenable position for feminists (and historians) who know that power is constructed on and so must be challenged from the ground of difference.[109]

The politics of difference and solidarity is not easily maintained, and accounts of failures to maintain openness to different strategies and critiques are found in many resistance narratives. Toni Cade Bambara and Toni Morrison, for example, are among those who depict the pain caused by the denial of fluid identities, and the strong commitment to develop social structures that value diversity. Listening and grieving, loving and raging, moral discernment occurs as we act and think together, accepting accountability for our people's violations of the integrity of others, moving from grief at "all that has been lost" to committed action, rebuilding, healing, and celebrating communities of resistance and solidarity.

8

A Theology of Resistance and Hope

— ■ —

There are words I cannot choose again:
humanism   androgyny

Such words have no shame in them, no diffidence
before the raging stoic grandmothers:

their glint is too shallow, like a dye
that does not permeate

the fibers of actual life
as we live it, now:

this fraying blanket with its ancient stains
we pull across the sick child's shoulder

or wrap around the senseless legs
of the hero trained to kill. . . .

My heart is moved by all I cannot save:
so much has been destroyed

I have to cast my lot with those
who age after age, perversely,

with no extraordinary power,
reconstitute the world.[1]

Adrienne Rich's poem is a declaration of dangerous memory. Challenged by the lives of "raging stoic grandmothers," she moves from self-critique to committed action. She grieves for lives lost and damaged by sexism, and she produces a poetry of mourning and rage.

While fully aware of the irreparable damage of injustice, Rich also holds fast to her love of life and creates a poetry of resistance and hope. She speaks of "the dream of a common language"—the ability of women to speak in words that reflect our deepest hopes for life, to speak in a genuine openness to each other as survivors of a deadly system of oppression.

It is this latter reality that she sees missing in the words "humanism" and "androgyny." Rich can no longer use these words to express her goals, because they fail to bear within them memories of defeat and memories of defiance, the dangerous memories of "raging stoic grand-mothers." She seeks a language that allows her to imagine a new world without forgetting the tragedies of the past. For Rich, hope is empowered and deepened by memories of "how much has been destroyed." Without such a memory, changes may be superficial: upper-class women are allowed entry into formerly all-male professions, yet they forget the many women still subject to sexual harassment, still victims of battering by men who understand love as possession, who understand violence as a legitimate means of control.[2] The memories Rich carries are continually challenging. Her memories of oppression and resistance lead her to make choices, lead her to stand with the ordinary doers of extraordinary deeds.

What Rich evokes in poetry, James Cone, Gustavo Gutierrez, Mary Daly, and others describe in passionate prose.[3] Our time is enriched and enlivened by the voices of liberation theologians, women and men who celebrate and seek to understand the dangerous memories of the oppressed.

The life and work of Martin Luther King, Jr., and the women and men involved in the civil rights movement can also be appropriated as a dangerous memory. In working with women and men who have long been active in the struggle against racism, I find courage, hope, and theological and political challenges to Euro-American middle-class activists. In this chapter I explore ways in which dangerous memories can be kept alive. I reflect on elements, symbols, and structures of our religious life that can empower an ethic of risk and effectively challenge oppressive elements in faith and society.

Johann Baptist Metz has identified the power of dangerous memories in resisting communities. My use of the term is derived from his exploration of the task of Christian theology, which he defines as "speaking about God by making the connection between the Christian message and the modern world visible and expressing the Christian tradition in this world as a dangerous memory."[4] Metz describes the Christian tradition as the bearer of "a dangerous memory of freedom." Christians remember the freedom of Jesus and the call of God to all people to be subjects before God.[5] According to Metz, this memory leads Christianity to a critique of what is commonly accepted as plausible; dangerous memory leads to political action.[6] Dangerous memories fund a community's sense of dignity; they inspire and empower those who challenge oppression. Dangerous memories are a people's history of resistance and struggle, of dignity and transcendence in the face of oppression.

Dangerous memories are stories of defeat and of victory, a casting of the past in terms of a present of joy, hope, and struggle. Memories of oppression and defeat become dangerous when they are used as the foundation for a critique of existing institutions and ideologies that blur the recognition and denunciation of injustice. Martin Luther King, Jr.'s, "Letter from Birmingham City Jail" is a powerful evocation of dangerous memories in this sense, challenging the ideology of those white ministers who argued for restraint and a slower pace of change with a vivid recounting of the costs of the past and the burdens of oppression. King wrote the letter while imprisoned for civil disobedience. He responded to the charge of eight liberal clergymen who called the campaign of nonviolent civil rights demonstrations "unwise and untimely":

> I guess it is easy for those who have never felt the stinging darts of segregation to say, "Wait." But when you have seen vicious mobs lynch your mothers and fathers at will and drown your brothers and sisters at whim; . . . when you see the vast majority of your twenty million Negro brothers smothering in an outright cage of poverty in the midst of an affluent society; . . . when you are humiliated day in and day out by nagging signs reading "white" and "colored"; . . . when you are forever fighting a degenerating sense of "nobodiness"; then you will understand why we find it difficult to wait.[7]

The memories evoked by King are indeed dangerous. They endanger the continued acceptance of racial injustice as they propel people to courageous acts of resistance. Similarly, memories of defiance and victory become dangerous as they serve as the spur to further action and critique, an ennobling reminder of the good that can be attained by ordinary people.

In the past twenty-five years many theologians have turned to an analysis of the theological dimensions of movements for political liberation. Liberation theologians (African-American, feminist, and third world), join poets and singers in a celebrative retelling of stories of solidarity and defiance. We name the divinity at work in our people's histories.

Because of the work of feminist historians and theologians, we can identify many dangerous memories that enable our resistance as women. With my sisters, I rejoice in memories of strong, creative women. I find it difficult, however, to identify the stories that would empower me as someone who has a certain degree of privilege (as white, American, and middle-class). As we have seen earlier, the memories that are constitutive of white, middle-class identity are hardly dangerous. They tend, rather, to reinforce the defense of privilege and often evoke despair or cynicism in the face of oppression.

Cynicism and despair need not have the last word. It is possible for middle-class people to work for justice, and a critical theology of liberation can do much to motivate and sustain us in our work for social transformation.

THEOLOGY AND TRANSFORMATION

I began this exercise from a particular vantage point, that of a member of the Euro-American middle class committed to lessening the threat of war. In working on this political problem with African-American women and men, I found my theological and political analyses fundamentally challenged. I was confronted by African-American women and men with a critique of militarism that was inseparable from a critique of my racism, the racism of the Euro-American middle class. I found myself involved in communicative ethics, a political involvement and dialogue that evoked a foundational critique of Western philosophical and theological understandings of responsible action.

Communicative ethics can lead to a critical theology of liberation, a theology that begins with an acknowledgment of the cultural and the political matrix of our thought as well as our particular location within a tradition. For example, it is important for middle-class Euro-American males to forthrightly analyze their experiences of sinfulness and transformation (not assuming this represents either the "Western" experience, much less a universal human reality) and to elucidate the ways in which their religious traditions have furthered their unwitting participation in structures of race, class, and sex oppression and, to name furthermore, how religious traditions have called them to conversion, to participate in individual and structural change. Attention to the specificity of the foundational experiences and the cultural-political matrix shaping our work brings both critical and constructive power to the theological task. It is then possible to examine thoroughly a particular element of human experience and the actual power of religion in shaping that experience.

A central assumption in my work is that ideas have effects of truth.[8] Whatever their intellectual credibility, ideas do shape the lives of those who are taught them. Even if a particular symbol or doctrine is partial in its incorporation of the scriptural tradition or unfair to the history of doctrine, it may still be powerful. Such symbols or doctrines may be believed by millions and thus affect the lives of believers and nonbelievers. A Euro-American theology of liberation would extend our critical work to this realm of reality, seeing that ideas have effects of truth, recognizing that their meaning includes the way the ideas are embodied and the structures of communal life they uphold.

The primary aim of a critical Euro-American theology of liberation, like that of other theologies of liberation, is the enhancement of processes of social transformation. The criterion of truth is also that which liberates. Beverly Harrison defines liberation as the attainment of justice, an achievement that is both a process and a particular state of affairs:

> Implicit in the experience of the liberation struggle is . . . a radically relational understanding of justice as rightly ordered relationships of mutuality within the total web of our several relations. The givenness of reciprocal, interdependent social relations must be presupposed in liberation moral theory. All of our norms must be reciprocal, stressing mutuality both of responsibility and of control. Genuine equality in this model must mean equal dignity-in-relation and in-power.[9]

The content of "liberation" is an expanding understanding of human possibilities, individually and structurally. The specific possibilities include a vision of a world free of racial discrimination, sexual violence, and economic exploitation. While these ends, and others, have been described by liberation theologians, they are not seen as exhaustive. The process of discerning the contours of a just society is ongoing. Liberation is also defined as a process of naming and analysis. It is a process in which dominated groups discover their history of oppression and resistance and articulate their concept of themselves and their vision of a just society. Liberation is a process in which oppressive groups acknowledge their responsibility for structures of domination and name the forces that lead to repentance and conversion.

A Euro-American theology of liberation is a revision of the method of correlation developed by Paul Tillich and David Tracy. Tillich's method of correlation requires the examination of the present situation (as described by philosophers, artists, and other intellectuals) to find the fundamental human problems, and then it turns to Christian faith for the answers to these questions.[10] Tracy revises this method, advocating critical correlation—the present situation is the source of answers as well as questions.[11] My method has a further twist: the source of theological problems is both the secular and the religious worlds. These worlds pose the problems for theologians, and the wealth of the human imagination (not merely religious traditions) provides the answers.

The first step of a critical theological method is the choice of a particular locus for work, then examination of the function of faith in a particular situation, the way in which faith maintains or challenges structures of oppression. The second step is a search for alternative symbols and structures of religious life that might effectively challenge oppressive manifestations of faith (symbols, rituals, polity, doctrines) and that might meet, in less oppressive ways, some of the needs being met by the problematic religious discourse.[12] The truth of such theological construction is not measured by its "coherence" or "adequacy" but by its efficacy in enhancing a particular process of liberation.

The truth claims made in this form of theological discourse are both verifiable and transitory.[13] It is possible to develop a liberating, and therefore true, understanding of eschatological hope, for example, but this particular eschatology is fundamentally transitory in two senses. First, it is true for a specific situation, but the same formulation may function oppressively or be ineffective in other situations. Second, even as "true," a particular theological construction contains the seeds of its eventual replacement. If a formulation is actually liberating, it helps create a new situation in which different problems and challenges arise, and other symbols and doctrines will be required to address the challenges and opportunities of that changed situation.

MATRIX IN THE BELOVED COMMUNITY: CELEBRATING LIMITS, CONTINGENCY, AND AMBIGUITY

Following this critical theological method has led to the critique in chapter 6 of liberal theology and ethics. In this chapter I will present an alternative theology, one that offers the hope of sustaining resistance to injustice.

As we saw earlier, the passion behind the use of the eschatological reservation by liberal theologians is a recognition of the need for self-criticism. The danger of this position is that the criteria used in much critique, comparison of the finite with the infinite or the absolute, does not merely prevent the absolutizing of particular social structures but also leads to enervation. The use of the eschatological reservation creates a mood of cultured despair, an intense awareness of the costs of injustice and of the limitations of all attempts to transform unjust social structures.

Alternative understandings of the interaction between limitations and resistance are found in the work of feminist and womanist writers and theologians. In *Sula* Toni Morrison, for example, describes two sorts of limits to human well-being—those posed by injustice and those posed by the vagaries of life (natural disasters and human conflicts emerging from difference but not from exploitation).[14] The latter set of limits are to be survived but not defeated. She depicts a creative endurance, not a definitive conquest of "natural" conflicts. In my earlier discussion of Toni Cade Bambara, Paule Marshall, and Mildred Taylor, I highlighted this distinction. Attempts to eradicate injustice are made, yet other limitations of human existence are accepted—the transitoriness of institutions, the need to let go of old pains and embrace new challenges with their attendant pain, and the limits of being finite and dependent on the earth.

In Native American traditions and in feminist theology (Carol Christ, Dorothee Soelle, Mary Daly, and Starhawk) one sees a similar distinction. Even the "final limit," *death,* is not an enemy. Death is understood as part of the cycle of life, an event to be mourned but also an event that can be accepted as good in that it makes it possible for others to live.[15] What is fiercely resisted is not death itself but *untimely death,* death caused by human folly or evil, by torture, environmentally induced cancer, war, occupational hazards, or malnutrition.

There are different kinds of limits to the well-being of all, those caused by the limits of finitude and those caused by injustice. Frequently, limitations caused by injustice are rooted in attempts to deny or control the limits of finitude. A Marxist explanation of the root of economic injustice is a case in point. The leisure of the upper class, the evasion of the limits entailed by having to work, are attained by binding others to little *but* work: consigning certain classes to cleaning, factory production, service work, clerical work, and garbage collection. Another form of this exploitation is the male appropriation of female labor: in patriarchal societies men avoid the limits of life by relegating the maintenance work of cooking, childcare, cleaning, and mending to women.[16] Thus physical limits are transcended through the exploitation of other people or of nature. This illusion, that the task of self-maintenance can be avoided without costs, has led to the degradation and exploitation of nature and of millions of human beings.

Injustice can be eliminated, but human conflicts and natural limitations cannot be removed. The conflicts of social life and the limitations of nature cannot be controlled or transcended. They can, however, be endured and survived. It is possible for there to be a dance with life, a creative response to its intrinsic limits and challenges. These conflicts and limitations are not the threat of nonbeing, as Tillich thought, but are, rather, the conditions of life, the matrix of creativity, community, and love. Tillich's description of the power of Being as that which "eternally conquer(s) its own nonbeing" seems plausible and innocuous until we realize what he means by nonbeing. While Tillich rarely specifies what he means by nonbeing, his description of one central aspect of nonbeing in *The Courage To Be* is revealing. He sees as a threat and as something to be conquered, the constituent elements of human life: our belonging to history and place and our dependence on a world that is itself changing and interdependent:

> One can show the *contingency of our temporal being*, the fact that we exist in this and no other period of time, beginning in a contingent moment, ending in a contingent moment, filled with experiences which are contingent themselves with respect to quality and quantity. One can show the *contingency of our spatial being* (our finding ourselves in this and no other place, and the strangeness of this place in spite of its familiarity); the contingent character of ourselves and the place from which we look at our world; and the *contingent character of the reality at which we look, that is, our world*. . . . Contingent does not mean causally undetermined but it means that the determining causes of our existence have no ultimate necessity. They are given, and they cannot be logically derived. Contingently we are put into the whole web of causal relations. Contingently we are determined by them in every moment and thrown out by them in the last moment.[17].

Tillich interprets our interdependence as threat. The fact that there is no necessity to our existence, that no law of nature would be violated had we never have been born, is seen by him as a threat to self-affirmation. In poetry, prose, and philosophy, feminists are celebrating another possibility, the acknowledgment of contingency, our belonging to the web of life, as a complex, challenging, and wondrous gift. Meaning and value, in this emerging world view, are not predicated upon either necessity or upon ultimate foundations. The dance of life, with all its contingency and ambiguity, can be good in itself. The many victories of injustice do not belie the richness of life that is possible when the alienation between humans, and between humanity and nature is overcome.

An appropriate symbol for the process of celebrating life, enduring limits, and resisting injustice is not the kingdom of God; it is the beloved community. The kingdom of God implies conquest, control, and final victory over the elements of nature as well as over the structures of injustice. The "beloved community" names the matrix within which life is celebrated, love is worshiped, and partial victories over injustice lay the groundwork for further acts of criticism and courageous defiance.[18]

From within the matrix of the beloved community, there is a solid basis for social critique and self-criticism: the life-giving love constitutive of solidarity with the oppressed and love of oneself. Resistance to oppression is often based on a love that transcends the limits of social systems, a love that leads us to value ourselves more, and leads us to hope for more than the established cultural system is willing to grant. June Jordan, a poet and activist, describes the revolutionary power of love: "It is always the love . . . that will carry action into positive new places, that will carry your own nights and days beyond demoralization and away from suicide."[19]

The love that heals is far from the spirit of self-sacrifice. It is founded in love of oneself, a difficult task for those who are judged as less rational, reliable, and honorable than white middle- and upper-class men. It is also difficult for ruling-class men to love themselves as finite human beings, limited in judgment and in action by time and place.

Jordan claims that the rigorous work of self-love, "cleans(ing) myself of the hatred and the contempt that surrounds and permeates my identity, as a woman, and as a Black human being" leads to passionate social critique:[20]

> I am entering my soul into a struggle that will most certainly transform the experience of all the peoples of the earth, as no other movement can, in fact, hope to claim: because the movement into self-love, self-respect, and self-determination is the movement now galvanizing the majority of human beings everywhere. This movement explicitly demands the testing of the viability of a moral idea:-that the health, the legitimacy of any status quo, any governing force, must be measured according to the experiences of those who are, comparatively, powerless.[21]

The "powerless" are valued because they are loved. Such love does not have to lead to the absolutizing of any political projects. To the extent that love remains strong, a movement is open to internal critique and is able to recognize the validity of the experiences of all people, thus realizing that liberating ideals are not yet extended to all. Love enables whites to recognize the grievances and aspirations of people of color; love enables those who are relatively affluent to recognize systematic inequities in the distribution of wealth. Jordan, for example, uses the criterion of love to challenge the sexism present among many men working against racism:

I cannot be expected to respect what somebody else calls self-love if that concept of self-love requires my suicide to any degree. . . . My Black feminism means that you cannot expect me to respect what somebody else identifies as the Good of The People, if that so-called Good . . . requires the deferral or the diminution of my self-fulfillment. We *are* the people. And, as Black women, we are most of the people, any people, you care to talk about. And, therefore, nothing that is Good for The People is good unless it is good for me, as I determine myself.[22]

Jordan challenges the equation of love and self-sacrifice. She holds a vision of love that is both self-affirming and affirming of others, a love that denounces injustice, heals the wounds of exploitation, and builds a community of strong individuals.

Jordan's rejection of self-sacrifice as intrinsic to love is as appropriate for those who have economic and political power as it is for those who are exploited by such power. Self-sacrifice is an inadequate model of love even for those who are members of the dominant strata of society. Middle-class people can sustain work for justice when empowered by love for those who are oppressed. Such love is far more energizing than guilt, duty, or self-sacrifice. Love for others leads us to accept accountability (in contrast to feeling guilt) and motivates our search for ways to end our complicity with structures of oppression. Solidarity does not require self-sacrifice but an enlargement of the self to include community with others.

To work with others is not to lose oneself, but first and foremost, it is to find a larger self. The identification of solidarity and self-sacrifice is predicated on a faulty anthropology, though one with a solid philosophical and theological pedigree, the notion of the self as foundationally individualistic. Feminist theologians and philosophers have argued, however, that we are foundationally social beings:[23]

Not only are our bodies ourselves (rather than being something that we as minds, possess), but the bodies, intellects, emotions, souls, characters, and configurations of relationships that we are can be understood only in relation to one another. . . . A person is an historical being whose history is fundamentally a history of relationships to other people.[24]

Our bodies are formed from the bodies of two other people; our personalities are created by the regard given us by others. If we begin with a social anthropology and imagine a self constituted by our connection with the earth and with other people, the motivation for work for justice is wholly positive. Realizing we are of the earth, born of woman, and defined by the regard of others for us, establishing "right relations" (Carter Heyward) with all others does not require self-sacrifice but is, rather, a movement in which the self is enlarged.

The dichotomy between love of self and love of others is a dangerous one, created by alienation and sustained by structures of alienation. To choose one or the other option is destructive. Feminist theologians and psychologists have depicted the costs of choosing love for others alone:

> The language of self-sacrifice conflicts with personhood and becomes destructive when it suggests that the struggle to become a centered self, to achieve full independent selfhood, is sinful. In this case, theology is not irrelevant to women's situation but rather serves to reinforce women's servitude. . . . Valerie Saiving states this point very clearly. The woman who believes the theological advocates of sacrificial love . . . will stifle in herself the desire to be a separate person. . . . She will devote herself wholly to the needs of her family. . . . "She learns . . . that a woman can give too much of herself, so that nothing remains of her own uniqueness; she can become merely an emptiness, almost a zero, without value to herself, to her fellow men. . . ."[25]

Equally, the theological, philosophical, and moral tradition has been inadequate in its definition of the self as essentially independent and in its assumption that the loss of that independent self is the means of salvation. In the work of Emmanuel Levinas, for example, we find a profound depiction of the richness of recognizing other people, accompanied by a disturbing account of regard for others as a move of self-denial. Levinas draws the distinction between "infinity and totality," two ways of viewing others. Within the scheme of totality, people are regarded as manifestations of an essence or process, be it Hegel's Geist, Whitehead's principle of concrescence, or Freud's Oedipal complex.[26] The frame of understanding is here one of universal comprehension, seeing the individual as the manifestation of a larger principle.

Levinas prefers another scheme of understanding, one more in line with poets and the Romantic tradition than with systematic philosophy or systematic theology. Here the concern is with infinity. Each individual and each group is understood from the perspective of seeing and acknowledging the infinite possibilities of that life, the innumerable ways in which humanity is expressed.[27] From the perspective of infinity, no one is seen solely as victim but is seen fully as alive, new, engaging in an infinite number of possibilities. Or, as Gloria Naylor describes, humans can be seen as the mating of "unfathomable will and unfathomable possibility."[28]

Levinas argues that our encounter with other people is foundationally ethical and that "responsibility [is] the essential, primary and fundamental structure of subjectivity."[29] He provides a phenomenology of subjectivity in terms of "a phenomenology of the face." While the

"Other" is valued by Levinas, his description of the call to responsibility conveys a primary hostility to others and a fundamental individuality. The "face" is *first* seen as something that he could kill. "There is first the very uprightness of the face, its upright exposure, without defense. The skin of the face is that which stays most naked, most destitute. . . . The face is exposed, menaced, as if inviting us to an act of violence. At the same time, the face is what forbids us to kill."[30]

In describing responsibility to this vulnerable yet commanding Other, Levinas combines care with control. He maintains that responsibility is "non-symmetrical," that the idea that the Other is also responsible for you is irrelevant to the experience of intersubjectivity.

> *Ph.N.:* But is not the Other also responsible in my regard?
>
> *E.L.:* Perhaps, but that is *his* affair . . . the intersubjective relation is a non-symmetrical relation. It is precisely insofar as the relationship between the Other and me is not reciprocal that I am subjected to no Other; and I am "subject" essentially in this sense. It is I who support all. You know that sentence in Dostoevsky: "We are all guilty of all and for all men before all, and I more than the others." This is . . . because I am responsible for a total responsibility, which answers for all the others and for all in the others, even for their responsibility.[31]

Levinas's equation of responsibility with control is fundamentally dangerous. The danger is manifest in his own writings in the initial hostility that is felt toward another person. In Paule Marshall's analysis of racism, we saw the further consequences of such an asymmetrical understanding of responsibility in Marshall's depiction of the character Harriet. Denying that others are also responsible to oneself leads to errors in judgment and alienation from the resources that sustain responsible action. Errors in assessing both the needs of others and of how those needs could best be met inevitably follow from the patronizing stance of working for others rather than working with them. Marshall depicts whites who give the wrong things—inequitable irrigation projects, the imposition of their cultural mores—and who realize that more is demanded. They are unable to give what is required, because giving is experienced only as loss. Without the joy and support that comes from acknowledging the mutuality of responsibility, from experiencing being loved as well as loving, the will for fundamental change cannot be sustained.

Psychologists at the Stone Center for Developmental Services and Studies are developing a comprehensive theory of the relational self. Janet Surrey develops an alternative to models of power as being essentially domination (as in Tillich and Levinas). In an empowering interaction, each [person] feels "heard" and "responded to" and able to "hear," "validate," and "respond to" the other. Each feels empowered through creating and sustaining a context which leads to increased awareness and understanding. Further, through this process, each participant feels enlarged, able to "see" more clearly, and energized to move into action. The capacity to be "moved," and to respond, and to "move" the other, represents the fundamental core of relational empowerment.[32]

People are empowered to work for justice by their love for others and by the love they receive from others. While such work often entails grave risks and dangerous consequences, the costs of mutual empowerment are not adequately described by the language of self-sacrifice. The concept of self-sacrifice is faulty in two fundamental ways. First, the term "sacrifice" is "reviewer-language": it reflects how an outside observer sees someone's actions, and it rarely is used by those actually bearing the costs of resistance.[33] To those resisting, the primary feelings are those of integrity and community, not sacrifice. Second, what is lost in resistance is precisely *not* the self.[34] One may be deprived of the accoutrements of a successful self—wealth, prestige, and job security—but another self, one constituted by relationships with others, is found and maintained in acts of resistance. When we begin from a self created by love for nature and for other people, choosing *not* to resist injustice would be the ultimate loss of self.

Love provides the resiliency of commitment, vision, and hope when efforts for change either are defeated repeatedly or are shown to be insufficient. As I have argued earlier, the recognition that we cannot imagine how we will change society is the beginning point, not the end, of an ethic founded on love for oneself and others. Resistance to injustice and the creation of intrinsically temporal and limited social structures are acts of love, affirmations of the delightfulness and profundity of life. Such acts declare the tragedy of what is lost because of injustice, and they celebrate the satisfaction of life lived under conditions of justice. A deep joy accompanies the cycle of providing shelter and food, nurturing the young, and celebrating the beauty of life in art, music, and poetry.

The Marxist critique of love as a basis for social action is helpful at this point. Marx and Engels were

> equally disdainful of the intoxication with brotherly sympathy, of universal forgiveness, and of the "old cant love one another, fall into each other's arms." Socialism will introduce a "really human morality which transcends class antagonisms." . . . Socialist ethics will rest on material conditions which will permit higher standards of human conduct.[35]

Marxists offer a pertinent critique of concern that is limited in two ways—limited to compassion for those who are worthy, and limited in action, leading to works of charity and merely ameliorating the costs of a social system without changing the structures that produce those social costs. Sheila Collins, for example, describes women "mopping up the wounds of advanced capitalism," helping victims but not being allowed to change the social structures that created those wounds:

> Women in churches have provided the nurturance and emotional release for their families and community that the workplace could not provide. They have been used to mop up the wounds created by the cruelties of industrial capitalism—for example, in making bandages during wartime, sending mittens and canned goods to Peru after American companies have stripped that country of its ability to support its own people; and giving Thanksgiving baskets to the local poor because, in the richest country in the world, we are unable to provide meaningful employment for all our people.[36]

Marxists are right—love for individuals is not enough. Structural change is required. Yet, if the motive of love for all people is lost, programs for social change become idealized as ends in themselves, and groups of people are oppressed in the name of the greater good. The liberal critics of revolutionary fervor are right in their fear of tyranny in the name of the people. The cause of such absolutism is not, however, revolutionary hope; it is the loss of revolutionary love. Its source is not unwarranted hope; it is the isolation and elitism of a revolutionary vanguard.

Michel Foucault, a philosopher and social critic working within the Marxist tradition, challenged other socialists to carefully examine why the gulag, the suppression of political dissent, afflicts so many governments ostensibly committed to social change on behalf of the people.[37] Like Rosa Luxemburg, I would argue that the suppression of dissent occurs when a revolutionary vanguard, a group committed to the good of all, becomes isolated from other people and begins to see itself as the primary bearer of revolutionary vision.[38] The idolatry of a particular political program, rightly criticized by liberals, does not emerge directly from hope for change; it emerges from a hope cut loose from its moorings in community with people of many backgrounds when love for people and respect for the wisdom of people is lost in working for the masses instead of working with people.

Kim Chernin's account of her mother's lifelong commitment to social change is a case of revolutionary fervor without fanaticism. Rose Chernin was a labor organizer who prevented the deportation of many other activists during the McCarthy era and who worked for racial justice.[39] The following passage is a representative account of Rose Chernin's compassion and commitment, of work for social change grounded in love for people. Imprisoned during the McCarthy era for her work as a Communist, she finds, even in prison, the healing, sustaining joy of community. She describes a birthday party given in prison that became the occasion for acknowledging the wonder of human love.

> "They were singing songs and they had presents to give. Now you must wonder what these women could possibly give to anyone, and I will tell you. They had nothing. Nothing. But they managed to get something together. One woman crocheted a tiny set of teacups and saucers. A work of art. The other women, gave, for instance, a few hairpins, a scarf that one of them knitted. A hairnet, the few pennies one of them had. We had a party. We sang. But suddenly there was weeping. Everyone was weeping. Yes, believe me. Everyone."
>
> . . . "Never tear yourself from the people," she said. And her voice was not more than a whisper. "For us, our strength is with the people. This is our meaning. This is how we survive."[40]

An ethic based in love for self and for others can provide self-critique and social critique without the enervating cynicism of the eschatological reservation. A deeply felt, abiding love is the foundation for a resilient, dynamic hope without the fanaticism and idolatry of a revolutionary vanguard.

THE JOY OF COMMUNAL RESISTANCE

One alternative to the cynicism of the eschatological reservation is a constructive relativism and a passionate commitment to "learn innocence." (Mary Daly) Such "constructive relativism" is grounded in love. It is the recognition that we have to make the valued real. Our values are not eternal guarantees of right decisions or of proper analyses; they are calls to action. As Dorothee Soelle states:

> The question for Bultmann and for any theology is whether it makes men more capable of love, whether it encourages or obstructs the liberation of the individual and the community. Expressed scientifically that is the verification principle: expressed biblically, the proof of the Spirit and of power (1 Cor. 2:4).[41]

Relativism is the assertion that reality is fundamentally shaped by relationships of power. Constructive relativism is the assertion that power takes many forms. Coercive or manipulative power is undoubtedly the victor in many places, a significant shaper of reality. Healing power is undoubtedly the victor at other times: people free each other from bonds of isolation and oppression and are then freed to face further challenges. Love and justice are not all powerful, but they do, at times, grace our lives.

Middle-class people can be challenged by the fragile power of love and justice to move from cultured despair to learned hope. With this shift, critique can serve as a foundation for more nuanced strategies of resistance and a catalyst for further work. We move from critique to action and back to critique, maintaining our hope and our vision if our critique occurs in the context of working with others for justice. Separated from such practice, critique becomes all encompassing and enervating. There is a simple reason for the repeated emphasis on practice by liberation theologians. Without working with others on projects geared toward social change, it is impossible to maintain the vision and energy necessary to sustain long-term work. If one engages in critique in isolation from those who are the victims of social systems, critique can become despairing and cynical. If one does not know anyone who is unemployed or trying to live on a poverty-level income, if one does not know anyone laid off because of industrial relocation or displaced because of the farm crisis, it is easy to become cynical or numb in the face of continued social critique. Middle-class numbness is a luxury of being able to avoid direct interaction with victims. Middle-class cynicism is a way, then, of maintaining rage in the distorted form of giving up hope for change.

Cynicism emerges from seeing victims *only* as victims. Cynicism is a product of isolation, for knowing people suffering from unemployment or underemployment includes knowing their courage and liveliness as well as their pain. Knowing refugees or the poor makes it possible to sustain rage, because one is aware of the value of the lives being so unnecessarily damaged or destroyed. As long as critique occurs in the context of work for justice, it is possible to experience the essential factor in maintaining resistance—love for oneself, for the oppressed, and for those working against oppression.

An ethic based on a welcoming of diversity and interdependence is characteristic of the work of feminists creating new spiritualities. Starhawk, for example, describes the foundation of ethics as erotic love for the particular:

> All is relationship. Perhaps the ultimate ethic of immanence is to choose to make that relationship one of love; love of self and of others, erotic love, transforming love, affectionate love, delighted love for the

myriad forms of life as it evolves and changes . . . love for all the eternally self-creating world, love of the light and the mysterious darkness, and raging love against all that would diminish the unspeakable beauty of the world.[42]

A similar celebration can be found in the works of Susan Griffin, Mary Daly, and Paula Gunn Allan. Susan Griffin writes of the joy of "nature seeing nature," a joy constituted by the recognition that what is seen is both part of us and escapes our comprehension:

> The red-winged blackbird flies in us, in our inner sight. We see the arc of her flight. We measure the ellipse. . . . And yet the blackbird does not fly in us but is somewhere else free of our minds. . . . When I let this bird fly to her own purpose, . . . the light from this bird enters my body, . . . I fly with her, . . . I live in the body of this bird whom I cannot live without, . . . all that I know speaks to me through this earth and I long to tell you, you who are earth too, and listen as we speak to each other of what we know: the light is in us.[43]

In all of these writers I find expressed the ethos central to feminist spirituality and ethics—a deep and abiding joy in the wonder of life.[44] Mary Daly writes of the transformative happiness possible in life—a happiness borne of love for oneself, the earth, and others. She describes memories of childhood wonder and contentment:

> A woman who can evoke her childhood experiences of gazing at the moon and stars on clear nights, or lying on the grass, or listening to the sea, or watching the sunset is Elementally inspired. When she can recall early experiences of the smell of leaves on an October day, the taste of raspberries at a picnic, the feel of sand warmed by the sun, she is empowered. Energized by her own unique Elemental memories, she can break through the maze of "adult categories."[45]

Daly criticizes the social forces that destroy this joy, substituting for it an illusory "fulfillment" and holding as an ideal a state of stasis rather than a dynamic, ever-changing process of responding to the wonder and challenge of life.[46]

The fact of change, of transitoriness, is not necessarily a cause for despair. Seasons change and the activities that exercised all of one's abilities last year are no longer challenging. Friends change, children grow older, and even the inevitable coming of death—all these forms of transitoriness are not necessarily the cause of dismay, but they can be the shape of life so passionately valued.

The French writers Luce Irigaray and Helene Cixous and the African-American writer Audre Lorde have explored the nature of women's joy and claim that it is constituted by delight in diversity and change.

Lorde speaks of the critical power resident in the experience of the erotic, in the experience of transformative physical, intellectual, and emotional pleasure. In the male psychoanalytic tradition it is only recently, in the work of Jacques Lacan, that this aspect of women's lives has been analyzed. Yet here the analysis is partial. Lacan refers to female *jouissance* but claims that *jouissance* can never be brought to speech. He posits an ecstatic, mute female experience.[47]

Jouissance is brought to speech in the work of Lorde, Cixous, and Irigaray. In their work we find a partial reason for Lacan's inability to hear women's speech. According to Cixous, the language of *jouissance* challenges the categories of Western logic and the limits of capitalism and bureaucratic socialism:

> Because the "economy" of her drives is prodigious, she cannot fail, in seizing the occasion to speak, to transform directly and indirectly *all* systems of exchange based on masculine thrift. Her libido will produce far more radical effects of political and social change than some might like to think.[48]

Irigaray claims that the experience of women's knowing and loving cannot be contained in patriarchal depictions of logic or in patriarchal descriptions of a love predicated on a clear distinction between the self and other. She writes of the challenge of speaking without utilizing a static logic: "How can we speak so as to escape from their compartments, their schemas, their distinctions and oppositions. . . . Disengage ourselves *alive* from their concepts? . . . you know that we are never completed, but that we only embrace ourselves whole."[49] Irigaray describes the fluidity of life, a fluidity incomprehensible if one searches for "solid ground," if one has as a standard of knowing the ability to name that which is the same.

> You are moving. You never stay still. You never stay. You never "are." How can I say "you," when you are always other? How can I speak to you? You remain in flux, never congealing or solidifying. What will make that current flow into words? It is multiple, devoid of causes, meanings, simple qualities. . . . These movements cannot be described as the passage from a beginning to an end. These rivers flow into no single, definitive sea. These streams are without fixed banks, this body without fixed boundaries. This unceasing mobility. This life—which will perhaps be called our restlessness, shams, pretenses, or lies. All this remains very strange to anyone claiming to stand on solid ground.[50]

This life, with its unceasing mobility, cannot be comprehended in categories that imagine a "one," or even the "one and the many":

We are luminous. Neither one nor two. I've never known how to count. Up to you. In their calculations, we make two. Really, two? Doesn't that make you laugh? An odd sort of two. And yet not one. Especially not one. Let's leave *one* to them: their oneness, with its prerogatives, its domination, its solipsism. . . . And the strange way they divide up their couples, with the other as the image of the one.[51]

Irigaray writes of a love that does not require sacrifice of "one" to "another." She speaks of a love that emerges from plenitude, not from lack. "We are not lacks, voids, awaiting sustenance, plenitude, fulfillment from the other."[52] The love that emerges from plenitude enlarges the world, and the joy that is achieved in such love is not static: its movement is the product of pleasure. "When you kiss me, the world grows so large that the horizon itself disappears. Are we unsatisfied? Yes, if that means we are never finished. If our pleasure consists in moving, being moved, endlessly. Always in motion: openness is never spent nor sated."[53]

In the work of Audre Lorde there is a further description of *jouissance* (here named the erotic) and further evidence of why the speaking of the erotic cannot be heard in patriarchal categories:

The erotic . . . [provides] the power which comes from sharing deeply any pursuit with another person. The sharing of joy, whether physical, emotional, psychic, or intellectual, forms a bridge between the sharers which can be the basis for understanding much of what is not shared between them, and lessens the threat of their difference . . . the erotic . . . [functions in] the open and fearless underlining of my capacity for joy. In the way my body stretches to music and opens into response, hearkening to its deepest rhythms, so every level upon which I sense also opens to the erotically satisfying experience, whether it is dancing, building a bookcase, writing a poem, examining an idea.[54]

The erotic is a form of power that challenges the very core of capitalism:

The principal horror of any system which defines the good in terms of profit rather than in terms of human need, or which defines human need to the exclusion of the psychic and emotional components of that need—the principal horror of such a system is that it robs our work of its erotic value, its erotic power and life appeal and fulfillment. Such a system reduces work to a travesty of necessities, a duty by which we earn bread or oblivion for ourselves and those we love.[55]

Lorde refuses to accept repression of creative energy as the only form of order possible. She posits a different ordering, one that builds from the power of the erotic, the energy that comes from the delight in relatedness, an energy that can be part of work just as it is part of love:

> For once we begin to feel deeply all the aspects of our lives, we begin to demand from ourselves and from our life-pursuits that they feel in accordance with that joy which we know ourselves to be capable of. Our erotic knowledge empowers us, becomes a lens through which we scrutinize all aspects of our existence, forcing us to evaluate those aspects honestly in terms of their relative meaning within our lives. And this is a grave responsibility, projected from within each of us, not to settle for the convenient, the shoddy, the conventionally expected, nor the merely safe.[56]

The alternative understanding of communion articulated by feminists provides deep joy and the strength required for sustained resistance to oppression. It is possible to combine skepticism about the likelihood of certain, total victory over injustice, and persistent, energetic work for justice. The key is a complex, fluid, concrete love: love for the earth, for oneself, for those who are oppressed, and for those who work against oppression. It is our love for life that enables the critique of particular strategies for further resistance. It is our love for life that enables us to maintain rage and vision in the face of the disclosure of more forms of oppression.

THE IMMANENCE OF THE DIVINE

In 1973 Mary Daly argued that the participation of women in processes of self-definition beyond the strictures of patriarchal cultures was participation in the movement of God the Verb.[57] Other liberation theologians have also claimed that the love that gives birth to hope and to work for justice is holy. We participate in divinity as we delight in the beauty of humankind, as we rage against all that destroys the dignity and complexity of life. The ability to love and to work for justice is profoundly spiritual. Carter Heyward argues that the capacity for "right relations," with others, with nature, and with ourselves, is the gift of God:

> For god is nothing other than the *eternally creative source* of our relational power, our common strength, a god whose movement is to empower, bringing us into our own together, a god whose name in history is love—provided we mean by "love" not just simply a sentiment or unfocused feeling but rather that which is just, mutually empowering, and co-creative.[58]

While Heyward claims that "god" is the source of our relational power, I argue that the divine *is* that relational power, and that it is neither necessary nor liberating to posit a substance or ground that exists outside of relational power.

The power of compassion is divine: the compassion expressed in simple acts of acknowledging each others' fear and pain, standing with a baby with colic, caring for a friend dying of AIDS, acknowledging, without diminishment, the pain that others feel; the power of saying "Your pain is real, your cries are heard, your anger is just, and along with you are many others who mourn and rage." This power of compassion and anger is holy.

Resilient connections with other people and the earth bring joy, pain, and wisdom. These resilient connections are the presence of grace. Grace can move us from resignation, bitterness, and despair to passionate love and determined action. Alice Walker describes the movement from cynicism to resistance, what I would call the movement of grace, in her essay, "Only Justice Can Stop a Curse." Walker explains her initial inability to actively oppose nuclear war. She depicts a cynical reaction to the complex reality of oppression: so much evil has been wrought by whites against the planet and against people of color that perhaps it would be best if the earth and all people were destroyed in a nuclear war. "Fatally irradiating ourselves may in fact be the only way to save others from what Earth has already become. And this is a consideration that I believe requires serious thought from every one of us."[59]

Walker then briefly and eloquently depicts the love for life that enables her to move from cynicism and the desire for revenge to hopefulness and work for justice:

> However, just as the sun shines on the godly and the ungodly alike, so does nuclear radiation. And with this knowledge it becomes increasingly difficult to embrace the thought of extinction purely for the assumed satisfaction of—from the grave—achieving revenge. Or even of accepting our demise as a planet as a simple and just preventive medicine administered to the universe. Life is better than death, I believe, if only because it is less boring, and because it has fresh peaches in it. In any case, Earth is my home—though for centuries white people have tried to convince me I have no right to exist, except in the dirtiest, darkest corners of the globe.
>
> So let me tell you: I intend to protect my home. Praying—not a curse—only the hope that my courage will not fail my love. But if by some miracle, and all our struggle, the Earth is spared, only justice to every living thing (and everything is alive) will save humankind.
>
> And we are not saved yet.
>
> *Only justice can stop a curse.*[60]

Walker's essay expresses a solid foundation for ethical action—love, courage, and rage. We are moved to moral action by love and hope, not by guilt or duty. It is painful to learn that we have caused others harm, either as individuals or as members of a dominant social group. Change occurs when the response to this knowledge is not guilt but repentance, a deep commitment to make amends and to change patterns of behavior. Such changes are not losses but gains, opportunities to live out our love and respect for others.

Mary Daly describes this process as "learning innocence." She states that the root of the word innocence is *innocere,* "to not harm." "Not harming" is something we learn, a continual task that expands as our ability to affect the lives of others expands.[61] We will always need to learn innocence. As our social worlds change and our individual responsibilities change, there will be more opportunities for harm, thus the necessity of learning again how to respect and honor the life around us.

The need for continual learning is not a sign of weakness or depravity; it is born of the complexity and dynamism of life. The healing response of whites to racism, of men to sexism, is quite simple—repentance. Out of love for others, out of love for oneself, as a person who respects all people, it is possible to admit fault, to examine social patterns that perpetuate racism and sexism, and to begin the careful work of making amends, of building egalitarian social structures. This latter process is not a torturous, life-denying one, but is life-giving. It can be the finding of a larger self and a deeper joy in the challenge of mending the rifts of injustice.

It is difficult to acknowledge complicity in structures of oppression. This difficulty is mitigated when our acknowledgment is grounded in strength, in the eager search for a self made larger through the challenge of accountability. Accountability, not guilt, is the response to critique when our selves are constituted by love for others.

This love for others is holy and is rightly referred to as grace, a power that lifts us to a larger self and a deeper joy as it leads us to accept blame and begin the long process of reparation and re-creation. Grace brings joy, not shame, the finding of self in a larger community. Grace is not the opposite of works; it is the gift of being loved and loving that enables work for justice. The connotations of grace are many, and there are many that I want to affirm—grace is a power or an intensity of relationship that is more than we can predict or produce solely by our own volition. This surplus connoted by grace—the deep joy of loving and being loved, the amazing changes possible in peoples' lives—is sometimes interpreted as a gift from outside, grace being the gift of a force or person, grace as the gift of God or the Goddess. I would argue that grace is not the manifestation of the divine in our lives, the gift of a separate or foundational being; but that grace is all there is or need be of the divine.

The healing connections of grace are both profoundly life-giving and undeniably fragile. The resiliency of grace, of the divine, healing power of relatedness has led many to claim that grace is grounded in substance, a force or person outside the web of life who is at times present in that web and at times absent. In this conception, times of absence such as the Holocaust or the bombing of Hiroshima and Nagasaki, are tragic and difficult to understand, but they do not call into question the continued existence, or undergirding of existence, by that which is the source of grace.

I cannot deny the comfort that such ideas about God or the Goddess provide. Yet I find myself drawn, for several reasons, to a different interpretation of the resiliency and fragility of grace. In the first place, the triumph of evil in much of history makes untenable the claims of classic theism. The basic question of theodicy—Given the existence of so much evil in the world, how can God be both loving and all-powerful?—is not a new one. In examining this problem I concur with those who find that the existence of evil falsifies the claim of omnipotence. Furthermore, with the modern critics of classical theism (Paul Tillich, Gordon Kaufman, Charles Hartshorne, and others), I find the god of classical theism irrational and unworthy of worship. Mark C. Taylor provides a concise description of the concept of God that has been thoroughly criticized by nineteenth- and twentieth-century theologians and philosophers. When theologians speak of "the death of God" and the rejection of "ontotheology," it is this concept of God that is at stake:

> According to the tenets of classical theism, God, who is One, is the supreme Creator, who, through the mediation of His divine Logos, brings the world into being and providentially directs its course. This Primal Origin (First Cause or *Arche*) is also the Ultimate End (Final Goal or *Telos*) of the world. Utterly transcendent and thoroughly eternal, God is represented as totally present to Himself—in text. He is, in fact the omnipresent font, source, ground, and uncaused cause of presence itself.[62]

Feminist thealogians such as Mary Daly and Emily Culpepper are critical of many of these tenets of classical monotheism when they are applied to the symbol of the Goddess. Culpepper points to the dangerous reifications at work in this type of thinking—the tendencies to have *an* image of *the* Goddess, an image which for white women is, disturbingly, often white, heterosexual, and maternal. Culpepper decries the tendencies to elevate these aspects of some women's lives as definitive for all women. She describes several central distortions operative in describing the Goddess as the Great Mother.

> All women are not mothers. . . . Birth is an inadequate symbol for many forms of creativity. . . . The Great Mother inadequately challenges the model of female self-sacrifice. . . . The Mother Goddess obscures the presence of single women, of spinsters. . . . The Goddess is too easily a white Goddess.[63]

The alternative Culpepper advocates is the creation of multiple images and symbols of all that is holy: "Feminists create pantheans of symbols as one tool for recreating and changing our Selves and the World. . . . Pluralism is more likely to help us to recognize our differences as positive and to explore what Mirtha Quintales has called 'our different primary emergencies.'"[64]

I affirm with Culpepper, Daly, and other women the plurality of images of divinity and experiences of divinity, a plurality best acknowledged by referring to divinity, not as a noun or even a verb, but as an adjective or adverb. Divinity then connotes a quality of relationships, lives, events, and natural processes that are worthy of worship, that provide orientation, focus, and guidance to our lives.[65] Feminist spirituality at this point appears to be similar to the theologies developed by men working with the critical tools of deconstruction (Thomas J. J. Altizer and Mark C. Taylor) and to the theological positions developed by Ludwig Feuerbach, but it is significantly different in valence. Taylor, for example, extols an affirming love for the world in the absence of the god of classical theism. Although Taylor does not cite Daly, he uses her metaphor of amazing thought and love. "Mazing grace opens 'a way of totally loving the world, and not only a way of loving the world but also a way of [writing] love itself in a time and world in which God is dead.'"[66]

While affirming the possibility of such love, I disagree with Taylor's description of its effects and costs. He describes grace as belonging to a network of relations but finds this belonging confusing and bewildering.

> Through unexpected twists and unanticipated turns, erring and absence show the death of God, disappearance of self, and end of history to be the realization of *mazing grace*. . . . To maze is to bewilder, perplex, confuse, daze or stupefy . . . a maze is a labyrinth. . . . Mazing grace situates one in the midst of a labyrinth from which there is no exit. . . . Every line that seems to promise escape further entangles the drifter in a complex network of relations.[67]

For Taylor, participation in mazing grace requires the crucifixion of the self: "The play of the relational network both destroys the integrity of the autonomous self and exposes the pretensions of the all-knowing *cogito.* "[68] The alternative to egocentricity is a sacrificial generosity.[69] Taylor assumes, but does not explain, resistance to relationships. What I and other women see as delightful, as that which constitutes the self, he describes as violent and as a crucifixion of the self. The peculiarity of such resistance, the Western, male, possibly even white, middle- and upper-class nature of this resistance to interdependence, is not addressed.

My emphasis on divinity as a quality of relationships, lives, events, and natural processes appears similar to the immanent theology of Feuerbach. He argues that "the fact is not that a quality is divine because God has it, but that God has it because it is in itself divine."[70] Feuerbach also identifies human relationships as divine: "Man and man, the unity of I and Thou, is God."[71] Yet what is valued in humanity by Feuerbach is not our complex finitude but "the *infinity* of the human species in contrast to the finitude of the human individual."[72] "All divine attributes . . . are attributes of the [human] species— attributes which in the individual are limited, but the limits of which are abolished in the essence of the species. . . . The history of mankind consists of nothing else than a continuous and progressive conquest of limits. . . ."[73]

Like Tillich, Feuerbach sees "limit" in itself as a threat, or, as he describes it, "the sense of limitation is painful," and we free ourselves from it by participation in that which is without limits.[74] Like Taylor and Levinas, Feuerbach experiences relationships as an affront, an initial obstacle to identity which must be overcome. While Feuerbach values human relationships to the point of seeing them as divine, they are first experienced as an obstacle: "The first stone against which the pride of egoism stumbles is the *thou,* the *alter ego.* "[75] Relationships are accepted not because of their intrinsic delight but because they are the avenue to the individual's experience of infinite power: "In isolation human power is limited, in combination it is infinite."[76]

In contrast to Taylor's valorization of sacrifice and Feuerbach's glorification of unlimited power, I celebrate a presence that is both healing and fragile, constitutive of life and unambiguously present in the human condition, as well as unambiguously absent in the atrocities of history and in humankind's despoliation of the earth. Kate Rushin has evoked this form of presence in her poem, "The Black Goddess." She is denying the attributes of the monotheistic goddess of presence—perfection, completion, and omnipotence—and celebrating the incomplete, yet undeniably real power of transformation and liberation.

I am not a Black Goddess,
I am not a Black Goddess,
Look at me
Look at me
I do what I can
That's about it
Sometimes I make it Sometimes I don't . . .

I still get Night Terrors
And sometimes it takes me weeks to
Answer a letter or make a phone call
I am not a Black Goddess
I am not a Black Goddess

Once though   I was Harriet Tubman[77]

Divinity is not a mark of that which is other than the finite. Grace is not that which comes from outside to transform the conditions of finitude. Divinity, or grace, is the resilient, fragile, healing power of finitude itself. The terms *holy* and *divine* denote a quality of being within the web of life, a process of healing relationship, and they denote the quality of being worthy of honor, love, respect, and affirmation.

The need for continued critique and transformation does not mean that the impulse and power present in work for justice is not divine. The fact that we experience moments of defeat, of being outmaneuvered, does not mean that the power in our movements for justice is not divine. If divinity is understood as an absolute, this is the case. But divinity is not only transcendent and life-giving, it is also fragile. The power of relatedness can be destroyed and has been destroyed in the Nazi Holocaust and in the many genocides of Western history. The divinity of these forces does not lie in their absolute power but in the quality of life they enable. Worship of nature, love, and interdependence does not ensure success but does offer the possibility of a life of belonging and resistance. The power which is holy is also fragile. We are constituted by it; it is sustained by us.

Such fragility is intrinsic to creative power. Central to its working is the eliciting of responses from others and courageous openness to novelty and creativity. Creative power, the power of love and the power of the web of life, can never guarantee the results of its operation. When freed to be creative, people's responses can delight or dismay, but they always escape our control.

In solidarity with others, in work for justice, we remain human. Our vision is ever-growing. Our strategies for change have partial successes and require continual critique and revision. Yet this work, though partial in its depth and scope, is divine. We who are feminist theologians find much that is divine—work for justice, love, creativity itself, the web of life, joy, and beauty. Innumerable states and qualities of acting are divine. By naming joy as divine, we affirm that these aspects of human existence are worthy of worship. Attentiveness to the web of life, to the exuberance of children, to the beauty of nature, provides a sense of peace, of belonging, of exultation and ecstasy. Attentiveness to these forces provides energy, focus, and a challenging reorientation of our lives.

A theology of immanence does provide the benefits of a theology of transcendence without the social costs. There is an imperative for ethical action, one grounded in love and accountability. Love and accountability also produce a type of transcendence. This theology is transcendent in four ways. First, there is the ability to see clearly the complexity of life. Humanity is not merely immersed in natural processes, responding to them blindly, but is aware of the complex patterns of life and the ways in which life's richness exceeds our intellectual grasp. We "transcend" instinct but need to learn that nature also transcends us. Our actions have consequences far greater than our ability to predict. We are not condemned to a foolish, hasty mode of acting; we can act deliberately in awareness of these limits.[78]

Second, the human community can celebrate the wonder and beauty of life. Native American religious traditions exemplify this sort of transcendence. To celebrate the cycles of nature is not to be imprisoned in a static pattern. Celebration implies seeing, honoring, and rejoicing—all acts of transcendence. This celebration is not merely romantic, for it can provide the resources necessary for resistance. Maya Angelou, Toni Morrison, and Alice Walker, for example, describe the beauty of nature glimpsed in the midst of oppression and the power such recognition evokes.[79]

A third aspect of transcendence is the transcending of conditions of oppression through loving life, self, and others despite social forces that deny the value of all of these. This type of transcendence is celebrated in the novels discussed earlier. Love for life, what Daly calls "Pure Lust," is an act of profound transcendence in a culture that sees the world, human and natural, solely in terms of use value, as commodities, things to be developed and marketed.[80]

The fourth form of transcendence is the movement of social transformation. The last century has seen masses of people demanding social change, refusing to accept their oppression as natural. We can look to the labor movement, the civil rights movement, the peace movement, and the women's movement as models. All of these are holy. They are manifestations of transcendence, of the love of life and self leading to work for social change. In Africa there has been the ouster of colonial powers and, now, the determined resistance of the majority to oppressive white rule in South Africa. The mass movements in the Philippines, Korea, and Nicaragua are all manifestations of a holy transcendence, love of life enabling the transcendence of social structures that destroy life.

All of these movements are holy; all of them are flawed. Their gains are incomplete: aims for social justice are hindered by exploitive forces within the movements, and hindered by oppression from without. Middle-class people can be empowered by a recognition of the power of divine love and healing at work in our communities of resistance. Our efforts are partial, yet they are divine in their love and courage. They bear witness to the transcendent, healing power of love; they bear witness to the beauty and wonder of life. They are a dangerous memory.

Notes

———— ■ ————

1. The Ethic of Control

1. Sharon Parks has discussed this apparent anomaly. She found that many of her students felt optimistic about their own lives but pessimistic about the possibilities of any sort of justice in the larger world. (Personal conversations, Cambridge, Massachusetts, 1990). She, along with her co-authors, explores what it takes to have hope for the larger world in *Common Fire: Lives of Commitment in a Complex World*, Laurent A. Parks Daloz, Cheryl H. Keen, James P. Keen, Sharon Daloz Parks (Boston: Beacon Press, 1996).

2. Barbara Crossette, "The World Expected Peace, It Found a New Brutality." *New York Times*, January 24, 1999.

3. Shamshad Ahmad, "The Nuclear Subcontinent: Bringing Stability to South Asia," *Foreign Affairs*, 78/4 (July/August 1999), 123-25.

Elizabeth Becker described the U.S. House of Representatives vote to build an antiballistic missile defense system, and the limited critiques of that system: "The Pentagon has budgeted $10.5 billion over the next six years to create a workable system. . . . Representative Vernon J. Ehlers of Michigan was the lone Republican voting against the measure. As a trained physicist, Mr. Ehlers said, he could not vote for something that cost so much—perhaps an additional $75 billion—and seemed to have such a small chance of succeeding." Elizabeth Becker, "Congress Passes Antimissile Defense Policy," *New York Times,* May 21, 1999.

4. Emilie M. Townes, *Breaking the Fine Rain of Death: African American Health Issues and a Womanist Ethic of Care* (New York: Continuum, 1998), p. 26.

5. Jane Braaten, "From Communicative Rationality to Communicative Thinking: A Basis for Feminist Theory and Practice," in *Feminists Read Habermas,* ed. Johanna Meehan (New York: Routledge, 1995), pp. 139, 142.

6. Cynthia Willett, *Maternal Ethics and Other Slave Moralities* (New York: Routledge, 1995).

7. Garth Kasimu Baker-Fletcher, *Xodus: An African-American Male Journey* (Minneapolis: Fortress Press, 1996), p. 7.

8. Katie Geneva Cannon, *Katie's Canon: Womanism and the Soul of the Black Community* (New York: Continuum, 1995), p. 61.

9. See, for example, the work with Asian feminist groups and Asian religious traditions reflected in Rita Nakashima Brock and Susan Brooks Thistlethwaite, *Casting Stones: Prostitution and Liberation in Asia and the United States*

(Minneapolis: Fortress Press, 1996). See also the work of Virginia Fabella and Lee-Park Sun Ai, *We Dare to Dream: Doing Theology as Asian Women* (Hong Kong: Asian Women's Resource Center for Culture and Theology, 1988); in another venue, Ada María Isasi-Díaz, *Mujerista Theology: A Theology for the Twenty-first Century* (Maryknoll, N.Y.: Orbis Books, 1996).

10. Diane I. Meyers and Eva Feder Kittay, eds., "Introduction," *Women and Moral Theology* (Totowa, N.J.: Rowman and Littlefield, 1987), p. 3.

11. Kathryn Tanner provides a critical assessment of care ethics in "The Care That Does Justice: Recent Writings in Feminist Ethics and Theology," *Journal of Religious Ethics*, 24/1 (Spring 1996), pp. 171-91. Emilie Townes develops a womanist ethic of care that is different from the feminist ethic of care in her attention to race, gender, and class: "The attempt to understand gender-based distinctions, while helpful, is much too narrow a focus for analyzing the dynamics of care and developing an interstructured moral theory of care." Townes, *Breaking the Fine Rain of Death*, p. 1.

12. Beverly Wildung Harrison, *Making the Connections: Essays in Feminist Social Ethics*, ed. Carol S. Robb (Boston: Beacon Press, 1985), p. 255.

13. Jonathan M. Feldman, "Public Choice, Foreign Policy Crises, and Military Spending," in *The Socio-Economics of Conversion from War to Peace*, ed. Lloyd J. Dumas (Armonk, N.Y.: M.E. Sharpe Studies in Socio-Economics, 1995). See also John Hillen, "Defense's Death Spiral," *Foreign Affairs*, 78/4 (July/August 1999), pp. 2-7.

14. For an analysis of the complexity of economic conversion, and the political and economic resistance to it, see Dumas, ed., *The Socio-Economics of Conversion*; Gregory A. Bischak, "The Political Economy of an Alternative Security and Disarmament Policy for the United States," *Towards a Peace Economy in the United States: Essays on Military Industry, Disarmament and Economic Conversion*, ed. Gregory A. Bischak (New York: St. Martin's Press, 1991), pp. 121-58. Jonathan Feldman examines the political power of warmaking institutions and economic dependency created by long-term military spending in "Constituencies and New Markets for Economic Conversion: Reconstructing the United States' Physical, Environmental and Social Infrastructure," in Bischak, ed., *Towards a Peace Economy*, pp. 202-41.

15. For an analysis of successful conversion, see Jonathan M. Feldman, "Civilian Diversification, Learning and Institutional Change: Growth through Knowledge and Power," *Environment and Planning*, 31/10 (October 1999) pp. 1805-24.

16. Crossette, "The World Expected Peace," p. 1.

17. John Hillen, "Defense's Death Spiral," *Foreign Affairs*, 78/4 (July/August 1999), p. 2.

18. Ibid., p. 4.

19. Ibid., p. 7.

20. Edward N. Luttwak, "Give War a Chance," *Foreign Affairs*, 78/4 (July/August 1999), p. 37.

21. Ibid., pp. 36, 44.

22. Michael Hirsh, "At War with Ourselves: In Kosovo, America Confronts Its Own ideals," *Harper's Magazine*, July 1999, pp. 60, 61.

23. Ibid., p. 60.

24. Ibid., p. 69.

25. Ibid.

26. Ibid., p. 68.

27. Joseph S. Nye Jr., "Redefining the National Interest," *Foreign Affairs*, 78/4 (July/August 1999), p. 26.

28. Ibid., p. 32.

29. David Rief, "The Precarious Triumph of Human Rights," *New York Times Magazine*, August 8, 1999, p. 39.

30. Nye, "Redefining," pp. 31-32.

31. Ibid., p. 24.

32. Michael Lerner, "Compassion with Teeth: Caring Requires Intervention" *Tikkun*, 14/3 (May/June 1999), p. 8.

33. Noam Chomsky, "Stop U.S. Intervention: An Interview with Noam Chomsky," *Tikkun*, 14/3 (May/June 1999), p. 6.

34. Cynthia Enloe, "Cynthia Enloe and Vivian Stromberg on Militarism and Making Peace," *Ms.*, August/September 1999, p. 21.

35. Semour Melman, *The Demilitarized Society: Disarmament and Conversion* (Montreal: Harvest House, 1988), p. 8.

36. Amitai Etzioni, "Preface," in Dumas, ed., *The Socio-Economics of Conversion*, pp. ix-x.

37. Vojtech Matny, "Did NATO Win the Cold War? Looking over the Wall," *Foreign Affairs*, 78/3 (May/June 1999), p. 188.

38. Micheal J. Glenna, "The New Interventionism: The Search for a Just International Law," *Foreign Affairs*, 78/3 (May/June 1999), p. 6.

39. "Global Action to Prevent War: A Coalition-Building Effort to Stop War, Genocide, and Other Forms of Deadly Conflict," April 1999, Revision 10 (Cambridge, Mass.: Institute for Defense and Disarmament Studies), p. 2. Among the many organizations working for nonviolent conflict resolution are International Alliance of Lawyers against Nuclear Arms, International Physicians for the Prevention of Nuclear War, Toda Institute for Peace Studies, World Order Models Project, Union of Concerned Scientists, University of Copenhagen Peace Research Institute, Korea Peace Research Association, U.N. Institute for Disarmament Research, Geneva, Institute for Defense and Disarmament Studies. Some of the women's groups working for peace, as reported in *Ms.*, August/September 1999, pp. 22-23, include in Africa: Federation of African Women's Peace Organizations (Rwanda); Women's Movement for Peace in Sierra Leone, Sudanese Women's Voice for Peace, African Women Committee on Peace and Development (Ethiopia); in Asia and Middle East: Association of Women of the Mediterranean Region, Jerusalem Link, Cyprus Link, Women's Solidarity for Human Rights (Indonesia); South Asia Forum for Human Rights, Revolutionary Association of the Women of Afghanistan (exiled women organized against Taliban and helping refugee women and children), TransCaucasus Women's Dialogue Project; in South America: Conamus (National Coordinating Committee of Women in El Salvador); Mujeres por Colombia; International: Grandmothers for Peace International, Hunt Alternatives, Women against Military Madness, Women in Black against War, Women's International League for Peace and Freedom.

40. Deborah Sontag, "Now That the Wars Are Over, Utopia Seems More Distant," *New York Times*, July 18, 1999.

41. "Overriding objections from a number of countries that contribute peacekeeping troops to the United Nations, Secretary General Kofi Annan has ordered that all forces operating under the organization's command abide by international laws protecting civilians and governing the conduct of soldiers in

war.... In this decade, peacekeeping troops, which are supposed to be neutral, began to be entangled in vicious civil wars that turned even peacekeeping into a violent free-for-all at times ... some of the most publicized cases involved Belgian, Canadian and Italian troops in Somalia from 1993 to 1995. But many United Nations operations have drawn accusations of theft, rape, torture and other abuses against citizens...." Barbara Crossette, "Global Rules Now Apply to Peacekeepers, U.N. Chief Declares," *New York Times,* August 12, 1999.

42. Nye, "Redefining," p. 24.

43. Michael Howard, "An Unhappy Successful Marriage: Security Means Knowing What to Expect," *Foreign Affairs,* 78/3 (May/June 1999), p. 172.

44. Cynthia Enloe, *Bananas, Beaches and Bases: Making Feminist Sense of International Relations* (London: Pandora, 1989); *idem, The Morning After: Sexual Politics after the Cold War* (Berkeley: University of California Press, 1993); Miriam Cooke and Angela Woolacott, *Gendering War Talk* (Princeton: Princeton University Press, 1993); Jill Steans, *Gender and International Relations: An Introduction* (New Brunswick, N.J.: Rutgers University Press, 1998); J. J. Pettman, *Worlding Women: A Feminist International Politics* (New York: Routledge, 1996); Christine Sylvester, *Feminist Theory and International Relations in a Postmodern era* (Cambridge: Cambridge University Press, 1994).

45. Nye, "Redefining," p. 25.

46. David A. Sanger, "America Finds It's Lonely at the Top," *New York Times,* July 18, 1999.

47. Ibid.

48. Nye, "Redefining," p. 27.

49. John and Karl Mueller, "Rethinking Sanctions on Iraq: The Real Weapons of Mass Destruction," *Foreign Affairs,* 78/3 (May/June 1999), pp. 43-53.

50. David Bernstein, "A Force Now in the World, Citizens Flex Social Muscle," *New York Times,* July 10, 1999.

51. Robert E. Hunter, "Maximizing NATO: A Relevant Alliance Knows How to Reach," *Foreign Affairs,* 78/3 (May/June 1999), p. 192.

52. G. John Ikenberry, review of *Security Communities,* ed. Emanuel Adler and Michael Barnett (New York: Cambridge University Press, 1999), in *Foreign Affairs,* 78/4 (July/August 1999), p. 129.

53. Ibid.

54. Ibid.

55. I am not, of course, making the claim that this ethic is found in the writings of all African Americans, nor that it is reflected in the lives of all African American women and men. For a cogent critique of this essentialist over-generalization, see the work of Victor Anderson, *Beyond Ontological Blackness* (New York: Continuum, 1995).

56. Karen Baker-Fletcher, *A Singing Something: Womanist Reflections on Anna Julia Cooper* (New York: Crossroad, 1994); *idem, Sisters of Dust, Sisters of Spirit: Womanist Wordings on God and Creation* (Minneapolis: Fortress Press, 1998); Emilie M. Townes, *A Troubling in My Soul* (Maryknoll, N.Y.: Orbis Books, 1993); *Embracing the Spirit: Womanist Perspectives on Hope, Salvation and Transformation,* ed. Emilie M. Townes (Maryknoll, N.Y.: Orbis Books, 1997); Emilie M. Townes, *In a Blaze of Glory: Womanist Spirituality as Social Witness* (Nashville: Abingdon Press, 1995); Marcia Y. Riggs, ed., *Can I Get a Witness? Prophetic Religious Voices of African American Women: An Anthology* (Mary-

knoll, N.Y.: Orbis Books, 1997); Marcia Y. Riggs, *Arise, Awake, and Act! A Womanist Call for Black Liberation* (Cleveland: Pilgrim Press, 1994); Delores S. Williams, *Sisters in the Wilderness: The Challenge of Womanist God-Talk* (Maryknoll, N.Y.: Orbis Books, 1993). Traci C. West, *Wounds of the Spirit: Black Women, Violence and Resistance Ethics* (New York: New York University Press, 1999).

57. Cannon, *Katie's Canon*, pp. 23, 25.

58. Emilie Townes, *In a Blaze of Glory*, p. 11.

59. Ibid., pp. 11, 79-85.

60. Peter J. Paris, *The Spirituality of African Peoples: The Search for a Common Moral Discourse* (Minneapolis: Fortress Press, 1995); Anthony B. Pinn, *Why Lord? Suffering and Evil in Black Theology* (New York: Continuum, 1995); Robert Michael Franklin, *Liberating Visions: Human Fulfillment and Social Justice in African-American Thought* (Minneapolis: Fortress Press, 1990); Enoch H. Oglesby, *Born in the Fire: Case Studies in Christian Ethics and Globalization* (New York: Pilgrim Press, 1990); Garth Baker-Fletcher, *Somebodyness: Martin Luther King, Jr., and the Theory of Dignity* (Minneapolis: Fortress Press, 1993); Karen Baker-Fletcher and Garth Kasimu Baker-Fletcher, *My Sister, My Brother: Womanist and Xodus God-Talk* (Maryknoll, N.Y.: Orbis Books, 1997); Dwight N. Hopkins, *Introducing Black Theology of Liberation* (Maryknoll, N.Y.: Orbis Books, 1999); James H. Cone, *The Spirituals and the Blues: An Interpretation* (Mary Knoll, N.Y.: Orbis Books, 1992).

61. Pinn, *Why Lord?* p. 141.

62. Ibid., p. 140.

63. Ibid., p. 141.

64. Cannon, *Katie's Canon*, p. 58.

65. Townes, *In a Blaze of Glory*, p. 48.

66. Delores S. Williams, "Straight Talk, Plain Talk: Womanist Words about Salvation in a Social Context," *Embracing the Spirit*, ed. Townes, p. 105.

67. Patricia J. Williams, *Seeing a Color-Blind Future: The Paradox of Race* (New York: Farrar Straus and Giroux, 1997); Chalmer E. Thompson and Helen A. Neville, "Racism, Mental Health, and Mental Health Practice," *The Counseling Psychologist*, 27/2 (March 1999), pp. 155-223; bell hooks, *Killing Rage: Ending Racism* (New York: Henry Holt & Company, 1995); Derrick Bell, *Faces at the Bottom of the Well: The Permanence of Racism* (New York: Basic Books, 1992); Garth Kasimu Baker-Fletcher, *Xodus: An African American Male Journey* (Minneapolis: Fortress Press, 1995).

68. Delores S. Williams, "Straight Talk, Plain Talk," pp. 97-121.

69. Marcia Riggs, *Awake, Arise, and Act!*; Garth Kasimu Baker-Fletcher, *Xodus*; Emilie Townes, *Breaking the Fine Rain of Death*, p. 151.

70. Peter Paris, *The Spirituality of African Peoples*, pp. 12-13.

71. Cheryl Townsend Gilkes, "A Conscious Connection to All That Is: *The Color Purple* as Subversive and Critical Ethnography," *Embracing the Spirit*, ed. Townes, p. 277.

72. Ibid.

73. Karen Baker-Fletcher, *Sisters of Dust, Sisters of Spirit*, pp. 9-10.

74. Townes, *In a Blaze of Glory*, pp. 72-73.

75. Ibid., p. 118.

76. Ibid., p. 138.

77. Aaron Thompson, personal communication, Columbia, Missouri, August 1999. Aaron Thompson is the author, with Erma Jean Lawson, of

Black Men and Divorce, (London: Sage Publications, 1999).

78. Cheryl A. Kirk-Duggan, "Justified, Sanctified, and Redeemed," p. 143.

79. Ibid.

80. Townes, *In a Blaze of Glory,* p. 178.

81. Ibid., p.114.

82. Townsend Gilkes, "A Conscious Connection to All That Is," p. 279.

83. Karen Baker-Fletcher, *Sisters of Dust, Sisters of Spirit,* p. 122.

84. Townes, *Breaking the Fine Rain of Death,* p. 175.

85. Ibid., p. 178.

86. Ibid., p. 181.

2. Narratives of Healing and Transformation

1. Piven and Cloward provide an analysis of movements for social change in the United States and give an extensive bibliography (Frances Fox Piven and Richard A. Cloward, *Poor People's Movements: Why They Succeed, How They Fail* [New York: Vintage Books, 1979]).

2. Jane Caputi provides disturbing evidence of increasing violence against women in her book *The Age of Sex Crime* (Bowling Green, Ohio: Bowling Green University Popular Press, 1987).

3. A similar analysis can be found in Henry Giroux, *Theory and Resistance in Education: A Pedagogy for the Opposition* (South Hadley, Mass.: Bergen and Garvey Publishers, Inc., 1983).

4. Katie G. Cannon, "The Black Woman's Literary Tradition as a Source for Ethics," in *Black Womanist Ethics* (Atlanta: Scholars Press, 1988), pp. 75-98. The works analyzed by Cannon and others range from the rediscovered writings of Zora Neale Hurston, Lucy Terry, Phyllis Wheatley, and Harriet E. Wilson to contemporary writers such as Maya Angelou, Toni Cade Bambara, Gwendlyn Brooks, Alice Childress, Lucille Clifton, Mari Evans, Mikki Giovanni, Rosa Guy, Gayl Jones, June Jordon, Audre Lorde, Paule Marshall, Toni Morrison, Gloria Naylor, Carolyn Rodgers, Sonia Sanchez, Ntozake Shange, Mildred Taylor, Joyce Carol Thomas, Alice Walker, and Margaret Walker.

5. Barbara Christian, *Black Feminist Criticism: Perspectives on Black Women Writers* (New York: Pergamon, 1985); Mari Evans, ed., *Black Women Writers (1950-1980): A Critical Evaluation* (Garden City, N.Y.: Doubleday Anchor Books, 1984).

6. Henry Louis Gates, Jr., "Reclaiming Their Tradition," *New York Times Book Review,* October 1987, p. 34.

7. Mary Helen Washington, *Invented Lives: Narratives of Black Women 1860-1960* (New York: Doubleday, Anchor Press, 1987). Reading this material as a representative testament raises a host of critical methodological problems. In chapter 7 I discuss my method of reading, one that is dependent on feminist literary criticism and the critical theory of Michel Foucault. I place this strategy of reading in the context of current debates in critical theory. I describe the way in which this reading is a postmodern strategy and the ways in which it differs from two other developments within postmodernism, deconstruction, and structuralism.

8. Christian, *Black Feminist Criticism,* p. 159. Cf. the similar characteri-

zation of the black aesthetic by Addison Gayle, Jr. Gayle cites another critic who describes the writing of black men and women as "the act of creation of the self in face of the self's historical denial by our society." Gayle goes on to argue that such work should be evaluated less in terms of its beauty and more in terms of "the transformation from ugliness to beauty that the work of art demands from its audience" (Addison Gayle, Jr., *The Black Aesthetic* [Garden City, N.Y.: Doubleday, 1972], pp. ix, xxii).

9. Ibid., pp. 159–60.

10. Ibid., p. 116.

11. John McCluskey, Jr., "And Call Every Generation Blessed: Theme, Setting and Ritual in the Works of Paule Marshall," in Evans, *Black Women Writers*, p. 316.

12. Ibid., p. 317.

13. Eugenia Collier, "The Closing of the Circle: Movement from Division to Wholeness in Paule Marshall's Fiction," in Evans, *Black Women Writers*, p. 296.

14. Toni Cade Bambara, "Salvation Is the Issue," in Evans, *Black Women Writers*, p. 46.

15. Ibid., p. 47.

16. Ibid., p. 42.

17. Ibid., p. 41.

18. See bell hooks, *Ain't I a Woman: Black Women and Feminism* (Boston: South End Press, 1981), p. 6; and Mary Helen Washington, "Black Women Image Makers," *Black World,* Aug. 1974, pp. 10–18.

19. Toni Cade Bambara, *The Salt-Eaters* (New York: Vintage Books, 1981), p. 265.

20. Jonathan Schell makes a similar point in his discussion of the moral costs of accepting current nuclear weapons policies. Schell, *Fate of the Earth,* p. 148.

21. Bambara, *Salt-Eaters,* p. 266.

22. Alice Walker, Revolutionary Petunias and Other Poems (New York: Harcourt Brace Jovanovich, 1973).

23. June Jordan, quoted in Walker, *Revolutionary Petunias,* p. 67.

3. Memory and Accountability

1. Paule Marshall, *The Chosen Place, The Timeless People* (New York: Random House, 1984). References to this work are provided hereafter parenthetically in the text.

2. John McCluskey, Jr., "And Call Every Generation Blessed: Theme, Setting and Ritual in the Works of Paule Marshall" in Mari Evans, ed. *Black Women Writers (1950–1980): A Critical Evaluation* (Garden City, N.Y.: Doubleday, Anchor Books, 1984), p. 317.

3. Marshall, *The Chosen Place, The Timeless People,* frontispiece.

4. Barbara Christian, *Black Women Novelists: The Development of a Tradition, 1892–1976* (Westport, Conn.: Greenwood Press, 1980), p. 106.

5. It is revealing that Marshall's treatment of structural oppression is marred by her unwitting repetition of two other abuses of power: homophobia and sexism. I find two serious difficulties with Marshall's analysis of power—her negative portrayal of gay and lesbian life and her blame of white

women for the power of white men. The one gay man in the novel is portrayed as tortured, unable to acknowledge and name his love for men. The lesbian experience of the protagonist is thoroughly exploitive (not unlike many heterosexual relationships) and "cured" by the love of a strong man. The second difficulty, Marshall's portrayal of white women, is also skewed by her inattention to structures of sexism. She describes white women, not white men, as those directly responsible for the past and present evils of capitalism and racism. The person who perpetrates the legacy of slavery is a woman, and the money she uses was made in the slave trade by another woman. This is a dangerous equation of white women with the evils of racism and capitalism, ignoring the fact that most wealth is in the hands of white men, that white women's inclusion in the power of the upper class is marginal—a by-product of their relationship to men and not something independently gained. While many white women have been oppressive, their power has been derivative. The primary holders of power, white men, do not play a central role in this novel. The danger here is that white men are not held responsible for the systems that operate primarily for their benefit. For a further discussion of lesbianism by African-American women, see Barbara Smith, ed., *Home Girls: A Black Feminist Anthology* (New York: Kitchen Table Press, 1983); Alice Walker, correction to review of *Gifts of Power: The Writings of Rebecca Jackson,* in *The Black Scholar,* Nov.–Dec. 1981, p. 80; Barbara Christian, *Black Feminist Criticism: Perspectives on Black Women Writers* (New York: Pergamon Press, 1985).

6. Barbara Christian, "Trajectories of Self-definition: Placing Contemporary Afro-American Women's Fiction" in *Conjuring: Black Women, Fiction and Literary Tradition,* ed. Marjorie Pryse and Hortense Spillers (Bloomington: Indiana University Press, 1985); Eugenia Collier, "The Closing of the Circle: Movement from Division to Wholeness in Paule Marshall's fiction" in Evans, *Black Women Writers.*

4. A Heritage of Persistence, Imagination, and Solidarity

1. Barbara Christian, *Black Women Novelists: The Development of a Tradition, 1892–1976* (Westport, Conn.: Greenwood Press, 1980), p. 138.

2. Toni Morrison, *The Bluest Eye* (New York: Holt, Rinehart and Winston, 1970), p. 55. References to this work are provided hereafter parenthetically in the text.

3. Mildred Taylor, "Preface: Newberry Award Acceptance Speech," *Let the Circle Be Unbroken* (New York: Bantam Books, 1983). p. iii. References to this work are provided hereafter parenthetically in the text.

4. Mildred Taylor, *Roll of Thunder, Hear My Cry* (New York: Bantam Books, 1984), pp. 40–41. References to this work are provided hereafter parenthetically in the text.

5. The Healing Power of Love

1. Angela Jackson, review of *The Salt Eaters, The Black Scholar,* Fall 1982, p. 57.

2. Gloria T. Hull, "What It Is I Think She's Doing Anyhow: A Reading of Toni Cade Bambara's *The Salt Eaters,*" in *Home Girls: A Black Feminist Anthology,* ed. Barbara Smith (New York: Kitchen Table Press, 1983), p. 124.

3. Toni Cade Bambara, *The Salt-Eaters* (New York: Vintage Books, 1981). References to this work are provided hereafter parenthetically in the text.

6. The Ideology of Cultured Despair

1. See Melissa Everett, *Bearing Witness, Building Bridges: Interviews with North Americans Living and Working in Nicaragua* (Philadelphia: New Society Publishers, 1986).

2. See the works of James Cone, Cornell West, Jon Sobrino, Gustavo Gutierrez, Rosemary Ruether, Mary Daly, Judith Plaskow, Carter Heyward, and Carol Christ for an introduction to theologies of liberation.

3. George Lindbeck, *The Nature of Doctrine: Religion and Theology in a Postliberal Age* (Philadelphia: Westminster Press, 1984), pp. 22, 31–41.

4. See the works of Edward Farley, David Tracy, Schubert Ogden, Langdon Gilkey, Van Harvey, and Gordon Kaufman.

5. Edward Farley, *Ecclesial Reflection: An Anatomy of Theological Method* (Philadelphia: Fortress Press, 1982), p. 163.

6. David Tracy, *The Analogical Imagination: Christian Theology and the Culture of Pluralism* (New York: Crossroad, 1981), p. 78.

7. Gordon Kaufman, *The Theological Imagination: Constructing the Concept of God* (Philadelphia: Westminster Press, 1981); *Theology for a Nuclear Age* (Philadelphia: Westminster Press, 1985).

8. Lindbeck, *Nature of Doctrine*, p. 32.

9. This critique is found in the work of James Cone, Cornell West, Mary Daly, Judith Plaskow, and Carter Heyward.

10. Gordon Kaufman has a similar critique in *Theology Today*, 42d ser., no. 2 (July 1985): 240–41.

11. Sarah Harasym, "Practical Politics of the Open End: An Interview with Gayatri Chakravorty Spivak," *Canadian Journal of Political and Social Theory*, vol. 12, nos. 1–2 (1988).

12. Gayraud Wilmore (*Last Things First,* [Philadelphia: Westminster Press, 1982], pp. 31–39) describes a shift in theological interpretations of eschatology from a focus on biblical prophecies about the end of time, or "last things" (Johannes Weise, *Jesus' Preaching on the Kingdom of God;* Albert Schweitzer, *The Mystery of the Kingdom of God* and *The Quest for the Historical Jesus*) to the "transcendental eschatology" of Karl Barth (the final truth about human lives exists in our relation to that which is eternal) and the "existential eschatology" of Bultmann. Eschatology as a category for interpreting political struggle has been developed by Jürgen Moltmann, James Cone, and Juan Luis Segundo among others. Francis Schüssler Fiorenza also explores "the intersubjective force and interactive pragmatic" of eschatology in *Foundational Theology: Jesus and The Church* (New York: Crossroad, 1986), p. 117.

13. For example, see John B. Cobb, Jr., *Process Theology as Political Theology* (Philadelphia: Westminster Press, 1987).

14. Johannes Metz, *Theology of the World,* trans. William Glen (New York: Seabury Press, 1969), p. 153, as cited by Dennis P. McCann, *Christian Realism and Liberation Theology: Practical Theologies in Creative Conflict* (Maryknoll, N.Y.: Orbis Books, 1981), p. 162.

15. McCann, *Christian Realism,* p. 162.

16. Ibid., p. 163.

17. Juan Luis Segundo, S.J., *The Liberation of Theology,* trans. John Drury (Maryknoll, N.Y.: Orbis Books, 1976), p. 145.

18. Ibid., p. 147.

19. Ibid., p. 65.

20. Rachel Carson, *Silent Spring* (New York: Fawcett Crest, 1962).

21. Timothy Weiskel, "The Anthropology of Environmental Decline," Statement for Hearings of the Committee on Environment and Public Works, United States Senate, September 14, 1988.

22. Jeremy Rifkin, *Declaration of a Heretic* (Boston: Routledge and Kegan Paul, 1985), Part 2.

23. Susan Griffin, *Woman and Nature: The Roaring Inside Her* (New York: Harper & Row, 1978).

24. Jürgen Habermas, *Communication and the Evolution of Society* (Boston: Beacon Press, 1979), pp. 121–22.

25. McCann, *Christian Realism,* p. 4.

26. Ibid., p. 179.

27. Ibid., p. 178.

28. Gustavo Gutierrez, *Power of the Poor in History* (Maryknoll, N.Y.: Orbis, 1986); Janice G. Raymond, *A Passion for Friends* (Boston: Beacon Press, 1986). The Marxist critique of an ethic of rights is based on the charge that so-called "genuine limit-situations" are often not genuine but are, rather, the product of political and economic exploitation. See Steven Lukes, *Marxism and Morality* (Oxford: Clarendon Press, 1985), pp. 33–34.

29. June Jordan, "Where is the Love?" *Civil Wars* (Boston: Beacon Press, 1981), p. 142.

30. McCann, *Christian Realism,* p. 179.

31. Gustavo Gutierrez, *A Theology of Liberation* (Maryknoll, N.Y.: Orbis, 1973); Phillip Berryman, *The Religious Roots of Rebellion* (Maryknoll, N.Y.: Orbis, 1986).

32. Rosemary Radford Ruether, *New Woman/New Earth* (New York: Crossroads, 1975); Judith Plaskow, *Sex, Sin and Grace* (Washington, D.C.: University Press of America, 1980); Mary Daly, *Beyond God the Father* (Boston: Beacon Press, 1973).

33. Ruether, Plaskow and Daly make the same argument in their works.

34. Alfred North Whitehead, *Process and Reality: an Essay in Cosmology* (Darby, Penn.: Darby Books, 1983), p. 342.

35. My concept of the erotics of domination is dependent on Jessica Benjamin's discussion of erotic domination and Michel Foucault's exploration of the colonization of desire. Although the terms are the same, Benjamin's usage differs from mine. She describes a fantasy of rational violence present individually in sadomasochism and culturally in the public-private split of capitalism. See Jessica Benjamin, *Psychoanalysis, Feminism, and the Problem of Domination* (New York: Pantheon Books, 1988).

36. Augustine, De civ. Dei, 14.12, as cited by Elaine Pagels, "The Politics of Paradise: Augustine's Exegesis of Genesis 1–3 Versus That of John Chrysostom," *Harvard Theological Review,* 78:1–2 (1985), pp. 78–79.

37. Ibid., p. 68.

38. Ibid., p. 85.

39. Ibid., p. 90.

40. Ibid., p. 93.

41. Ibid.

42. Ibid., p. 89.

43. Ibid., p. 97.

44. Ibid., p. 98.

45. Dietrich Bonhoeffer, *Letters and Papers from Prison: The Enlarged Edition*, "After Ten Years: A Reckoning Made at New Year 1943," ed. Eberhard Bethge (New York: Macmillan Co., 1972), p. 4.

46. Ibid.

47. Ibid., p. 8.

48. Ibid., pp. 8–9.

49. Ibid.

50. Thomas Ferguson and Joel Rogers, "The Myth of America's Turn to the Right," *The Atlantic*, vol. 257, no. 5 (May 1986): 43–53.

51. Ibid., p. 44, 45.

52. Ibid., p. 49.

53. Ibid., p. 50.

54. Ibid., p. 51.

55. Ibid., p. 49.

56. Ibid., pp. 50, 52–53.

57. Anselm, *Proslogium III*, in *Basic Writings*, trans. S. N. Deane (La Salle, Ill.: Open Court, 1962), pp. 8–9.

58. H. Richard Niebuhr, *Radical Monotheism and Western Culture: With Supplementary Essays* (London: Faber and Faber, 1960), p. 37.

59. Ibid., p. 53.

60. Ibid.

61. Karl Barth, *The Humanity of God* (Richmond: John Knox Press, 1960), p. 41.

62. Paul Tillich, *The Courage to Be* (New Haven, Conn.: Yale University Press, 1952), p. 179.

63. Ibid., pp. 43–44.

64. Paul Tillich, *Systematic Theology*, vol. 3 (Chicago: University of Chicago Press, 1963), p. 405.

65. Barth, *Humanity of God*, p. 48.

66. Paul Tillich, *Systematic Theology*, vol. 1 (Chicago: University of Chicago Press, 1951), p. 136.

67. Ibid., p. 137.

68. Tillich, *Systematic Theology*, 3:310–11.

69. Ibid., p. 341.

70. Ibid., p. 311.

71. Ibid., p. 340.

72. Ibid., p. 385.

73. Ibid., p. 264.

74. Ibid., p. 263.

75. Ibid., pp. 263–64.

76. Niebuhr, *Radical Monotheism*, p. 37.

77. Ibid., pp. 121–22.

78. Ibid., pp. 122–23.·

79. Ibid., p. 123.

80. Tillich, *Systematic Theology*, 3:397.

7. *An Ethic of Solidarity and Difference*

1. Stephen Fowl, "The Ethics of Interpretation or What's Left After the Elimination of Meaning," presentation at the annual meeting of the Society of Biblical Literature, Chicago, Ill., November 22, 1988, p. 9.

2. Ibid.

3. Ibid., pp. 9–20. Fowl argues that the professional societies to which biblical scholars belong adhere to the principle of pluralism. The valuing of pluralism leads to questions regarding the actual degree of openness of academic discussions.

4. Ibid., pp. 11, 13.

5. Ibid., p. 14.

6. Alastair MacIntyre, *After Virtue: A Study in Moral Theory,* 2d ed. (Notre Dame, Ind.: University of Notre Dame Press, 1984), p. 14.

7. Ibid.

8. Michel Foucault, *The Use of Pleasure: The History of Sexuality, Volume Two,* trans. Robert Hurley (New York: Pantheon Books, 1985), p. 22.

9. Ibid., p. 80.

10. Ibid., p. 70.

11. Ibid., p. 75.

12. Ibid.

13. Ibid., p. 76.

14. Ibid.

15. For a further description of the ethically sanctioned domination of women and slaves see Foucault, *The Use of Pleasure,* Part 3 and pp. 215–16.

16. MacIntyre, *After Virtue,* p. 162.

17. Ibid., p. 159.

18. Ibid., p. 148. Emphasis mine.

19. Robert Farris Thompson, *Flash of the Spirit: African and Afro-American Art and Philosophy* (New York: Random House, 1983), p. 222.

20. Seyla Benhabib, "The Generalized and the Concrete Other: The Kohlberg-Gilligan Controversy and Feminist Theory," in *Feminism as Critique: On the Politics of Gender,* ed. Seyla Benhabib and Drucilla Cornell (Minneapolis: University of Minnesota Press, 1987), p. 87.

21. Ibid.

22. Beverly Wildung Harrison, *Making the Connections: Essays in Feminist Social Ethics,* ed. Carol S. Robb (Boston: Beacon Press, 1985).

23. Ibid.

24. Sandra Harding, *The Science Question in Feminism* (Ithaca, N.Y.: Cornell University Press, 1986), p. 191.

25. Jürgen Habermas, "Questions and Counterquestions" in *Habermas and Modernity,* ed. Richard J. Bernstein (Cambridge, Mass.: MIT Press, 1985), p. 194.

26. Jürgen Habermas, "What is Universal Pragmatics?" in *Communication and the Evolution of Society,* p. 3, as cited in Bernstein, *Habermas and Modernity,* p. 18.

27. Anthony Giddens, "Reason Without Revolution? Habermas's *Theorie des Kommunikativen Handelns*" in Bernstein, *Habermas and Modernity,* p. 97.

28. Ibid., p. 97.

29. Ibid., p. 105.

30. Habermas, "Historical Materialism and the Development of Normative Structures," in *Communication and the Evolution of Society,* p. 97, cited in Bernstein, *Habermas and Modernity,* p. 20.

31. Jürgen Habermas, *Knowledge and Human Interests* (Boston: Beacon Press, 1971), pp. 43–63, 301–17.

32. Habermas, "Questions and Counterquestions," p. 214.

33. Giddens, "Reason Without Revolution?", pp. 117–19.

34. Ibid., pp. 117–18.

35. Richard Katz, *Boiling Energy: Community Healing Among the Kalahari Kung* (Cambridge, Mass.: Harvard University Press, 1984).

36. Giddens, "Reason Without Revolution?", pp. 116–17.

37. Paule Marshall, *The Chosen Place, The Timeless People* (New York: Random House), 1984.

38. Giddens, "Reason Without Revolution?", p. 105.

39. Harding, *The Science Question in Feminism,* p. 191.

40. Benhabib, "Generalized and Concrete Other," p. 78.

41. Harding, *The Science Question in Feminism,* p. 32.

42. Ibid., p. 193, and Iris Marion Young, "Impartiality and the Civic Public: Some Implications of Feminist Critiques of Moral and Political Theory", in Benhabib and Cornell, eds., *Feminism as Critique,* p. 60.

43. Young, "Impartiality and the Civic Public," p. 60.

44. Ibid., pp. 60–61.

45. Andreas Huyssen, "Mapping the Postmodern," *New German Critique* 33 (Fall 1984): 5–52.

46. Harding, *The Science Question in Feminism,* p. 191.

47. Ibid., p. 192.

48. For a concise summary of the literature in feminist scholarship addressing this point, see Mary Lowenthal Felstiner, "Seeing The Second Sex Through the Second Wave," *Feminist Studies,* 6th ser., no. 2 (Summer 1980).

49. Ann Cameron, *Daughters of Copperwoman* (Vancouver: Press Gang Publishers, 1981).

50. Barbara Harlow, *Resistance Literature* (New York: Methuen, 1987), pp. 64–65.

51. Nadine Gordimer, "Guarding the 'Gates of Paradise': a Letter from Johannesburg," *New York Times Magazine,* September 8, 1985, p. 34, cited in Harlow, *Resistance Literature,* p. 179.

52. Jean Francois Lyotard writes of the end of "grand narratives" in *The Postmodern Condition: A Report on Knowledge,* trans. Geoff Bennington and Brian Massouri, foreword by Frederick Jameson (Minneapolis: University of Minnesota Press, 1984).

53. Iris Young, "The Ideal of Community and the Politics of Difference," *Social Theory and Practice,* vol. 12, no. 1 (Spring 1986): 76. Emphasis mine.

54. Ibid.

55. Ibid.

56. Barbara Christian makes the same argument in "The Race for Theory" *Feminist Studies,* 14th ser., no. 1, (Spring 1988): 67–80.

57. Harlow, *Resistance Literature,* pp. 55, xvi.

58. Ibid., pp. 85–86.

59. Ibid., p. 86.

60. Ibid., p. 116.

61. Ibid., p. 73.

62. Ibid., pp. 72–73.

63. Sarah Graham-Brown, *Palestinians and Their Society* (London: Quartet England, 1981) cited by Harow, *Resistance Literature*, p. 83.

64. Ibid., p. 82.

65. Graham-Brown, cited by Harlow, *Resistance Literature*, p. 83.

66. Ibid., p. 182.

67. Ibid., p. 80.

68. Ibid., p. 96.

69. Ibid., p. 75.

70. Julio Cortazar, "Apocalypse at Solentiname," p. 122, cited in Harlow, *Resistance Literature*, p. 76.

71. Ibid., p. 125, in Harlow, *Resistance Literature*, p. 77.

72. Ibid., p. 78. Emphasis mine.

73. Harlow, *Resistance Literature*, p. 95.

74. Ibid., p. 79.

75. Ibid., pp. 35–36.

76. Cited in Harlow, *Resistance Literature*, p. 17.

77. Cited in Harlow, *Resistance Literature*, pp. 165–66.

78. Gioconda Belli, cited in Harlow, *Resistance Literature*, p. 198.

79. Iris Young, "The Ideal of Community and the Politics of Difference," pp. 1–26. See also Patricia Hill Collins, "Learning from the Outsider Within: The Sociological Significance of Black Feminist Thought," *Social Problems*, vol. 33, no. 6 (December 1986).

80. E. Ann Kaplan, *Postmodernism and Its Discontents: Theories, Practices* (London: Verso, 1988), p. 5. See also Craig Owens, "The Discourse of Others: Feminists and Postmodernism" in Hal Foster, ed., *The Anti-Aesthetic: Essays on Postmodern Culture* (Port Townsend, Wash.: Bay Press, 1983), pp. 57–82.

81. For a critique of Lyotard see Seyla Benhabib, "Epistemologies of Postmodernism: A Rejoinder to Jean-Francois Lyotard," *New German Critique* 33 (Fall 1984): 103–27.

82. Michel Foucault, "The real strength of the women's liberation movement is not that of having laid claim to the specificity of their sexuality and the rights pertaining to it, but that they have actually departed from the discourse conducted within the apparatuses of sexuality" (*Power/Knowledge: Selected Interviews and Other Writings 1972–1977* [New York: Pantheon Books, 1980], pp. 219–20).

83. Terry Eagleton, "Capitalism, Modernism and Postmodernism," *New Left Review* 152 (July–Aug. 1985): 70. .

84. Joan Scott, "Deconstructing Equality-versus-Difference: or, The Uses of Poststructuralist Theory of Feminism," *Feminist Studies*, 14th ser., no. 1 (Spring 1988): 33.

85. Ibid., pp. 33–34.

86. Hal Foster, "Postmodernism: A Preface," *The Anti-Aesthetic,* p. ix.

87. "Nowhere does the break with modernism seem more obvious than in recent American architecture. Nothing could be further from Mies van der Rohe's functionalist glass curtain walls than the gesture of random historical citation which prevails on so many postmodern facades. Take, for example, Philip Johnson's AT&T highrise, which is appropriately broken up in to a neoclassical mid-section, Roman colonnades at the street level, and a Chippendale pediment at the top" (Huyssen, "Mapping the Postmodern," p. 12).

88. "[T]hese current designs for fortified skyscrapers indicate a vogue for battlements not seen since the great armoury boom that followed the Labour Rebellion of 1877. In so doing, they also signal the coercive intent of postmodernist architecture in its ambition, not to hegemonize the city in the fashion of the great modernist building, but rather to polarize it into radically antagonistic spaces." (Mike Davis, cited by Harlow, "Resistance Literature," p. 15).

89. Foster, "Postmodernism," p. x.

90. Ibid., pp. xi–xii.

91. Lyotard, *Postmodern Condition*, p. 76.

92. Eugene Rochberg-Halton, *Meaning and Modernity: Social Theory in the Pragmatic Attitude* (Chicago: The University Press, 1986), p. x.

93. Richard J. Bernstein, "Introduction," *Habermas and Modernity*, p. 31.

94. Irene Diamond and Lee Quinby, *Feminism & Foucault: Reflections on Resistance* (Boston: Northeastern University Press, 1988); Benhabib and Cornell, eds., *Feminism as Critique*.

95. Lyotard, *Postmodern Condition*, p. 66.

96. Ibid., p. 67.

97. For a more detailed discussion of Foucault's treatment of the insurrection of subjugated knowledges and its utility for feminist critique, see my *Communities of Resistance and Solidarity: A Feminist Theology of Liberation* (Maryknoll, N.Y.: Orbis Books, 1985).

98. Jean-Francois Lyotard and Jean-Loup Thebaud, *Just Gaming* (Minneapolis: University of Minnesota Press, 1985), p. 23.

99. Michel Foucault, *The Order of Things* (New York: Vintage Books, 1973).

100. Ibid., p. 386.

101. Michel Foucault, "What Is an Author?" *Language, Counter-memory and Practice: Selected Essays and Interviews,* ed. and trans. Donald F. Bouchard (Ithaca, N.Y.: Cornell University Press, 1980).

102. Ibid., pp. 116–17.

103. Cf. Diamond and Quinby, *Feminism and Foucault.*

104. Foucault, "What Is an Author?" p. 138.

105. Ibid.

106. For a further critique of Foucault's concept of "the end of man" see Reiner Schürmann, "On Constituting Oneself as an Anarchistic Subject," *Praxis International* vol. 6, no. 3, October 1986, pp. 294–310.

107. Benhabib and Cornell, eds., *Feminism and Critique.*

108. "Milkman's ambivalence is an example of what the legal theorist Martha Minow has labeled in another context 'the difference dilemma.' Ignoring difference in the case of subordinated groups, Minow points out, 'leaves in place a faulty neutrality,' but focusing on difference can underscore the stigma of deviance. 'Both focusing on and ignoring difference risk recreating it. This is the dilemma of difference.' What is required, Minow suggests, is a new way of thinking about difference, and this involves rejecting the idea that equality-versus-difference constitutes an opposition. Instead of framing analyses and strategies as if such binary pairs were timeless and true, we need to ask how the dichotomous pairing of equality and difference itself works. Instead of remaining within the terms of existing political discourse, we need to subject those terms to critical examination. Until we understand how the concepts work to constrain and construct

specific meanings, we cannot make them work for us." Scott, "Deconstructing Equality," p. 39.

109. Ibid., p. 48.

8. *A Theology of Resistance and Hope*

1. Adrienne Rich, "Natural Resources," *The Dream of a Common Language: Poems 1974–1977* (New York: W.W. Norton, 1978), pp. 66–67.

2. For a description of the increasing violence against women, see Jane Caputi, *The Age of Sex Crime* (Bowling Green, Ohio: Bowling Green State University Popular Press, 1987).

3. James Cone, *For My People: Black Theology and The Black Church* (Maryknoll, N.Y.: Orbis Books, 1984); Gustavo Gutierrez, *A Theology of Liberation* (Maryknoll, N.Y.: Orbis Books, 1973); Mary Daly, *Pure Lust: Elemental Feminist Philosophy* (Boston: Beacon Press, 1984).

4. Johann Baptist Metz, *Faith in History and Society: Toward a Practical Fundamental Society* (New York: Seabury Press, 1980), p. 89.

5. Ibid., pp. 90, 236.

6. Ibid., p. 90, 77.

7. Martin Luther King, Jr., "Letter from Birmingham City Jail," in *A Testament of Hope: The Essential Writings of Martin Luther King, Jr.,* ed. James M. Washington (New York: Harper & Row, 1986), pp. 289, 292–93.

8. This idea is derived from the work of Michel Foucault, *Power/Knowledge: Selected Interviews and Other Writings 1972–1977,* ed. Colin Gordon (New York: Pantheon Books, 1980).

9. Beverly Wildung Harrison, *Making the Connections: Essays in Feminist Social Ethics,* ed. Carol S. Robb (Boston: Beacon Press, 1985), p. 253.

10. Paul Tillich, *Systematic Theology,* vol. 1 (Chicago: The University of Chicago Press, 1951).

11. David Tracy, *Blessed Rage for Order: The New Pluralism in Theology* (New York: Seabury Press, 1975), pp. 43–56.

12. Mark Muesse suggested this type of critical work in his analysis of fundamentalism. Unpublished dissertation prospectus, Harvard Divinity School, spring 1984.

13. This approach has affinities with the pragmatism of John Dewey and William James but is more similar to the work of Richard Rorty.

14. Toni Morrison, *Sula* (New York: New American Library, 1973).

15. Carol Christ, *The Laughter of Aphrodite: Reflections on a Journey to the Goddess* (San Francisco: Harper & Row, 1987), pp. 217–27.

16. For a detailed analysis of the male appropriation of female labor see Christine Delphy, *Close to Home: A Materialist Analysis of Women's Oppression,* trans. and ed. Diana Leonard (Amherst: The University of Massachusetts, 1986).

17. Paul Tillich, *The Courage to Be* (New Haven, Conn.: Yale University Press, 1952), pp. 43–44. Emphasis mine.

18. While many theologians have described and defended the communal matrix of Christian faith, my use of the term "beloved community" is dependent on the political and theological work of Martin Luther King, Jr. Unlike Christian theologians, my referent is not primarily the Christian community. For a discussion of the communal nature of Christian faith see Josiah Royce, *The Problem of Christianity* (New York: Macmillan Company, 1913), vol. 2,

lecture 10. For an example of Martin Luther King, Jr.'s use of the term "beloved community," see "An Experiment in Love" in *A Testament of Hope,* p. 18.

19. June Jordan, "Where Is the Love?" *Civil Wars* (Boston: Beacon Press, 1981), p. 142.

20. Ibid.

21. Ibid.

22. Ibid., p. 144.

23. Cf. Evelyn Fox Keller, *Reflections on Gender and Science* (New Haven: Yale University Press, 1985) chaps. 5 and 6; Alison M. Jagger, *Feminist Politics and Human Nature* (Totowa, N.J.: Rowman and Allanheld, 1983); Catherine Keller, *From a Broken Web: Separation, Sexism, and Self* (Boston: Beacon Press, 1987). Nona Plessner Lyons, "Two Perspectives on Self, Relationship and Morality" in Carol Gilligan, Janie Victoria Ward, Jill McLean Taylor with Betty Bardige, eds., *Mapping the Moral Domain* (Cambridge, Mass.: Harvard University Press, 1988), pp. 21–48.

24. Caroline Whitbeck, "A Different Reality: Feminist Ontology" in *Perspectives on Women and Philosophy,* ed. Carol C. Gould (Totowa, N.J.: Rowman and Allanheld, 1983), p. 73.

25. Valerie Saiving, "The Human Situation: A Feminine View," *Journal of Religion* 40 (April 1960): 108, 110. Cited by Judith Plaskow, *Sex, Sin, and Grace: Women's Experience and the Theologies of Reinhold Niebuhr and Paul Tillich* (Washington, D.C.: University Press of America, 1980), pp. 87–88.

26. Emmanuel Levinas, *Totality and Infinity* (Pittsburgh: Dusquesne University Press, 1969), p. 26.

27. Emmanuel Levinas, *Otherwise Than Being* (Netherlands: Martinus Nihoff, 1981), p. 146.

28. Gloria Naylor, *Linden Hills* (New York: Ticknor and Fields, 1985), pp. 288–89.

29. Emmanuel Levinas, *Ethics and Infinity: Conversations with Philippe Nemo* (Pittsburgh: Dusquesne University Press, 1985), p. 95.

30. Ibid., p. 86.

31. Ibid., pp. 98–99.

32. Janet L. Surrey, "Relationship and Empowerment," *Work in Progress #30* (Wellesley, Mass.: Stone Center Working Papers Series, 1987) p. 7. See also in the Stone Center Working Papers Series: Jean Baker Miller, "What Do We Mean By Relationships," *Work in Progress #22* (1986); J. Jordan, "Empathy and Self-boundaries," *Work in Progress #16* (1984); J. Surrey, "The 'Self-in Relation': A Theory of Women's Development," *Work in Progress #13* (1984); J. Jordan, "The Meaning of Mutuality," *Work in Progress #23* (1986).

33. Margaret Miles, conversation, October 1988.

34. Janet Farrell Smith, conversation, October 1988.

35. M. M. Bober, *Karl Marx's Interpretation of History,* 2d ed., rev. (New York: W.W. Norton and Company, 1965), p. 146.

36. Sheila Collins, "Theology in the Politics of Appalachian Women," in *Womanspirit Rising,* ed. Carol Christ and Judith Plaskow (San Francisco: Harper & Row, 1979), pp. 149–50.

37. Foucault, *Power/Knowledge,* p. 137.

38. See Dick Howard's description of Rosa Luxemburg's work in *The Marxian Legacy* (New York: Urizen Books, 1977), pp. 41–65.

39. Kim Chernin, *In My Mother's House: A Daughter's Story* (New York: Harper & Row, 1983), p. 301. While depicting her mother's joyful commitment to social change, Chernin misnames its source, stating that her mother was motivated by an ideology—communism. Chernin does not see the significance of what she so faithfully records—her mother's consistent affirmation of the wonder of human life as the passion that directed her work.

40. Ibid., pp. 256–60.

41. Dorothee Soelle, *Political Theology* (Philadelphia: Fortress Press, 1974), pp. 5–6.

42. Starhawk, *Dreaming the Dark: Magic, Sex and Politics* (Boston: Beacon Press, 1982), p. 44. See also Starhawk, *Truth or Dare: Encounters with Power, Authority & Mystery* (New York: Harper & Row, 1988).

43. Susan Griffin, *Woman and Nature: The Roaring Inside Her* (New York: Harper & Row, 1978), pp. 226–27.

44. See the work of Paula Gunn Allen, *The Sacred Hoop: Recovering the Feminine in American Indian Traditions* (Boston: Beacon Press, 1986); Gloria Anzaldua, *Borderlands/La Frontera: The New Mestiza* (San Francisco: Spinsters Aunt Lute, 1987); Gloria Anzaldua and Cherrie Moraga, eds., *This Bridge Called My Back: Writings by Radical Women of Color* (Watertown, Mass.: Persephone Press, 1981); Judith Plaskow and Carol P. Christ, eds., *Weaving the Visions: New Patterns in Feminist Spirituality* (San Francisco: Harper & Row, 1989).

45. Daly, *Pure Lust,* p. 356.

46. Ibid., pp. 356–61.

47. Jacques Lacan, *Feminine Sexuality,* ed. Juliet Mitchell and Jacqueline Rose (New York: W.W. Norton, Pantheon Books, 1985), pp. 137–48.

48. Helen Cixous, "The Laugh of Medusa," in *New French Feminisms: An Anthology,* ed. Elaine Marks and Isabelle de Courtivon (Amherst, Mass.: University of Massachusetts Press, 1980), p. 252.

49. Luce Irigaray, *This Sex Which Is Not One,* ed. Catherine Porter and Carolyn Burke (Ithaca, N.Y.: Cornell University Press, 1985), p. 212.

50. Ibid., pp. 214–15.

51. Ibid., p. 207.

52. Ibid., p. 209.

53. Ibid., p. 210.

54. Audre Lorde, *Sister Outsider: Essays and Speeches* (Trumansberg, N.Y.: The Crossing Press, 1984), pp. 56–57.

55. Ibid., p. 55.

56. Ibid., p. 57.

57. Mary Daly, *Beyond God the Father: Toward a Philosophy of Women's Liberation* (Boston: Beacon Press, 1973), p. 33.

58. Carter Heyward, *Our Passion for Justice* (New York: Pilgrim, 1984).

59. Alice Walker, *In Search of Our Mother's Gardens: Womanist Prose* (New York: Harcourt Brace Jovanovich, 1983), p. 341.

60. Ibid., pp. 341–42. Emphasis mine.

61. Mary Daly, *Gyn/Ecology: The Metaethics of Radical Feminism* (Boston: Beacon Press, 1978), pp. 413–14.

62. Mark C. Taylor, *Erring: A Postmodern A/Theology* (Chicago: University of Chicago Press, 1984), p. 7.

63. Emily Erwin Culpepper, "Contemporary Goddess Thealogy: A Sympathetic Critique," in *Shaping New Visions: Gender and Values in American*

Culture, ed. Clarissa W. Atkinson, Constance H. Buchanan, Margaret R. Miles (Ann Arbor, Mich.: University of Michigan Research Press), 1987.

64. Ibid., 62–66.

65. Gordon D. Kaufman, *The Thealogical Imagination: Constructing the Concept of God* (Philadelphia: Westminster Press, 1981), pp. 28–30.

66. Taylor, *Erring,* p. 168.

67. Ibid., p. 136.

68. Ibid., p. 143.

69. Ibid., p. 34.

70. Ludwig Feuerbach, *The Essence of Christianity,* trans. George Eliot (New York: Harper & Row, 1957), p. 21.

71. Feuerbach, cited by Karl Barth, "An Introductory Essay," *The Essence of Christianity,* p. xvi.

72. Feuerbach, cited by Barth, ibid., p. xvii.

73. Feuerbach, *Essence of Christianity,* p. 152.

74. Ibid., p. 153.

75. Ibid., p. 182.

76. Ibid., p.83.

77. Donna Kate Rushin, "The Black Goddess," Barbara Smith, ed., *Home Girls: A Black Feminist Anthology* (New York: Women of Color–Kitchen Table Press, 1983), pp. 328–30 as cited by Culpepper, "Contemporary Goddess Thealogy," in *Shaping New Visions,* ed. Atkinson, et al., p. 68.

78. The basic insight of the "deep ecology" movement, for example, is awareness of the limitations of human action due to the interdependence of all aspects of nature. See Bill Devall and George Sessions, *Deep Ecology* (Salt Lake City: Peregrine Smith Books, 1985).

79. Maya Angelou, *And Still I Rise* (New York: Random House, 1978); Alice Walker, *In Search of Our Mother's Gardens* (New York: Harcourt Brace Jovanovich, 1983); Toni Morrison, *Beloved* (New York: Alfred A. Knopf, 1987).

80. Mary Daly, *Pure Lust,* pp. ix, 5.

Index

———————— ■ ————————